11.

MW00806706

From

Dave & Amy

BATTLEFIELDS OF NEBRASKA

BATTLEFIELDS OF NEBRASKA

THOMAS D. PHILLIPS

CAXTON PRESS
Caldwell, Idaho
2009

ISBN 978-0-87004-471-7

Library of Congress Cataloging-in-Publication Data

Phillips, Thomas D.
Battlefields of Nebraska / Thomas D. Phillips. -— 1st ed.
   p. cm.
ISBN 978-0-87004-471-7 (pbk.)
   1. Nebraska—History, Military. 2. Indians of North America—Wars—Nebraska. 3. Nebraska—History—Civil War, 1861-1865. 4. Nebraska—History, Local. 5. Battlefields—Nebraska. 6. Historic sites—Nebraska. I. Title.

F666.P48 2009
355.4'7782—dc22

2008050637

Cover

by Jim D. Nelson.
www.jdnelsonportraits.com

Lithographed and bound in the United States of America

CAXTON PRESS
Caldwell, Idaho
177547

DEDICATION

To my friends and fellow Nebraskans who share my love for the state, its people, and its history.

TABLE OF CONTENTS

Appendices

Illustrations

Maps

THOMAS D. PHILLIPS

FOREWORD

Battlefields in Nebraska?
Surprisingly, perhaps, there are several. Many of them are unique in our nation's annals, impressive in scope, and significant in their consequences. Luminous names from America's past graced our landscape and fought notable battles here—Custer, Cody, Red Cloud, Crazy Horse, and many others. The intensity of the engagements fought between the Army and Indians was such that 15 Medals of Honor were awarded for actions within Nebraska's borders.[1]

The full display of Nebraska's military history is long, rich, and enormously exciting. Nebraska was the scene of:

- A battle fought almost 300 years ago that for all practical purposes ended a Great Power's attempt to exert its authority over a substantial portion of the North American continent;[2]
- The earliest encounter between the U.S. Army and the Plains Indians;
- The first clash of the Indian War of 1864;
- The last significant battle between Native tribes;
- The first engagement between U.S. forces and the Plains Indians following the battle of the Little Big Horn;
- The last great charge of the U.S. Cavalry;
- The death of the Native American leader whose passing signaled the end of the conflict on the plains.

These and an incredible number of additional encounters were fought east to west and north to south throughout the state. Many of them are little known, misunderstood, or unappreciated for their significance.

Speaking specifically of a single facet of Nebraska's military history, the Indian Wars, one historian said:

Although many other states have placed greater emphasis upon their participation in Indians wars, Nebraska may claim a similar era in her history—one which was often as vivid and stirring as that of any other state. Notable expeditions marched through Nebraska's river valleys and over her plains, battles were fought on her soil, and military posts protected her burgeoning population. Yet the sites of these events are often unmarked, and the names of the men who participated in them are only dimly remembered.[3]

As I traveled to Nebraska's battle sites and researched the fascinating events associated with them, I came to share the conviction expressed in that paragraph. The state indeed possesses a long, rich, and important military history that is "vivid and stirring" but too often only "dimly remembered."

This book is an attempt to help us remember.

SPECIAL THANKS

I am beholden to the many scholars whose work I have drawn upon while preparing this book. I have tried to acknowledge their contributions and many kindnesses in the "End Notes" sections of the chapters that reflect their involvement.

I am especially grateful to Margaret E. Wagner, Editor, Publishing Office of the Library of Congress for her gracious correspondence. Ms Wagner helped identify sources and provided information on the six Nebraska regiments organized during the Civil War. It was an added delight to find that she has ties to Nebraska.

Thomas R. Buecker, Superintendent, Fort Robinson State Historical Park, and Roye Lindsay and his staff at Fort Hartsuff State Historical Park provided superb insights to the sections of this book touched by their areas of expertise. Tom Buecker's unselfish help regarding events associated with the death and capture of Crazy Horse, the Cheyenne Outbreak, and other important pieces of history linked to Fort Robinson were most appreciated. Roye Lindsay is the state's acknowledged expert regarding the Battle of the Blowout. Mr. Lindsay's correspondence regarding the battle was particularly helpful.

Sarah Polak, Director, Mari Sandoz High Plains Heritage Center, in Chadron, Nebraska, spent long hours researching my request for information regarding Lost Chokecherry Canyon, a key refuge site used by the Northern Cheyenne during their "Cheyenne Autumn" flight from Indian Territory. For many years, there was a great deal of uncertainty among scholars regarding the location of the canyon. After an exhausting search, Ms. Polak discovered a letter written by Mari Sandoz that pinpoints the site with great specificity. I am enormously grateful to Ms. Polak for her extraordinary work.

Doctor Alexander M. Vielakowski, Department of Military History, Army Command and General Staff College, Fort Leavenworth, Kansas, graciously responded to my questions regarding an aspect of Native culture that may have ties to the present day military.

Among the many who read and critiqued the manuscript, special thanks go to Dr. Roger Berger, Ames, Iowa, and Edward Jones, San Antonio, Texas, for their dedication to this effort, and, most especially, for their thoughtful comments and wise counsel.

Most of all, thanks to Nita for her wisdom and marvelous photography. . .and for making this journey with me.

* * *

A major purpose of this book is to identify, locate, and describe battles fought on the soil of present-day Nebraska, and for the first time to present information about them in a single, comprehensive reference.

Battlefields of Nebraska contains information about clashes big and small waged inside the borders of the present state. Every attempt has been made to make the list of battles as inclusive as possible and the accounts of them as accurate as scholarship allows when recounting events that in every case occurred more than a century in the past.

Assembling a definitive list of all the incidents that took place in the state is an unattainable standard. To begin with, some of that information is unknowable. Oral traditions have faded or been lost over the years as have documents contemporaneous to the time. Many encounters were probably not written about at all. Secondly, available information sometimes changes as new sources—pioneer diaries, correspondence, and so forth—are discovered that describe episodes previously unknown or shed new light on events already comprehended, although perhaps dimly, in the present day.

With these cautions acknowledged, this account is as complete as the author could make it. For instances such as the Great Sioux Uprising – when attacks across Nebraska's frontier were so widespread and occurred so frequently that all of the individual episodes associated with it will perhaps never be known—illustrative events from that period are cited to provide a representative picture of conditions at the time.

Categorizing the many clashes that were fought on the land that forms present day Nebraska is necessarily a subjective process.

Those selected as "Major Battles and Campaigns"* (Part I) were chosen because in substantial ways they met the following criteria:

- The size of the forces involved was exceptionally large or their composition unusual;
- The outcome of the battle directly shaped the course of major events that followed;
- The encounter was of exceptional significance in the history of the state or the nation;
- The battle is attested to by multiple sources.

"Significant Encounters" (Part II) includes engagements that contained many of the following characteristics:

- The battle had unique consequences associated with its outcome or special notoriety attached to its participants;
- The engagement involved numbers of contending forces often more sizable than was typical for the time;
- The major features of the battle are well documented.

The final section, Part III ("Skirmishes, Incidents, and the Shadows of History") highlights military events that fall into the following categories:

- The episode was smaller in scale than most more notable battles;
- The impact was transitory or less than consequential over the long term—or it was part of a larger campaign or a more extensive chain of events;

- The attestation is sketchy, sometimes consisting of a passing reference—often from a single source—or relayed only through oral traditions.

* The military history of the Republican River Valley provides a unique set of circumstances. Although individual encounters fought in the valley were sometimes not large or decisive, their cumulative effect was of enormous significance historically. The shared objective of the series of expeditions—to pacify the valley or force the Native tribes out of the stronghold area—makes it useful to discuss the years of fighting along the river as a single, comprehensive chapter in the "Major Battles and Campaigns" section. The "Terror Across the Plains: The Guns of August (1864)" chapter presents a similar circumstance. While some of the incidents involved large numbers of combatants, many did not. All, however, were part of a single, larger campaign and the aggregate impact of the numerous clashes was of considerable historical importance.

Introduction Notes

1. R. Eli Paul, Ed., The Nebraska Indian Wars Reader 1865-1877, (Lincoln and London: University of Nebraska Press, 1998) p. 217
2. Robert M. Manley, Platte Valley Chronicles, (Grand Island: Hall County Historical Society, 2001) p. 21
3. Paul, p. 1

MAJOR BATTLES AND CAMPAIGNS

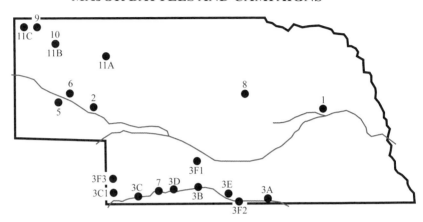

| 1. Villasur's Expedition | August 14, 1720 | Columbus, near Loup-Platte junction. |
| 2. Battle of the Blue Water | September 3, 1855 | 6 mile N.W. of Ash Hollow, near Lewellen. |

Republican River Campaigns

3A. Reconnaissance	Summer 1858	Along valley, N to Ft. Kearny.
3B. Reconnaissance	Summer 1860	Battle near Cambridge.
3C. Custer in Nebraska	June 24, 1867	Battle S of Benkelman.
3C1. Custer in Nebraska	June 24, 1867	Battle near Haigler.
3D. Carr's first expedition	Autumn 1868	4-day running fight along valley.
3E. Sappa Creek	Spring 1869	Battle S of Orleans.
3F1. Republican R. Expedition	June 12, 1869	Along Deer Creek.
3F2. Republican R. Expedition	June 15, 1869	4 Miles N of Prairie Dog Creek.
3F3. Republican R. Expedition	July 8, 1869	SW Panhandle, E of Colorado border.

4. Plum Creek Massacre	August 8, 1864	10 miles S of Lexington.
5. Battle of Mud Springs	February 4-6, 1865	25 miles NW of Sidney.
6. Battle of Rush Creek	February 8-9, 1865	15 miles NE of Mud Springs.
7. Massacre Canyon	August 5, 1873	Near Trenton.
8. Battle of the Blowout	April 28, 1976	NW of Burwell.
9. Battle of Warbonnet Cr.	July 17, 1876	Near Montrose.
10. Death of Crazy Horse	September 5, 1877	Ft. Robinson.

Odyssey of the Northern Cheyenne

11A. Lost Chokecherry Can.	Winter 1878-79	Snake R. Valley, Sheridan County.
11B. Breakout	January 9-21, 1879	Fort Robinson.
11C. Final battle	January 22, 1879	17 miles N of Harrison.

PART 1

MAJOR BATTLES
AND
CAMPAIGNS

VILLASUR'S EXPEDITION

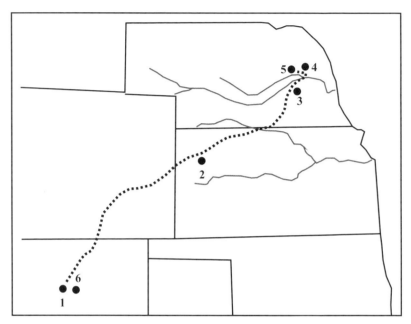

1. Mid-June, 1720: Villasur's army—42 soldiers, 3 armed settlers, a priest, an interpreter, a scout, and 60 Pueblo Indian allies—departs Santa Fe.
2. July 1720: Villasur halts momentarily at a location in present-day Scott County, Kansas, to rest and recruit Apache guides for the remainder of the campaign.
3. Early August, 1720: Villasur crosses the Platte River, probably near present-day Grand Island, and eventually moves north across the Loup River.
4. August 13, 1720: Concerned by the presence of large numbers of potentially hostile Indians near present-day Linwood and Bellwood, Villasur pulls back, recrosses the Loup, and makes camp along the south bank near the junction of the Loup and the Platte.
5. August 14, 1720: A force of 500 or more Pawnees and Otos attacks Villasur's camp, annihilating his army.
6. September 6, 1720: Survivors reach Santa Fe.

Chapter One

VILLASUR'S EXPEDITION

In the eighteenth century, Spain and France were among the foremost of the world's Great Powers. Spain's claim to an immense expanse of the North American continent west of the Mississippi River to the Pacific Ocean conflicted with France's competing ambitions for a share of the same territory.

Worried about French incursions, Spain attempted to assert its claim over what is now the north central portion of the United States by dispatching a major military expedition commanded by Don Pedro de Villasur. Villasur's journey led him to a climactic battle that changed the face and future of the continent.

* * *

Columbus, Nebraska, seems an unlikely site for a battle that would influence the destiny of a Great Power. However, shortly after sunrise on August 14, 1720, just south of the present day city, a large force of Pawnees and Otos—perhaps aided by French traders—overwhelmed a company of Spanish soldiers and their Pueblo Indian allies and the implausible became reality.[1]

The losses suffered by the Spanish on that blood-soaked morning remain the greatest sustained by white men in any battle on Nebraska soil.[2] Beyond the numbers, the battle's consequences were enormous. Never again would Spanish military forces venture so deeply onto the Great Plains[3] nor, in a concerted way, would they again attempt to control the northern frontiers of their vast American empire.[4]

The journey that led the Spanish forces to their destruction began in Santa Fe, New Mexico, in June 1720. The "Villasur Expedition" as it came to be known, was sent as a reconnaissance in force to check suspected French incursions into the northern plains.[5]

France's involvement in areas claimed by Spain was viewed as a persistent and growing threat by Spanish authorities. French presence in Spanish regions had been confirmed as early as 1699 when a Navajo war party brought back French weapons, clothing, and other equipment taken during a raid on the Pawnees.[6] By 1703, the French were trading regularly with Indians in eastern Nebraska and were providing their Indian allies with guns and steel weapons.[7] Over the years, the frequency and depth of French advances grew more visible and alarming. French traders, explorers, and commercial interests ranged hundreds of miles down the Missouri River; French settlers from Louisiana moved to the Red River in Texas, while others journeyed even further to the west and south. The year 1719 brought war between France and Spain in Europe and word of a potentially menacing French-Pawnee alliance in the northwest.[8]

Spanish authorities responded to the news by organizing an expedition the following summer. Appointed to lead the company was Don Pedro de Villasur, second in command to the Governor of New Mexico. Villasur had held a variety of administrative posts,[9] but his military background was not extensive, a circumstance that would later become a central focus of the investigation that followed.

There was no question, however, that Villasur selected a formidable company of troops to take with him on his journey. Forty-two seasoned, experienced soldiers accompanied him when the party left Santa Fe, as did three armed settlers and sixty Pueblo Indian allies. The cadre included a priest, an interpreter, and a noted explorer and scout, Jose Naranjo.[10] Naranjo's role was especially important: he may have made as many as three previous trips to the Platte River in Nebraska.[11]

The expedition was well provisioned. In addition to ample food and military supplies for the company, Villasur took with him "maize, short swords, knives, sombreros, and a half mule load of tobacco" to reward his own guides and give as gifts along the way.[12] Altogether, six pack animals loaded with goods were taken on the journey.[13]

After leaving Santa Fe, Villasur's army marched first to an outpost in what is now Scott County, Kansas, a distance of about 350 miles. There they rested and Villasur recruited a dozen or so Apaches to serve as guides for the remainder of the journey.[14]

The route from Santa Fe and the outpost tracked consistently north and east and in early August eventually brought the company to

Nebraska State Historical Society

The hide tapestry above shows Spanish soldiers surrounded and under furious attack. Below, today a small commercial area adjoins the neatly-trimmed meadow east of the Loup River Bridge where the Spanish fought for their lives in "grass higher than the stature of a man."

Photo by Nita Phillips

the South Platte River (called the Rio Jesus Maria by the Spanish[15]) probably near present day Grand Island.[16] Villasur and his men had covered more than 600 miles and had not yet seen any indication of French presence. The absence of any signs prompted Villasur to call a meeting of his officers to discuss whether to continue the search or halt there and wait further orders from authorities in Santa Fe. The council decided to press on until contact with the Pawnees might establish whether there were French in the region and, if so, where they were located.[17]

Villasur crossed to the north side of the Platte and soon after sent Jose Naranjo out with a company of scouts to reconnoiter the ground ahead. When Naranjo returned from his reconnaissance, he reported having seen a Pawnee village with a war dance in progress. Villasur then crossed a second stream (the Loup) that had just merged with the South Platte and sent a Pawnee captive, a personal servant of an officer in the party, to win the confidence of the villagers and present gifts to them.

The Pawnee servant eventually located a large village accessible by a nearby ford. Standing by the stream, he attempted to parley with a sizable number of Pawnee warriors who had gathered on the opposite bank. His efforts were greeted belligerently by the warriors who, by brandishing tomahawks and war clubs, signaled their hostility and caused Villasur's emissary to hurry back to his own camp. The following day, Villasur moved his army, placing his forces opposite the village on the far bank of the stream.[18]

An ambiguous series of meetings and conversations then took place. A group of about twenty-five Pawnees first ventured to the edge of the stream expressing their desire to talk peace and requesting the services of the Pawnee interpreter. Villasur sent the Pawnee servant to meet with them and gave him some tobacco to distribute.[19] Later, the servant appeared on the opposite bank saying that he was being well treated but the Pawnees would not allow him to leave. He said that the Pawnees in the village claimed not to have seen any Frenchmen. The next day, however, a group of Pawnees visited Villasur's camp and made reference to contact with at least one "white man."[20]

Villasur responded by having a member of his party write a note in French for the visiting Pawnees to take back to their village. They did so, and then returned the following day with an old linen flag and a paper covered with illegible writing. It is possible that later a second letter, this time written in Spanish, was prepared for delivery to the village. If so, no reply was received.[21]

Frustrated, Villasur called another meeting of his officers during which he proposed to cross the river and, if necessary, coerce the Pawnees into providing the desired information. Several of his officers objected, believing the detention of the Pawnee servant was a warning. At about the same time as the council, Pawnees seized some of Villasur's Pueblo Indian allies who were bathing in the river. Two or three struggled free, but one was taken captive.[22]

Increasingly concerned by these events and by the large numbers of Indians in the area—their sizable villages were in proximity to present-day Linwood and Bellwood [23]—on the afternoon of April 13, Villasur pulled his forces back. Re-crossing the Loup, he halted on its south bank a few miles from the Pawnee village. The horses were put out to pasture and Pueblo Indians were assigned to guard the camp, which was made in a relatively flat meadow with very high grass.[24] The Pueblos settled down for the night close by but separated from the Spanish, and the horses were placed under guard a short distance from the Spanish troops' bivouac.

After dark, suspicious sounds were heard: guards reported a barking dog and noise possibly made by people crossing the river. This information was reported to Villasur, or by one account, to his second in command, Tomas Olguin, who alerted the sentinels guarding the horses and sent Pueblos to check for intruders along the stream. None were found and soon after, the Pueblos reported the absence of any threat.[25]

A short time later, not long after daybreak on August 14, Spanish dreams of sustaining the northern region of their vast American empire lay shattered on the soil of eastern Nebraska.

Taking advantage of the "thick grass higher than the stature of a man"[26] and a known pattern in the Spanish camp routine, an enormous force of Pawnee and Oto Indians variously estimated by survivors as numbering 500 or more,[27] possibly accompanied by French traders, attacked the camp and annihilated Villasur's army.

The attack was timed to occur after the Spanish horse herd was brought back to camp, but not yet saddled. Spanish veterans of combat on the Plains had noted that surprise attacks by their Indian foes typically occurred just after daybreak. Thus, several horses were normally left saddled through the night to respond to that contingency. Now, with the period of vulnerability apparently past, Villasur ordered the herd to be gathered and the horses unsaddled and exchanged for fresh mounts.[28]

On this morning, the Pawnees waited until the sun was up and the Spanish soldiers were busy tending the horses, collecting their gear, and making preparations for the morning's activities. Conjecture on the part of the few survivors was that the Pawnee servant sent as an emissary by Villasur, and then by outward appearances apparently detained in the village, had in fact defected and advised the Pawnees of the Spanish soldiers' usual preparations.[29]

What is certain is that the attack was delivered with complete surprise at a time when the Spanish camp was at its most vulnerable. From hiding places in the tall grass, using arquebuses, tomahawks, lances, war clubs, and bows and arrows,[30] the violent assault quickly carried into and through the encampment. Villasur and his personal servant were struck down immediately. Both died near Villasur's tent, killed before either could reach their weapons. Villasur's interpreter, Juan de l'Archeveque, also fell during the first volley. Although desperately injured and bleeding from seven wounds, l'Archeveque's servant was one of the few who managed to escape.[31]

The noise and confusion of the initial onslaught caused the horse herd to bolt. In desperation, handlers struggled successfully to overtake the runaways, but almost immediately after halting the stampede, the small group came under furious attack by large numbers of Pawnees. During the clash, a few soldiers managed to mount their horses and repulse several sorties made against their position.[32]

In the meantime, the situation inside the camp was becoming increasingly desperate. The massive attack quickly overwhelmed the Spanish at the perimeters of the camp, several of whom were killed immediately by the intense fire. During the chaos that followed, as pressure increased from all sides, the remaining Spanish, pushed by the cresting strength of the attackers and weakened by their own losses, retreated into an ever-tightening ring.

This portion of the battle is depicted in a marvelous 17-foot-long hide painting, a replica of which hangs in the Nebraska State Historical Society.[33] The painting contains remarkable detail—the clothing and

Nebraska State Historical Society

The hide painting shows Pawnee warriors fording the river where the Loup flows into the Platte. The spot near Columbus where the two rivers join is still wooded and undeveloped.

Photo by Nita Phillips

9

weapons are accurately portrayed—and so closely coincides with the accounts of survivors that it was likely painted by an eye-witness. The central focus of the painting shows the battle in its final stage: there, amidst tents, saddles, and packs, engulfed in the chaos of a furious struggle, a group of soldiers clustered in a tightly compressed circle wages a desperate last stand. Their position bristles with rifles and lances; some have apparently had time to gather shields and armor. The numerous casualties from both sides shown strewn across the landscape reflect the intensity of the combat. The small party of soldiers is surrounded by overwhelming numbers of Indians moving in a close circle around them. The statement of one survivor describes "Indians riding in a circle."[34] While the tapestry does not show Indians on horseback, it is known that Spanish horses from the southwest were in Nebraska by 1690,[35] so the possibility exists that some of the attackers were mounted.

As the tiny cluster of soldiers struggled in growing peril, a remarkable act of heroism occurred. After fighting off attacks on his own position with the horse herd, a cavalry corporal gathered two or three companions and, taking extra horses, charged into the fray, dashing through the smoke and dust toward where they could hear the desperate shouts of their encircled colleagues. Incredibly, they managed to fight their way through the mass of Indians and save perhaps as many as seven of their comrades, two of whom were severely wounded. The corporal and one of his men were killed during the course of the rescue.[36]

The Pueblos, camped a short distance from the Spanish, also came under severe attack and suffered heavy casualties, although it seems that the major focus of the Pawnees' assault was on the Spanish forces.[37] The battle probably lasted less than an hour,[38] but during those terrible minutes the fighting was notable for its savagery. When it was over, Villasur's army, and Spain's aspirations for controlling the vast northern region of her empire, were destroyed.

Left dead or dying in the meadow near Columbus were thirty-five Spanish, including the expedition's commander Don Pedro de Villasur, his second in command Tomas Olguin, and the noted frontiersman, Jose Naranjo. Eleven Pueblo Indians, allies of the Spanish, were also killed. Twelve Spanish, forty-nine Pueblos, and the Apache scouts, escaped.[39] Those who broke free from the killing field fled south to the outpost in Kansas, where they were given shelter and sustenance by friendly Apaches.[40] They reached Santa Fe on September 6, 1720, twenty-four days after the battle.[41]

The survivors insisted that although taken by surprise, the Spanish and their Pueblo allies had inflicted a considerable number of casualties on the attackers during the course of the battle. There is no way to determine how heavy the Pawnees' losses were, but the depiction in the tapestry and the fact that the survivors were apparently not pursued[42] and that they were able to take with them some portion of their horse herd[43] (a commodity of enormous value on the Plains), lends substance to the survivors' accounts.

When the few survivors struggled back with news of their ordeal, their report was greeted with great alarm by Spanish authorities. The crisis prompted the Viceroy to launch a tortuous investigation that eventually lasted seven years. Two questions formed the core of the inquiry. First, should the governor, Don Antonio Valverde, have led the expedition himself? Second, if he had lawful reasons to delegate that task, was he negligent in selecting Villasur, less experienced as a soldier, as leader? The investigator submitted a report that would have absolved Valverde. However, an official at a higher level disagreed with the initial conclusions, particularly those that had found no fault with Villasur's competence. The Viceroy eventually concurred with the dissenting official, and as punishment Governor Valverde was ordered to pay fines, including "fifty pesos for charity masses for the souls of the dead soldiers."[44]

Almost 300 years after the battle, the question of whether French soldiers or traders participated in the battle remains. Spanish sources are ambiguous. However, the hide painting may suggest an answer. The tapestry appears to show the presence of French civilians whose clothing and equipment are accurately depicted.[45]

* * *

Other than Nebraska State Historical Society Marker 305 located near the battle site, there are few reminders of the furious struggle that once took place there. An iron bridge carrying U.S. Highway 81 now spans the Loup near the point where Villasur crossed to the south side on the eve of the battle. Where grass in the meadow was "higher than the stature of a man" when the Pawnees attacked, today it is neatly trimmed by maintenance crews along Highways 81 and 30, which intersect just south of the river. There is a small commercial area running south along the east side of Highway 81 for a few hundred yards after the road crosses the river bridge. As the road continues in that direction along the path the survivors likely fled, there is a gravel quarry and then scattered residences before habitation thins into farms and cropland. To the east, near the "v" where the Loup joins the South Platte, the land remains undeveloped, wooded, and rough, still mirroring the appearance of the area depicted in the tapestry of the battle.

In 1998, a few traces of the struggle were found near Papillion. At a site known to have been occupied by Oto or Ioway Indians in the 1720s, archeologists discovered fragments of Spanish olive jars. They are the only known examples of eighteenth century Spanish pottery yet found in the central Great Plains. Otos participated in the attack on Villasur's army and the tribe's oral history speaks of tribesmen showing objects from the battle to French officials in Illinois. "Unless more convincing evidence is discovered, the Villasur battle is the most likely source. . ."[46]

Endnotes

1 James Hanson, *Spain on the Plains* in *Nebraska History,* Spring 1993, Vol 74, No. 1, p. 8.
2 "The Villasur Expedition," Nebraska State Historical Society Marker 305. See also Hanson, p. 8.
3 Ibid.
4 Robert B. Manley, *Platte Valley Chronicles* (Grand Island: Hall County Historical Society, 2001) p. 21.
5 James C. Olson and Ronald C. Naugle, *History of Nebraska, 3rd Edition* (Lincoln and London: University Nebraska Press, 1997) p. 30.
6 Olson and Naugle, p. 28.
7 Hanson, p. 7.
8 Alfred Barnaby Thomas, *After Coronado: Spanish Expeditions Northeast of New Mexico, 1697-1727 Documents from the Archives of Spain, Mexico, and New Mexico* (Norman: University of Oklahoma Press, 1935) p. 35-36.
9 Thomas, p.222-223 .
10 Thomas, p.36. Some sources cite 45 soldiers in Villasur's army. (See Hanson, p. 7).
11 Hanson, p. 7
12 Thomas, p. 37.
13 Hanson, p. 7.
14 Hanson, p. 7.
15 Thomas, p. 37.
16 Hanson, p. 8.
17 Thomas, p. 37.

18 Ibid.
19 Thomas, p. 133.
20 Thomas, p. 38.
21 Thomas, p. 163.
22 Thomas, p. 38.
23 Hanson, p. 8.
24 Ibid.
25 Thomas, p. 38.
26 Thomas, p. 184.
27 Thomas, p. 229.
28 Thomas, p. 164.
29 Hanson, p. 8.
30 Thomas, p. 242.
31 Thomas, p. 38.
32 Thomas, p. 230.
33 The original is in the Museum of New Mexico in Santa Fe.
34. Thomas, p. 38.
35. Hanson, p. 4.
36 Thomas, p. 165.
37 Hanson, p. 8.
38 Ibid.
39 Ibid.
40 Thomas, p. 39.
41 Hanson, p. 8.
42 Thomas, p. 39.
43 Thomas, p. 165.
44 Thomas, p. 41-43.
45 Hanson, p. 20.
46 Nebraska State Historical Society, News Release, January 29, 2003.

Other References

1. Louis F. Serna, Albuquerque, New Mexico, "The Sernas of New Mexico" Newsletter, Issue No. 50, February 1, 2003. The Newsletter is a publication of the Serna family. Capitan Cristobal de la Serna accompanied the Villasur expedition and was killed in Nebraska. This issue provides the family's information regarding his military career, the expedition, and the battle.

2. Felicia Lujan, Senior Archivist, New Mexico State Records Center and Archives, Santa Fe, New Mexico. Ms Lujan graciously acquainted me with the menu of the Spanish Archives of New Mexico that dealt with the Villasur episode and provided me with a copy of Spanish Archives of New Mexico, Series 11, Microfilm Roll #6, Frame #482, which pertains to the expedition. I am very grateful for her kind assistance.

3. My thanks also go to Mr. Steve Pierce, Lincoln, Nebraska, who translated the archival copies.

THE BATTLE OF THE BLUE WATER

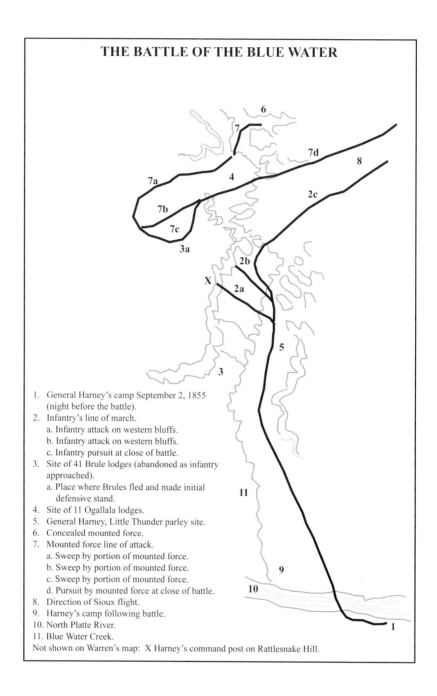

1. General Harney's camp September 2, 1855 (night before the battle).
2. Infantry's line of march.
   a. Infantry attack on western bluffs.
   b. Infantry attack on western bluffs.
   c. Infantry pursuit at close of battle.
3. Site of 41 Brule lodges (abandoned as infantry approached).
   a. Place where Brules fled and made initial defensive stand.
4. Site of 11 Ogallala lodges.
5. General Harney, Little Thunder parley site.
6. Concealed mounted force.
7. Mounted force line of attack.
   a. Sweep by portion of mounted force.
   b. Sweep by portion of mounted force.
   c. Sweep by portion of mounted force.
   d. Pursuit by mounted force at close of battle.
8. Direction of Sioux flight.
9. Harney's camp following battle.
10. North Platte River.
11. Blue Water Creek.
Not shown on Warren's map: X Harney's command post on Rattlesnake Hill.

Chapter Two

THE BATTLE OF THE BLUE WATER (ASH HOLLOW)

Despite a background of friction and occasional violence, during the early years of the mass migration to the west, the predominate relationship between emigrants and the Plains tribes was generally a guarded, often uneasy accommodation of each other's presence. For many settlers—possibly the majority in the early days—the Indians prompted a mixture of emotions: fascination, exasperation, fear, and, for some, compassion and sympathy. For the Indians, consternation with the enormous wagon trains moving through the lands that had always been theirs, the loss of buffalo, and other depredations eventually became "smoldering resentment which broke into sporadic clashes and finally open warfare."[1]

* * *

"One of the most savage of all encounters between red and white men"[2] took place on September 3, 1855 near Lewellen in the valley of a stream now called Blue Creek. By the usual standards of Plains warfare, the numbers involved were huge[3] and the casualties were high in a fight that eventually covered acres of ground both at the scene of the main combat and during the pursuit that followed.

The Battle of the Blue Water was the federal government's first military campaign against the Lakota Sioux.[4] The outcome was so decisive that for nearly a decade the overland trail was kept open and the Plains Indians remained relatively quiet.[5] That interlude was only temporary, however, and the Blue Water played a role in establishing "the pattern of violence that would be climaxed two decades later at the Little Bighorn."[6]

Although the significance of the battle has long been apparent, confusion remains regarding several of its features. For example, the encounter is increasingly referred to as the Battle of Ash Hollow. In reality, the battle occurred about six miles northwest of the famous site, across the North Platte River in a broad valley formed by a creek referred to in the 1850s as the Blue Water.[7] Also, the popular perception of the clash has changed over the years. The initial public reaction—widespread acclaim—was later followed by epithets such as "Harney's Massacre," in reference to General William S. Harney, who led the expedition. For a time, soldiers who fought in the battle were sometimes branded "butchers" and "squaw killers." In recent years, those harsh judgments have mostly reversed, and many current assessments conclude that Harney and his troops were unjustly accused.[8]

Adding further to the confusion is the fact that the 1855 battle was not the first or only encounter fought around Ash Hollow. At least three battles near the same site preceded it: a major fight in 1835 between the Pawnee and the Sioux[9]; an 1837 attack on an Oregon-bound expedition;[10] and an attack on a nearby U.S. mail station in 1854.[11]

Each of these "Battles of Ash Hollow" helped form the historical portrait of that storied region. None of them, however, carried the national impact or the lasting consequences of the 1855 encounter that has also come to bear the name.

The direct cause of the 1855 battle was an episode that came to be known as the Grattan Massacre. In 1854, a band of Ogallala and Brule Sioux led by Chief Conquering Bear was camped near Fort Laramie, about two miles from present-day Lingle, Wyoming,[12] awaiting allotments of food promised by an 1851 treaty.[13] The provisions were late in reaching them, by one account perhaps by as much as two months.[14] While the Indians were waiting, a contingent of Mormons on the way to Utah—the Hans Peter Olson Company—traveled through the region. When the party neared the Indian camp one of its livestock, "a sickly, half-starved cow," either wandered away or frightened, wound up in the Indian camp. The Mormons made no effort to have the cow returned to their herd. The Sioux regarded the animal as abandoned and killed and ate it.[15] When the Mormons reported the incident at Fort Laramie, the Indians—in accordance with the treaty provisions and in order to receive their annuities—at first promised to turn over the Indians who had killed the cow.

Other similar incidents—cows being taken and killed by Indians—had occurred during the summer. While not regarding the latest episode as being particularly serious, the commander of Fort Laramie eventually decided to send Second Lieutenant John Grattan to bring in the Indian perpetrators.

Grattan, a recent graduate of West Point, is described in some accounts as being inexperienced, quick tempered, and anxious for action.[16] Grattan took twenty-seven soldiers, another officer, an interpreter and two cannon with him. Some sources assert that Grattan was handicapped in that his interpreter, a man named Lucien Auguste, was thoroughly disliked by the Indians and quite possibly drunk when he accompanied Grattan. By one account, a local trader warned the lieutenant that Auguste could cause trouble at the Indian camp.[17] In later years, General Harney, who led the forces that fought in the battle precipitated by Grattan's actions, came to suspect that Grattan himself may have been drinking.[18]

When Grattan's force reached the encampment, Chief Conquering Bear, despite several attempts, was unable to get the Indian who had committed the offense to give himself up. Grattan then moved his men to the center of the camp and placed his cannon in position facing the lodge of the Indian who had killed the cow. One last, unsuccessful, attempt was made to secure his surrender. At that point, a gun went off. It is uncertain who fired it, Indian or soldier. The shot sparked a spasm of heavy firing by both sides. Volleys were unleashed from both cannons and Chief Conquering Bear fell almost immediately.[19]

When the melee eventually ended, Grattan and all but one of his men were dead. That one had his tongue cut out and died later at the Fort Laramie hospital.[20] The "Grattan Massacre" was the first time since the army's organization in 1775 that a military unit had been completely annihilated.[21] Chief Little Thunder, who would later confront General Harney on the Blue Water, was in the Indian's camp during the clash. Ironically, Little Thunder was apparently one of the pacifiers who, after Grattan and his party had been killed, talked some of the more violent and excited Indians out of attacking Fort Laramie and attempting to burn the post.[22]

In the immediate aftermath of the Grattan incident, an attempt was made to round up all "friendly and peaceable" Indians and shelter them near Fort Laramie.[23] Eventually, in hopes of diffusing the situation, the

Indian agent directed the Brule to move to the south side of the North Platte River.[24] Little Thunder's band did not comply with the orders. His group was thought to harbor participants involved in the recent robbery of a mail train and the murders of mail contractors. Many of those involved in the Grattan episode were with Little Thunder as well. Whatever considerations motivated them, the decision not to go to Fort Laramie violated the government's directive.[25]

In the meantime, a number of incidents quickly followed the Grattan affair. From August 1854 through August 1855, hostile Sioux bands (not the majority) launched a series of raids that involved murders, the theft of mules and mail, and the burning of hay, corrals, and stations.[26]

The public outcry from the Grattan incident and the depredations that followed compelled Congress to act. Secretary of War, Jefferson Davis—one of several names from the Civil War that would find their way to the pages of Nebraska's history—advised President Franklin Pierce to take military action. Davis's report, along with Commanding General of the Army Winfield Scott's recommendation for a punitive expedition[27] set in motion events that would bring General Harney and his troopers to west central Nebraska the following year.

On October 26, 1854, the War Department named General Harney to lead the campaign. Harney, on vacation in Paris, hurried back to the United States. After first meeting with President Pierce and General Scott, he moved on to Jefferson Barracks in St. Louis. There, he began assembling troops and supplies. Lieutenant Colonel Philip St. George Cooke, a veteran of the Mexican War and an experienced Indian fighter, was assigned to command the cavalry component of Harney's force.[28]

In early August, 1855, having first moved to Fort Leavenworth, Kansas, Harney was ready to begin. With 600 cavalry, infantry, and artillerymen consisting of the Second Dragoons, five companies of the Sixth Infantry, one company from the Tenth Infantry, and a battery of the Fourth Artillery,[29] Harney began his journey, tracking north and west into Nebraska. When he left Fort Leavenworth on that mid-summer day, he took with him the largest force that had ever entered Indian territory.[30]

Harney's plan was ambitious: one wing of a giant pincer would travel north up the Missouri and establish a base at Fort Pierre; the

other, led by Harney himself, would
move along the "Great Platte River
Road" toward Fort Laramie. Eventually, the wings of the enormous
double envelopment would converge
"to squeeze the Sioux into submission."[31] Harney's aim was to find the
Indians and either force them to fight
or keep them on the move, disrupting
their activities and perhaps causing
the warriors to separate themselves
from the rest of the group. If the
latter occurred, the onset of winter
might cause the Indians to surrender
or face starvation.[32]

Wyoming Tales and Trails.com

General William S. Harney
Sioux Expedition commander

Delayed by torrential storms,
from Fort Leavenworth Harney first
moved his troopers to a camp near
Fort Kearny, Nebraska. Along the
route, Harney was unexpectedly joined by Lieutenant G. K. Warren,
a topographical engineer, and a party of seven men.[33] The addition of
Warren to the expedition was a fortunate occurrence, both for Harney
and for historians. Warren was a superb officer who participated
directly in the key events associated with the campaign and recorded
his observations in a daily journal. At the battle site, Warren drew a
much-reproduced map of the Blue Water battlefield that has become
famous in its own right.

On August 24, after a brief rest, Harney left the Fort Kearny
bivouac and continued his trek along the Platte River. Nine days later,
on September 2, his force crossed from the South to the North Platte,[34]
and reached the vicinity of the Blue Water Creek. By the time camp
was made that night in a flat meadow area west and a bit north of Ash
Hollow, Harney's horses and men were approaching exhaustion.[35]

Until that day, few Indians had been sighted. That circumstance
changed as Harney's force descended the gorge of Ash Hollow to
reach their campsite. From the bluffs in the Ash Hollow area, several
Indian lodges were visible in the distance via telescope. An eastbound
wagon train reported the presence of numerous lodges and identified

Little Thunder as the chief. Later still, the expedition's guide, Joseph Tesson, located the Indian's main camp on Blue Water Creek, a few miles distant to the north from both Ash Hollow and the North Platte River.[36] Undetected at the time was a second, smaller camp still further north on the west bank of the creek.

Harney's bivouac was on the south side of the North Platte River a short distance from where Blue Water Creek converges with it.[37]

They made a "cold" camp that evening; no fires were permitted so as not to disclose the location or size of the force. The men settled in for a short night after replenishing their canteens and eating wild grapes and plums that grew in abundance near the river.[38]

Harney met with his officers that evening and laid out an aggressive plan of attack that would strike the Indians from two directions. Colonel Cooke would set out early with his cavalry and some mounted infantry, moving east and north in a half circle until his force was on the other side of the Indian camp. There they would wait, hidden, until they heard firing, then attack the village from the rear. In the meantime, Harney's infantry would delay its start in order to approach the Indian camp at daybreak when Harney intended to launch a frontal attack. If the Indians retreated, they would be driven into Cooke's on-rushing cavalry. If they fought in place, they would eventually be surrounded as Cooke's force moved from the north to pin them against Harney's infantry and artillery.[39]

Despite having been warned of Harney's approach by an Indian agent, Little Thunder's band had chosen to ignore orders to move south or return to Fort Laramie. Encamped near Blue Water Creek, they were drying out buffalo meat taken during a recent hunt. Their decision not to move was likely influenced by the desire to stay in place until the meat was cured. Whatever the total combination of factors that went into their choice—which the chiefs had debated during a recent council—the Indians apparently misunderstood Harney's intentions and the strength of his contingent, "either thinking that Harney could not be serious about attacking, or else thinking that they could defeat any white force sent against them."[40]

On the morning of September 3, the Indians were clustered in two villages along the west side of Blue Water Creek. Forty-one Brule lodges were located four miles north of the North Platte River. An additional eleven Ogallala lodges formed a smaller camp three miles further north.[41]

By most contemporary accounts, in combination, the fifty-two lodges housed about 250 Indians. That would place about five Indians in each lodge. Some scholars have noted that the usual estimate is seven to eight individuals per lodge.[42] If the latter figure portrays the true picture at Blue Water, there may have been as many as 400 Indians encamped at the two locations.

Moving toward them in the early dawn hours were 500 troopers: infantry, cavalry, and artillery. (Harney's total force consisted of 600 soldiers. The figure of 500 for the attack subtracts out the number in the wagon train escort and those who dropped out during the march or were too lame to participate in the attack.[43])

National Museum of the American Indian
Smithsonian Institution
Chief Little Thunder

When the troops crossed the North Platte River, the terrain they moved through was shaped by the meanderings of the Blue Water Creek. At the time of the battle, the creek was "about 20 feet wide and 2 to 10 feet deep flowing over a rocky or sandy bottom." The banks were "abrupt and three to four feet high."[44] The stream makes a series of mostly mild curves back and forth along the east and west walls of a small valley as it runs its ten to eleven-mile course to the north.

The valley itself is about a half mile wide, bounded on the east by low sand hills. On that side, toward the north end of the valley, there is a gap between the sand dunes. At that point, hills momentarily soften and the ground levels out, falling away in a gradual slope to the east. The soil in this area has a springy, marshy texture associated with it. North of this meadow-like breach, the sand hills resume and continue with the stream until it ends a few miles in the distance. The hills

21

on the east are modest in height and have the appearance of gentle, rolling mounds.

There is little that is gentle about the bluffs that form the west wall. They are steep, rugged, cut by narrow ravines, and characterized by sharp outcroppings of rocks whose twisted crags form small caves or niches between the coarse formations. Small mesas periodically appear along the west face; the tops of the bluffs are relatively flat as they continue north through the valley.

Cooke's force moved out at 3 a.m. in order to be in place behind the Indian village prior to Harney's attack. Cooke took with him two companies of the Second Dragoons, one light company of the Fourth Artillery, and one company of the Tenth Infantry, about 150 men in all. The latter (artillery and infantry) were mounted on this occasion to enable them to reach their distant positions in time. Led by the scout Joseph Tesson, after crossing the river they trekked east behind the sand hills, skirting the far side to avoid detection.[45]

Harney delayed by a half hour his originally intended jump off time, deciding an extra thirty minutes would bring the village into clear view at the time his force arrived in front of it. At 4:30 a.m. along with his staff and five companies of the Sixth Infantry, Harney crossed the North Platte River. Keeping to the east side of the small valley, his troops moved north toward the Indian village.[46]

At the north end of the valley, events required a quick modification to Harney's plan. As Cooke's forces emerged from behind the sand hills and turned west to position themselves in back of the Brule encampment, they discovered the smaller Ogallala village. Saved by Tesson's scouting, they did not stumble into the camp. After already having traveled about five miles, Cooke moved still further north in order to place himself on the reverse side of what was now known to be a combined camp, larger and more extensive than expected. Still, soon after sunrise, he located a promising position on a ridge and the bank of a dry creek bed about a half mile north of the Ogallala village. Keeping his cavalry in readiness and out of sight, he placed his now dismounted artillerymen and infantry in prone positions to block the Indians' anticipated escape route. There he remained for the next two hours waiting to move into action at the sound of firing from Harney's attack.[47]

To the south, Harney's movement also met with unforeseen circumstances. About a mile into his march toward the Brule village, his approach was detected and, soon after, lodges were struck and the Indians began to withdraw quickly up the valley to the north. After moving some distance in that direction, they halted and a parley ensued between Harney and the village chiefs.[48]

As often occurs in the "fog of war," opinions differ regarding the meeting or meetings that followed. One version, said to come from Indian informants, was that Little Thunder asked for a conference to gain time to dismantle and move the camp. When Little Thunder, along with chiefs Spotted Tail and Iron Shell, rode from the village carrying a white flag, Harney —having fought Indians since the Seminole Wars in Florida—was not taken in by the ruse. While expressing his willingness to talk, he kept his infantry on the move. Alarmed, the chiefs broke off the talks and raced toward their camp at full speed. According to this account, soldiers fired at the chiefs as they galloped away.[49]

The journals of two officers, Captain J. B. L. Todd and Lieutenant G. K. Warren, and a separate newspaper article provide a somewhat different version. All agree that the Indians first asked for a parley that Harney ignored. Warren relates that at the time Harney's force reached Blue Water Creek, the Indians, on the opposite side of the stream, had moved a considerable distance up the valley. Concerned that he might lose contact with the Brules and not be able to bring them to battle, Harney sent his interpreter to talk with Little Thunder "in order to gain time and learn something of the disposition of the Indians."[50] Harney may have had another motive as well. By this time, he had received information that some of the ground traversed by Cooke's troops earlier that morning—especially the spongy soil near the gap area—was not conducive to cavalry.[51] Therefore, he may have agreed to a meeting to assure that Cooke's men had sufficient time to reach their positions and be in place to spring the trap.[52] Whatever Harney's intent, Little Thunder agreed to meet with him, but only if the troops were stopped.

Messages carried by the interpreter flowed back and forth until eventually both sides, infantry and Indians, halted with the creek separating them,[53] Indians to the west, Harney's infantry on the east side. Harney and Little Thunder met near a rock outcropping that projects from a low bluff on the east bank of the creek. The location was about a half mile downstream (south) of the large camp. While the talks were on-going, some of the Indians, possibly wary of a trap, began moving up the ravines and small canyons, seeking refuge in the caves and brush in the hills to the west.[54]

When the talks began, Harney dismounted in front of his skirmish line and waited for Little Thunder, who raced at full speed to meet him and stopped suddenly 30-40 feet away. The talks lasted for perhaps as much as an hour. Harney castigated the chief for the Grattan incident, the murders of the mail party, and the frequent attacks on wagon trains. Little Thunder replied that he could not contain the young people in his village, but that he himself was friendly and did not wish to fight. As the talks continued, Little Thunder became visibly more uneasy. By Warren's account, Harney told the chief that no attack would be launched until he returned to his camp and that if his young men wanted a battle, there would be one. Warren says Harney told Little Thunder that if he (Little Thunder) wanted sanctuary, he should leave the area immediately.[55]

Much remains uncertain about this series of meetings. Sioux lore asserts that the soldiers began firing while the chief was meeting with Harney under a white flag.[56] The journals of the officers involved in the parley are consistent in stating that the firing did not begin until Little Thunder returned to his camp.

Meanwhile, Cooke's forces, waiting at the north end of the valley, had also been discovered. An Indian woman and two children walking along the west side of the stream had seen the soldiers hidden in the grass. The woman hurried back to warn the encampment. Two young warriors immediately rode out and challenged the soldiers to fight. Cooke declined to do so, staying at the ready in accordance with Harney's plan, holding off his attack until he heard firing from the south.[57]

Sounds from Harney's battle were not long in coming. According to many accounts, after Little Thunder declined Harney's offer of safety and returned to his camp, the infantry advance resumed and the order to fire was almost immediately given.[58]

The din that reached Cooke's men came mostly from a heavy assault by two companies of Harney's infantry. Attacking diagonally west and north, they moved across Blue Water Creek and up the valley.

Fred H. Werner, from his book With Harney on the Blue Water

The hills west of the battlefield. Rattlesnake Hill, site of Harney's command post, is in the center of the photo.

Their spirited attack drove the Indians to the bluffs on the west side of the valley where they sought refuge and firing positions among the ragged outcroppings and limestone caves. As the Indians took shelter along the valley wall, the infantry companies sustained their attack, working up the steep slopes and through sharp ravines despite heavy fire.[59] While the two companies were charging the heights, a third was sent north along the creek in what turned out to be a mostly futile attempt to catch in the flank any Indians retreating toward the east from this first phase of the engagement.

Cooke's force, positioned north of the upper camp, moved out at the sound of the first volleys from Harney's battle, galloping "in a column of fours across the valley for the bluffs in the enemy's rear."[60] Cooke peeled off three companies and sent them on a sweep to the reverse side of the bluffs to close the west wall of the valley as an escape route. An additional company of mounted infantry was sent straight down the valley in an attempt to seal off the "gap" area which was correctly anticipated as a possible avenue for retreat.

As the cavalry raced south to meet the oncoming infantry, the Indians were pinned between the sides of Harney's rapidly closing vise. In a matter of minutes, as the trap swung shut, the valley of

Blue Water Creek and its adjoining western bluff became the scene of carnage.

Exposed to withering fire in the open and about to be overrun from the north and south, abandoning their possessions, most of the Indians fled initially to the caves and rocky outcroppings on the heights along the west side of the valley. There they were soon assaulted by the two companies of infantry moving up the valley floor and by the three companies of Cooke's cavalry coming over the tops of the bluffs behind them. Heavy fighting quickly spread across the hillsides as the Indians fired from rock formations and niches in the jagged limestone in a desperate attempt to repel attackers now enveloping them from both front and rear.

The first phase of the battle was notable for its fury. The infantry, employing new, recently issued long-range rifles (U.S. Rifle-Musket Model 1855, a .58 caliber muzzle loading percussion rifle; Harney's cavalrymen were armed with the Sharps Carbine, Model 1852, a .52 caliber breech-loading percussion rifle[61]), exacted a fearful toll as targets presented themselves along the hillside and in the crags, crannies, and underbrush on the faces and tops of the bluffs. It is possible that the Indians were surprised by the range of the new weapons and underestimated the extent of their lethal fire. Heavy broadsides into the caves and twisted rocks caused horrific casualties from ricochets as well as from direct fire.

Harney placed his artillery at the south end of the battle area on a small mesa at the base of the hills where the Indians had fled. That vantage point enabled the batteries to maintain a steady fire into the caves and rake the hillsides where a rain of arrows and bullets was coming from the Indian defenders.[62]

The fight along the bluffs was short but vicious as the Indians resisted fiercely, returning the concentrated fire being poured into their lodgments. Eventually, the fire from the cavalry shooting down from the top of the hills and the increasingly heavy assault by the infantry as more and more soldiers reached the bluffs, became too severe to withstand; the intensity of the attacks coming from both the front and the rear forced the Indians to abandon their positions. They fled—desperate, headlong, and mostly unorganized—away from the hillside, racing towards and then across the creek, seeking escape through the gap area between the sand hills on the east rim of the valley.

The report of one of the infantry company commanders describes the Indians being driven initially up the hillside where "the cavalry made its appearance directly in front of them. They turned and attempted to escape by the only avenue now left open to them, a ravine in front and to my right. As they passed, from a high commanding point we poured a plunging fire on them with our long range rifles. . . The party was compact, and as one of their people fell, others jumped from their horses and picked them up, replaced or carried them off. A few moments after, the cavalry came down and our worked ceased."[63]

Sent by Cooke to "the nearest practicable descent,"[64] a company of cavalry worked its way down the hillside and charged after the fleeing Brules and Ogallalas in an all out pursuit that carried through the gap and extended several miles beyond. The company of mounted infantry that Cooke had earlier dispatched down the valley as a blocking force was hampered by terrain, spongy soil, cumbersome infantry rifles, and the lack of experienced horsemen. Those factors as well as a poor choice of position reduced their effectiveness and prevented them from completely stopping the flow of retreating Indians who were already under continuous fire from the cavalry coming down the bluffs after them and from the infantry companies shooting from vantage points on the hillsides.[65]

The infantry company sent north along the creek by Harney at the outset of the battle in an attempt to catch the Indians in the flank along their anticipated line of retreat had little success. The distance was too great for the infantry to arrive in time to seal off the escape and too far also to reach with effective rifle fire. As the battle developed and flowed past their grasp to the north, commanders concluded that any effort to use the company in pursuit would be futile.[66] The major combat on the western hillsides and along the valley floor was over by mid-morning.[67]

The cavalry company sent by Cooke formed the vanguard of the pursuit outside the valley. Those troopers were soon joined by mounted infantry and other units dispatched by General Harney from his head-quarters on a high mesa called Rattlesnake Hill, midway along the west wall of the valley. The Indians fled down the slopes, through the gap and scattered into small parties, racing in every direction through the rolling table land. Those with fresher ponies often managed to escape, although "(t)here was much slaughter in the pursuit, which extended from five to eight miles."[68]

Viewing the pursuit from Rattlesnake Hill, Harney ordered a recall, fearing that the Indians' better knowledge of the terrain might place in jeopardy small groups of cavalry involved in a chase. However, many of his horsemen were too distant to hear the bugle and it was almost midday before all returned and were accounted for. The headcount revealed that one trooper—who had probably raced too far ahead of the rest of the pursuit—was missing.[69]

Harney's after action report cited eighty-six Indians killed, six wounded and more than fifty women and children captured.[70] Sioux tradition numbers the captives at 100 or more.[71] A few days later, the bodies of several Indians were found near the banks of the Platte River along the route of the bloody retreat from the Blue Water.[72] That consideration may account for another source's placing the Indian casualties at 136 killed.[73]

According the Harney, "(t)he casualties of my command amounted to 4 killed, 4 severely wounded, 3 slightly wounded, and one missing, supposed to be killed or captured by the enemy."[74] It is possible that one of the wounded soldiers later died. A journal entry written the following year by an emigrant on a wagon train traveling through Ash Hollow states: "We passed the graves of five soldiers who were killed in September, 1855 in an action between the Sioux and U.S. soldiers."[75] Cooke's mounted force sustained the majority of Harney's casualties, a reflection of the extent of their involvement and the intensity of the combat they engaged in.

Cooke's men claimed seventy-four Indians killed (six with age unspecified), five wounded, and forty-two women and children captured. The infantry declared twelve male Indians killed and ten or twelve women and children captured. Apparent from the statistics is that most male Indians who did not break out were killed.[76] Little Thunder, though wounded, was one of those who managed to escape, as did several other chiefs including Spotted Tail and Iron Shell.[77]

Hailed as heroes in the immediate aftermath of the conflict, Harney's troops later came under criticism particularly for alleged atrocities perpetrated against Indian women and children during the course of the battle. Over time, these actions sometimes drew comparison with the infamous "Sand Creek Massacre." In that incident, on November 29, 1864, near Sand Creek, Colorado, Colonel John Chivington led a group of Colorado volunteer militia in an attack on a peaceful village of Cheyenne and Arapaho. In the resulting slaughter perhaps as many as 300 Indians were killed, the majority of them women and children.[78]

The comparison between Blue Water and Sand Creek, Harney and Chivington, has been found to be unfortunate. The actions of Harney's regular army troops on that September day in 1855 bore little resemblance to the outrages inflicted by Chivington's militia nine years later. While at Blue Water adult male Indians and often boys "fought with great ferocity (and) were given no quarter,"[79] most recent researchers have concluded that, unlike Chivington's militia, the soldiers in Harney's expedition did not deliberately attack the innocent. There were casualties among the women and children in the crags and rock formations where they had sought haven along with braves who fired from the same positions in a futile attempt to fight off attackers and protect those sheltered with them. Others occurred on the hillside during efforts to flee "when distance or strangeness of dress or the camouflage of terrain sometimes prevented recognition of sex or age differences."[80]

Cooke's report states that "in the pursuit, women if recognized were generally passed by my men but that in some instances certainly these women discharged arrows at them."[81] However, after the battle that had been waged "with such intensity and high emotion" was over, the evidence is that captured women and children were treated with consideration and the wounded among them received all the medical care the soldiers could provide. The after action report of one officer describes the attack on Indians who "found defense positions in a rotten limestone formation filled with little caves covered by underbrush, from which they directed their fire."[82] First Lieutenant (later General) Richard C. Drum later described that officer's actions :

"In passing round his line giving directions and encouraging his men in their exposed position he heard the piercing cry of a child, and at once sounded the signal to cease fire. . . . This was the first indication that the women and children were concealed in the caves and under our fire. All the male Indians had, by this time, been killed except two who, seeing the men bring their

29

pieces to an order, jumped, raced, and thus got away. As it was, we killed 12 bucks and captured all the women and children in the caves, some of them being terribly wounded."[83]

Lieutenant G. K. Warren's report corroborates Drum's account:

"I aided in bringing in the wounded women and children who were found near the place to which the Indians first fled. These had secreted themselves in holes in the rocks in which armed men also took shelter, and by firing our men caused the destruction of the women and children, whom the soldiers were unable to distinguish in the confusion and smoke. Near one of these holes, 5 men, 7 women, and 3 children were killed and several wounded."[84]

After the battle, accounts indicate that General Harney was "prompt in detailing soldiers to recover the wounded"[85] on both sides. Lieutenant Warren's private diary recounts his participation in these efforts in considerable detail.

"At this time, the recall having sounded, I went with others in search of the wounded. The sight on top of the hill was heart-rending, wounded women and children crying and moaning, horribly mangled by bullets, most of this had been occasioned by these creatures taking refuge in the holes in the rocks, and armed Indians sheltering themselves in the same places. These later fired on our men, killing 2 men and wounding another . . . Our troops then fired in upon their retreat. Two Indians were killed in the hole and 3 children, 2 of them in their mothers' arms . . .

"One young woman was wounded in the left shoulder, the ball going in above and coming out below her arm. I put her on my horse. Another handsome young squaw was wounded just below her left knee, and same bullet her baby in the right knee . . . . I had a litter made, and put her and the child on it. I found another girl about 12 years old lying with her head down in a ravine, apparently dead. Observing her breath, I had a man take her in his arms. She was shot through both feet. I found a little boy shot thru the calves of his legs and thru his arms. I took him in my arms. He had enough strength left to hold me around the neck. . .

"With this piteous load we proceeded down the hill, and placing on the bank of the stream, I made a shelter to keep off the sun, and bathed their wounds in the stream. The same office was performed for those brought in wounded by the others in the morning, one little girl shot through the right breast, a boy in the thigh, another in his arm. A poor Ogallala woman was shot badly in the shoulder by a Dragoon after the fight was over. He saw her concealed in the grass and mistook her for a man. This woman and the one I brought down the hill on my horse were in some way left behind. All the others were brought to Dr. Ridgely, and from him and his assistants received all the attention that skill and humanity could bestow. I had endeavored to draw a topographical sketch of the scene, but the cause of humanity prevented my doing much."[86]

Contemporary reports indicate that most of Harney's men were appalled by the carnage, especially that inflicted on refugees in the rock crevasses where many women and children were killed by the soldiers as they sheltered there. These deaths do not seem to have occurred "deliberately or vindictively."[87] The expedition's medical officer was officially commended for being "indefatigable in his attention to the suffering wounded, both of our troops and the enemy."[88]

Indian accounts speak of mutilations and other atrocities committed by members of Harney's force.[89] Absent any written records—none of the soldiers' private journals speak of them—they are difficult to corroborate. If any occurred, the actions of Harney's troops that day represent both the best and the worst of the 1850s frontier army.

Few sites are as mournful as a battlefield in the aftermath of the fury. The scene at Blue Water was especially poignant. In the rush to the bluffs early in the battle and during the headlong flight at its conclusion, the Indians had abandoned their possessions: buffalo skins, parfleches, cradleboards, cooked meat, robes, tepees, lodge poles, pots—all the belongings that helped bring life to what scant hours before had been a large, busy, and productive village. Dead and wounded of both sides lay fallen across the rocks, scattered over the hillsides and along the escape route east across the valley to the space between the sand hills and beyond.

After the battle, Harney established a new camp close to the battlefield, near the North Platte River on the north side. There, his exhausted men and horses returned the night of September 3. The remainder of the day was spent policing up the battlefield and bringing in the dead and wounded. That horrific task was made all the more agonizing by a severe lightning and thunderstorm that drenched the detail parties that evening. Lightning flashes amidst the driving rain of a Great Plains storm added to the macabre scene as the soldiers in jolting army wagons struggled towards the North Platte, across ground still littered with Indian dead, where they would remain unburied. According to one officer's account, some of the wagons carrying Harney's dead and wounded did not reach camp until 10 o'clock that night.[90]

Other search parties found articles that established the presence of hostiles in Little Thunder's camp and confirmed their connection with the mail train murders and other atrocities. The concluding paragraph in Harney's report to headquarters contained the following statement:

"I enclose herewith several papers found in the baggage of the Indians ... (which) may show their disposition towards the whites. They were mostly taken, as their dates and marks will indicate, on the occasion of the massacre and plunder of the mail party in November, last. There are also in possession of officers and others, in camp, the scalps to two white females, and remnants of clothing, etc., carried off by the Indians in the Grattan massacre; all of which, in my judgment, sufficiently characterize the people I have had to deal with."[91]

Captain J. B. L. Todd's journal mentions that "one of the officers cut from the ornament of one warrior three tresses of different colors, the scalps of white women murdered on the plains."[92]

* * *

More than a century and a half after it occurred, fascination with the encounter at the Blue Water continues. Present on the field of combat that day were extraordinary personalities whose names shine through the pages of America's history.

A lieutenant named John Buford commanded Company H of the Second Dragoons. Eight years later, Brigadier General Buford, the first senior Federal officer on the field, would in the face of advancing Confederate forces make the decision to fight at a place called Gettysburg—and would then hold the position until the rest of the Union Army arrived. Michael Shaara, author of *The Killer Angels* wrote that "by his part in choosing the ground and holding it (Buford) save(d) not only the battle but perhaps the war."[93]

Another officer with Harney in Nebraska on September 3, 1855, was Lieutenant G. K. Warren, the topographical engineer who drew the famous map of the Blue Water battlefield. Warren's destiny also led to Gettysburg. There, on July 2, 1863, the second day of the battle, Brigadier General Warren, serving as engineering officer for General George G. Meade (Commanding General, Army of the Potomac), discovered that Little Round Top, a key height on the Union line, had been left unoccupied. With rebel forces approaching the base of the hill, acting on his own authority, Warren "deftly diverted a nearby brigade and artillery battery to this key point and saved the situation."[94] Had the Confederates taken Little Round Top, they likely could have rolled up the Union lines along Cemetery Ridge and changed the outcome of the battle.

Late in the evening of the battle at Blue Water, a young Lakota Sioux boy seeking friends and relatives in Little Thunder's camp came upon the battlefield. The boy was somewhere between ten and thirteen years old at the time. He was slender and had surprisingly pale skin and light hair. According to Lakota lore, as the youngster rode alone across the bluffs and the valley of the Blue Water, he came across the mutilated remains of fallen Indians. Eventually, he stumbled across a woman huddled in a small gully clutching a baby that had been born that day during her flight to safety. A second child, a small boy, lie dead along the trail beside her. The boy fashioned a travois, found a buffalo robe to cover the woman and infant and set out through the torrential rain, finally finding shelter the next day in the camp of his uncle, Spotted Tail, who had been wounded in the battle.[95]

At the time, the Lakota boy was called Curly. History would later know him as Crazy Horse.

* * *

The outcome of the Battle of the Blue Water had important consequences. "So shocked was the great Sioux nation by Little Thunder's disaster that the disorganized tribesmen, some 10,000 strong,

33

remained relatively peaceful for eight years, or until the uprisings of the middle 1860s."[96] While organized opposition ended for nearly a decade, overall conditions remained unsettled.[97] Eventually, in the face of building pressures, fighting erupted again. Encounters grew in size, frequency, and violence, exploding in a major way during the Civil War before reaching a crescendo at the Little Bighorn. Harney's battle against Little Thunder on the Blue Water Creek was the beginning of that larger conflict, "ushering in over twenty years of warfare on the Plains."[98]

* * *

Little Thunder and General Harney would still recognize the battlefield where they clashed a century and a half ago. Located about two miles northwest of Lewellen on private ranchland, the landscape remains generally unchanged from that September day in 1855 except for a few utility poles and working paths. The outcropping that was the site of the parley and Rattlesnake Hill where Harney made his headquarters are clearly identifiable. The caves and crevasses along the west wall of the valley remain as rugged and inhospitable as they were when Harney's shellfire ricocheted through them. The spongy area still exists; huge, rolled hay bales are sometimes visible in the sandhills pasture along the gap where many of the Indians fled. Over the years, cartridge cases, slugs and other artifacts have been found scattered across the battlefield, evidence even today of the desperate fight that took place there.

THE BATTLE OF THE BLUE WATER

Famous map of the Blue Water battlefield drawn by Lieutenant G. K. Warren, later a hero at the Battle of Gettysburg.

35

Endnotes

1 Merrill J. Mattes, *The Great Platte River Road*, (Lincoln: The Nebraska State Historical Society, 1969) p. 516.

2 Mattes p. 311.

3 Mattes p .318.

4 *The Battle of the Blue Water*, Nebraska State Historical Society Marker 403

5 Charles M. Robinson III, *A Good Year to Die: The Story of the Great Sioux War*, (Norman and London: The University of Oklahoma Press, 1996) p. 16. See also Mattes p 328-329.

6 Mattes p. 312.

7 Mattes p. 311.

8 Mattes p. 325.

9 Alan Boye, *The Complete Roadside Guide to Nebraska*, (St. Johnsbury Vermont: Saltillo Press, 1993) p. 359.

10 Mattes p. 285.

11 Mattes p. 310.

12 Eugene F. Ware, *The Indian War of 1864*, (Lincoln: The University of Nebraska Press, 1960) p. 464.

13 Geoffrey B. Dobson, *Indian Wars, Wyoming Tales and Trails* website http://www.wyomingtalesandtrails.com/custer.html. Material extracted from website February 24, 2005.

14 Fred H. Werner, *With Harney on the Blue Water: Battle of Ash Hollow, September 3, 1855*, (Greeley, Colorado: Werner Publications, 1988) p. 14.

15 Dobson, February 24, 2005.

16 Werner p. 12.

17 Werner p. 13.

18 Werner p. 49. The accusation of Grattan's drunkenness is in Harney's biography. Harney became one of the most respected friends of the Indians and served as a member of the peace commission that brought an end to the Red Cloud War in 1868.

19 Werner p. 11-14.

20 Dobson, February 24, 2005.

21 Robinson p. 11-12.

22 Werner p. 14.

23 Mattes p. 314.

24 Boye p. 361.

25 Mattes p. 314

26 Mattes p. 313-314. Also see Werner p. 21 for a separate list of incidents.

27 Werner p. 22

28 Werner p. 22,24

29 Dobson, February 14, 2005

30 Werner p. 24-25

31 Mattes p. 313

32 Werner p. 24

33 Mattes p. 315, 316

34 Werner p. 30

35 Mattes p. 315, 316

36 Mattes p. 316

37 Mattes p. 317

38 Werner p. 31

39 Werner p. 31

40 Mattes p. 314, 315

41 Mattes p. 317

42 Mattes p. 318

43 Mattes p. 318

44 Mattes p. 318. The quote is from the journal of Lieutenant G. K. Warren, the topographical engineer who accompanied Harney's expedition.

45 Mattes p. 319

46 Mattes p. 319, 320

47 Werner p. 56-59. Official report of Lieutenant Colonel Philip St. George Cooke.

48 Mattes p. 319,320

49 Mattes p. 319

50 Mattes p. 320. The quote is from the journal of Lieutenant G. K. Warren

51 Mattes p. 320
52 Werner p. 33
53 Mattes p. 320
54 Werner p. 33, 35
55 Mattes p 321
56 Mari Sandoz. *Crazy Horse: The Strange Man of the Oglalas,* (New York: Alfred A. Knopf, 1942) p. 79, 80
57 Werner p. 34
58 Mattes p. 321
59 Ibid
60 Werner p. 56-59. Official report of Lieutenant Colonel Philip St. George Cooke.
61 Margaret A. Wagner, Editor, *The Civil War Desk Reference,* (New York: Simon & Schuster, 2002) p. 492-493, 497
62 Werner p. 37
63 Werner p. 67, 70
64 Mattes p. 323
65 Ibid
66 Mattes p. 320
67 Mattes p. 327
68 Werner p. 56-59
69 Mattes p. 324
70 Mattes p. 321
71 Sandoz p. 80. Sandoz draws on Lakota oral tradition to recite these numbers, at least some of which are suspect. In the Lakota account, one chief, Spotted Tail, is credited with slaying as many as 13 soldiers. The total army casualties during the battle were four killed and eight wounded.
72 Werner p. 39
73 Robinson p. 15
74 Werner p. 50-53. Official report of General William S. Harney
75 Mattes p. 331
76 Mattes p. 323
77 Mattes p. 328
78 R. Ernest Dupuy and Trevor N. Dupuy, *The Encyclopedia of Military History, Second Revised Edition,* (New York: Harper & Rowe, 1986) p. 868
79 Mattes p. 325
80 Mattes p. 325
81 Werner p. 56-59. Official report of Lieutenant Colonel Philip St. George Cooke
82 Mattes p. 325
83 Mattes p. 326. The quote is from a statement by Lieutenant Richard C. Drum.
84 Mattes p. 326. The quote is from a statement by Lieutenant G. K. Warren
85 Mattes p. 326
86 Mattes p. 326. The quote is from Lieutenant G. K. Warren
87 Werner p. 41
88 Mattes p. 325
89 See Sandoz p. 74-79
90 Mattes p. 328
91 Werner P. 50-53. Official report of General William S. Harney
92 Mattes p. 328
93 Michael Shaara, *The Killer Angels,* (New York: Ballantine Books, 1975) p. 354
94 Dupuy p. 868
95 Sandoz p. 68-81
96 Mattes p. 329
97 R. Eli Paul, Editor, *The Nebraska Indian Wars Reader 1865-1877,* (Lincoln and London: University of Nebraska Press, 1998) p. 3
98 Mattes p. 310

Chapter Three

PLUM CREEK MASSACRE

While not a battle in the classic sense, history has assigned an attack on a wagon train near present-day Lexington—an encounter that came to be known as the Plum Creek Massacre—a place of special significance: it was the initial engagement of the Indian War of 1864.[1]

* * *

Trouble had long been brewing. Both sides had ravaged and killed; the Indians were angered by the government's failure to enforce existing treaties and alarmed at the steady encroachment of settlers into areas that had traditionally been their own. The Plains tribes were also aware of the titanic struggle then raging in the east. The Civil War, then in its fourth year, was absorbing much of the federal government's attention and resources.* With the government's focus elsewhere, many Indian leaders concluded that the time was right for action.

In early August 1864, war parties from several tribes—Cheyennes, Arapahos, and Sioux—launched raids on a massive scale. Within forty-eight hours of the strike at Plum Creek, every stage station, wagon train, and road 'ranche'** between Julesburg, Colorado, and Fort Kearny came under attack. From the Little Blue River in Nebraska to eastern Colorado, raiders swept across the plains killing large numbers of whites and kidnapping women and children. Within days, the Indians closed the trail to Denver. Travel beyond Fort Kearny ceased.[2] On August 15, 1864, a letter from a senior officer at Fort Kearny stated: "I find the Indians at war with us the entire District. . .from the South

---

* Appendix A provides additional perspective on the Civil War and the Great Sioux Uprising.
** See Appendix B for further information on ranches, stations, camps, and forts

Pass to the Blue, a distance of 800 miles or more, and have laid waste the country. . .and murdered men, women, and children."[3]

The date cited for that pivotal attack is variously given between 6-9 August, 1864.[4] The confusion likely stems from the fact that there were an enormous number of raids clustered within this time period. The date most frequently cited, and the one included on many historical markers in the state, is August 7.[5] Details of the attack are fairly well documented, based on testimonies from a survivor, other travelers nearby on the trail, and members of a cavalry unit that came upon the scene.

The evening before the attack, groups of travelers met at Plum Creek Station and joined together to form a twelve-wagon train,[6] most or all of the wagons pulled by four mules.[7] Plum Creek, about 35 miles west of Fort Kearny, was a favored stopping place: "the first wood and water of consequence after Kearny."[8]

The bluffs near Plum Creek, however, had acquired a reputation: they were regarded as the most dangerous part of the journey; "probably more men were killed here than at any other one point along the route"[9] according to an early account. At this location, the trail left the broad, open valley and passed through a funnel, steeply walled on both sides. Nearby timber and small canyons added to the prospects for concealment.

It is possible that the Indians used the bluffs to shield their approach, but the attack itself took place on a "level bench of prairie"[10] near where the Oregon Trail crossed Plum Creek. The massacre site is east of the Plum Creek Station on the south side of the Platte River, about ten miles from present day Lexington.[11]

The wagon train left the Plum Creek rendezvous at 6 a.m.[12] and began moving west along the trail. Before mid-morning, drivers noticed objects—soon to be identified as warriors "painted and equipped for battle"[13]—approaching the train from a distance. The Indians, thought to number about 100, were Oglala Sioux later believed to have been led by Chiefs Red Cloud and Big Bear.[14] So swift was the assault that the wagon drivers had no time to form a defensive stand. The Sioux carried the attack through and around the train. A survivor describes their "wild screams and yells," the noise of their firing, and the Sioux circling "round and round which frightened our teams so they became uncontrollable."[15] It seems from the latter account that any cohesion from the assembled train was soon lost. With the wagons separated, most would likely have been surrounded and overwhelmed in isolation.

The attack was violent, bloody, and probably did not last long. Armed only with revolvers and broken up into scattered pockets, the wagon drivers' resistance was futile. Many accounts put the number killed at eleven,[16] others cite the figure as twelve,[17] or "at least twelve."[18] Given the size of the train and the fact that almost surely all the adult males were killed, the higher figure is certainly within reason. Many, if not most, were killed outright. By at least one account, some were initially captured, tortured at the scene and then killed.[19]

From Massacre Along the Medicine Road
Captive Nancy Fletcher Morton.

After pillaging and burning the wagons,[20] the Indians rode away with captives. The numbers taken vary by source: one indicates two women and two children were made prisoners.[21] Most accounts confirm the capture of one woman and a twelve-year old male child.[22]

It is the story of the woman captive—Nancy Jane Fletcher Morton, the nineteen-year old wife of Thomas Morton, who owned the train's freight wagons—that is most often cited, and hers is the best account of the attack. Nancy Morton was held prisoner by the Indians until

From Massacre Along the Medicine Road
Massacre victim Frank Morton.

41

From Massacre Along the Medicine Road
The Plum Creek Massacre site today. A common grave lies hidden in the prairie grass in the center foreground.

December, when negotiations or ransom led to her release as well as that of the twelve-year old boy.[23]

Within hours, the news of the attack was widespread. The driver of a stage coach fleeing to the east shouted to travelers moving west up the trail after the wagon train, that "there were ten or twelve dead men lying in the road a little way (ahead)."[24] Soon after, a cavalry patrol from Fort McPherson raced along the trail and relayed a similar report.[25]

The Indians did not cut the telegraph lines and the presence of a telegraph station near Plum Creek enabled the word of the massacre to be rapidly sent up and down the trail. Quick reporting undoubtedly saved many lives. Although stations and road ranches between Julesburg and Fort Kearny would soon be attacked, because of the forewarning few lives were initially lost.[26]

Many more—on both sides—would be killed in the days ahead.

Several ranchers were soon slain, most of them as they worked away from the protection of ranch buildings. In September, men were killed while working at a nearby farm. At about the same time, soldiers from Fort McPherson on a work detail were surprised by Indians and "a number were killed and scalped."[27]

Several stage stations were burned to the ground. Frequent attacks on coaches and wagon trains continued all along the trail. For a time, mail delivery was disrupted, and when it did occur was made possible only in the presence of strong escorts. Wagon trains were held at Fort Kearny and released for travel only when military protection was available and/or the size of a combined train—often a hundred wagons or more—was sufficient to provide security. Some wagon masters began planning and rehearsing defensive procedures: "By pre-concerted arrangements, the wagons could, at the very first alarm, be placed in such a position as to form a perfect barricade. . . ."[28]

Initially, prices west along the route were pushed sky-high as the flood of goods was shut down. Eventually, precautions such as the wagon master described took effect and travel resumed, albeit warily, along the trail.

The hostilities that began with the massacre at Plum Creek would rage on for five long years. Finally, on July 11, 1869, Brevet Major General E. A. Carr, commanding a contingent of the Fifth U.S. Cavalry—aided immeasurably by the presence of 50 Pawnee Scouts led by Major Frank North,[29] and by the scouting of William F. Cody—inflicted a major defeat on the Indians near Summit Springs, Colorado.[30]

For a few years after Summit Springs, the frontier remained uneasily quiet. The period of relative tranquility lasted until 1876 when the discovery of gold in the Black Hills led to the outbreak of another war as prospectors flooded into the area reserved by treaty for the Indians.

* * *

About ten miles south of Lexington, near a small glen of trees surrounded by farm land, a marker commemorates the Plum Creek episode. The actual site—situated amid cornfields and other cropland —is a mile and a half east. Located on a "perfectly level tract," it is a mile from the stream that gave name to the massacre that began the Great Sioux Uprising.

Endnotes

1 Numerous sources attribute the attack as initiating hostilities in the war that followed: H.W. Foght, *The Trail of the Loup*, (Ord, Nebraska, 1906) p. 40; *Indian Troubles*, Andreas' History of the State of Nebraska—Lincoln County, Part 2 website www.kancoll.org/books/landreas_ne/ lincoln/lincoln- p.2. html, material extracted from website April 9, 2005; Phelps County History, website www.phelpsgov.org/about/history.htm, material extracted from website September 13, 2005.

2 James C. Olson and Ronald C. Naugle, *History of Nebraska*, (Lincoln and London: University of Nebraska Press, 1997) p. 135

3 Robert R. Manley, *Platte Valley Chronicles*, (Grand Island: Hall County Historical Society, 2001) p. 234

4 The earliest date, 6 August, is in History of the Project Area, website www.cnppd.com/History_ Central_P2.htm. Among many other sources, 7 August is cited as the date in Andreas' *History of the State of Nebraska-Dawson County* and in *Phelps County History*. August 9 is used by Frederick C. Luebke, *Nebraska: An Illustrated History*, (Lincoln and London: University of Nebraska Press, 1995) p. 75. Foght, in *The Trail of the Loup*, uses August 17 for the date of the attack, but this is surely incorrect or misprinted.

5 Among many other references, August 8 is cited in *Site of the Plum Creek Massacre*, Nebraska History and Record of Pioneer Days website www.rootsweb.com/~neresour/OLLi-brary/Journals/HPR/Vol05/nhrv05p6.html, Andreas' History of the State of Nebraska-Lincoln County, Part 2, and Merrill J.Mattes, *The Great Platte River Road*, (Lincoln: The Nebraska State Historical Society, 1969). The marker at the massacre site also uses the August 8 date (see website www.rootsweb.com/~nephelps/plum.html).

6 *The Plum Creek Massacre as told by Mrs. Thomas F. Morton*, Phelps County History website www.phelpsgov.org/about/history.htm. Material extracted from website September 28, 2005.

7 *Site of Plum Creek Massacre*, Nebraska History and Record of Pioneer Days website www. rootsweb.com/~neresour/OLLibrary/Journals/HPR/Vol05/nhrv05p6.html. Material extracted from website September 28, 2005

8 See discussion of the unique importantance of the Plum Creek location in Merrill J. Matthes, The Great Platte River Road, (Lincoln: The State Historical Society, 1969) p. 273-280.

9 Andreas' History of the State of Nebraska—Dawson County. Material extracted from website September 28, 2005

10 *Site of the Plum Creek Massacre*, Nebraska History and Record of Pioneer Days website.

11 Ibid.

12 *The Plum Creek Massacre as told by Mrs. Thomas F. Morton*, Phelps County History website

13 Ibid.

14 *Plum Creek Massacre*, Bertrand, Nebraska Website www.ci.bertrand.ne.us/tour.htm. Material extracted from website September 28, 2005.

15 *The Plum Creek Massacre as told by Mrs. Thomas F. Morton*, Phelps County History website

16 Eleven fatalities are cited in Andreas's *History of the State of Nebraska-Dawson County* and by Foght in *The Trail of the Loup* (p.40). The fewest fatalities mentioned by any source are nine, given in *History in the Project Area*.

17 *Site of the Plum Creek Massacre*, Nebraska History and Record of Pioneer Days. This source identifies those slain as "Frank Morton, owner of the outfit, of Sidney, Iowa, and ten white men drivers, and a colored cook." Gregory F. Michno also cites 12 in his book *Encyclopedia of Indian Wars*.

18 Frederick C. Luebke, *Nebraska: An Illustrated History* (Lincoln: and London: University of Nebraska Press, 1995) p. 75. See also www.rootsweb.com/~neresour/OLLibrary/collections/ vol19/v19p001.htm

19 *Plum Creek Massacre*, Phelps County, Nebraska. Website www.rootsweb.com/~nephelps/ plum.html. Material extracted from website September 28, 2005.

20 Andreas' *History of the State of Nebraska-Dawson County* website

21 *History in the Project Area* website

22 *Plum Creek Massacre, Phelps County, Nebraska* Phelps County Website

23 Luebke p. 75. The male child's name is most often given as Danny Marble. See also www. forttours.com/pages/plumcreek. Material extracted from website May 17, 2007.

24 *Site of the Plum Creek Massacre*, Nebraska History and Record of Pioneer Days website

25 Ibid.

26 Among many sources citing the importance of the rapid notification by telegraph are Andreas' *History of the State of Nebraska-Lincoln County* and Foght in *The Trail of the Loup*, Chapter Two.

27 Andreas' *History of the State of Nebraska-Lincoln County* website.

28 Andreas' *History of the State of Nebraska-Dawson County* website

29 James T. King, *The Republican River Expedition*, June-July 1869. I. On the March, Nebraska History, Volume 41, September 1960, p. 199

30 Foght, *The Trail of the Loup*, Chapter Two

TERROR ACROSS THE PLAINS: THE GUNS OF AUGUST (1864)

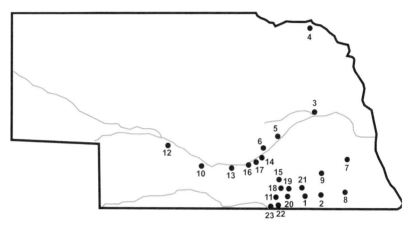

1. Thayer County Raids, Thayer County
2. Jefferson County Raids, Jefferson County
3. Stampede Through Columbus Columbus, Platte County
4. "The Great Stampede:" Cedar County
5. Desolation at Lone Tree Ranch, Merrick County
6. Grand Island Mobilizes for Battle Grand Island, Hall County
7. Yankee Hill Militia, Lancaster County
8. Gage County Scare, Beatrice and Gage County
9. Flight from Saline County, Saline County
10. Attack on Wagon Train 2 W of Plum Creek Stage Station
11. Attack on Oak Grove Ranch North of Nelson, Nuckolls County
12. Attack on Gillette's Ranch East of Fort McPherson
13. The Saga of Hopeville Ranch 18 W of Fort Kearny
14. Attack on Martin Ranch 18 S of Grand Island
15. The Fight at Pawnee Ranch SW corner of Clay County
16. Deaths along the Trail 15—20 E of Fort Kearny
17. Wagon Train Ambush E of Fort Kearny
18. Deaths near Pawnee Ranch SW corner of Clay County
19. Destruction of Constable Wagon Train, Little Blue Ranch 4 NW of Oak, Nuckolls County
20. Massacre of Eubanks Family 4 W of Oak Creek Ranch, Nuckolls County
21. Deaths near Kiowa Station 10 NW of Hebron
22. Deaths near Oak Grove Ranch 2 S of Oak Grove Ranch, Nuckolls County
23. Battle of the Little Blue Little Blue—Elk Creek area and beyond toward Republican River

** All incidents occurred early- to mid-August; most took place during the period 7/8—15 August. The Battle of the Little Blue was fought on August 15. While attacks also took place along Nebraska's western portion of the trail—indeed, at one point the route was said to have been shut down from Denver to the Little Blue—these incidents tended to be less well documented, perhaps due to the sparse early population and to the fact that many western counties were not yet organized. The encounters listed here are attested to in early histories or pioneer diaries.

Chapter Four

Terror across the Plains:
The Guns of August (1864)

ugust 1864 probably comes as close to total war as most Nebraskans past or present have ever experienced. In the days following the massacre at Plum Creek, violence exploded along the frontier. For distances stretching hundreds of miles, dwellings were attacked and burned, possessions destroyed, and the most savage tortures inflicted upon the victims. The total death count will likely never be known, but along the Little Blue River alone—the scene of particularly severe attacks—100 or more people were killed.[1] Entire counties were emptied of population and masses of refugees, wagons crammed with possessions, fled eastward in streams that sometimes reached several miles in length. For a time, the violence was so widespread and the situation so dangerous that travel along the trail was virtually halted.[2]

* * *

The extent and ferocity of the attacks, and the devastation that accompanied them, is apparent in descriptions drawn from the early histories of Nebraska's frontier counties.

Thayer County The *Hebron Journal* newspaper describes the aftermath of the first attacks: "At morn, the Government road was a traveled thoroughfare, dotted with prosperous and happy homes; at night, a wilderness, strewn with mangled bodies and wrecks, and illuminated with the glare of burning homes."

Jefferson County "Every ranch along the route (Overland Trail) except Pawnee Ranch at Big Sandy, was burned and the (residents) killed that could not make their escape." Accounts describe the Indians visiting ranches and stations "as they were in the habit of doing," and then "without the slightest warning they began shooting down the defenseless victims, mutilating their bodies, burning their homes, and carrying away what they could. . . ."

Phelps County: Stampede through Columbus

As the uprising emptied whole settlements, farms, and ranches, settlers fled in panic in the face of attacks that blanketed the region. The chaotic situation at Columbus, described below, was repeated in many of the small communities that dotted Nebraska Territory.

"The stampede from Wood River began to cross the Loup and pour down the valley into and much of it onward through Columbus. The whole county (i.e., Platte) was wild with alarm. The settlers came pouring in that evening. By next day it was a sight strange and painful, indeed, for hither came nearly every living being and thing—men, women, and children, with food and bed, cattle and horses—pell-mell, crawling into the little village and filling every square yard of space in the buildings, and in the gardens and streets. That day, an organization of Home Guards was (formed). . . ."

Cedar County: "The Great Stampede"

"In the year 1864, occurred what is called the great stampede. The Sioux, Cheyennes and other hostile tribes threatened the annihilation of the frontier settlements. Almost the entire population of the counties lying west of Cedar was fleeing before a supposed pursuing body of 10,000 warlike Indians. The settlers of Cedar County hastily consulted among themselves and decided to remain and defend themselves as best they could. At St. James, a fortification 100 feet square with an embankment nine feet high around the courthouse was constructed. The inhabitants of St. Helena also fortified themselves, four families in number, reinforced by quite a number of Norwegian families from across the Missouri River in Dakota. Thus they awaited an expected attack by Indians. . . .Portions of the Seventh Iowa Cavalry were stationed at St. Helena and the company remained about a year. . . ."

Merrick County: Desolation at Lone Tree Ranch

For a time during and after the August attacks, three men at Lone Tree Ranch in Merrick County were thought to be the only white population that remained between there and Central City. "Farms were abandoned and implements of agriculture left to rust and destruction. Only the more valuable varieties of stock were taken, such as horses and cattle; hogs and cats were turned loose to shift for themselves."

Hall County: Grand Island Mobilizes for War

As word of Plum Creek and other atrocities spread, settler families fled along the trail. One pioneer history recalls that by August 13 and 14, one continuous stream of wagons nearly twenty miles long passed through Grand Island.

Although the Platte Valley was virtually deserted, a few residents of Grand Island remained, determined to add to existing fortifications and resist an attack. Thirty-five persons gathered at the residence of a townsman named Stolley. Along the walls of his twenty-four-foot square house, Stolley had built twenty-five port holes that provided firing positions from inside the single, large room. A militia unit was organized and the members quickly busied themselves fortifying a large cattle yard, digging a well, and excavating an underground stable for horses.

A short distance away, another group decided to build fortifications around the "O.K. Store." (The location is about one and a half miles from the present courthouse.) Sod breastworks were put up around several buildings and "towers of green cottonwood logs" were erected at each corner. Sixty-eight men and 100 women and children clustered inside the barricades. Scouts were sent out daily and straw and brush piles—to be used as alarm fires—were placed at key locations. A requisition for munitions was quickly made to the territorial governor, but the arms were late in arriving and when they did reach the settlement, only seventeen weapons were provided.

On August 22, General Samuel R. Curtis arrived in Grand Island with a regiment of cavalry and a 10-pounder cannon. Deciding that the town was no longer under immediate threat, Curtis hurried on to Ft. Kearny but left the cannon at Grand Island to add to the settlers' arsenal.

Lancaster County Militia

Except for lethal flare-ups with Pawnees in 1858 and 1859, settlers in Lancaster County were generally spared the larger bloodshed that Nebraskans farther west were sometimes subjected to. However, the effects of fighting elsewhere in the state influenced the lives of Lancaster residents in the most profound ways. As with many counties in eastern Nebraska, refugees from the 1864 uprising flooded through the area. Although many remained, a considerable number of Lancaster settler families also took flight to the Missouri River. Those who stayed were promised by a small militia force at Yankee Hill that they would be warned in time if war parties were sighted.

Gage County

In normal times, Indian scares were rare for residents of Gage County in southeastern Nebraska. The Plum Creek Massacre and the massive uprising that followed changed all that. Streams of settler families fleeing the killing raids on the Upper Blue, Big Sandy, and Little Blue hurried into the county. For several days the refugees formed a large corral around an abandoned mill and prepared to defend themselves.

Meanwhile, fearing the possibility of a large attack if they took no action, on August 12, men from Gage County and settlers who had lost their homes formed a militia company and went west to meet the Sioux and Arapahos who were raiding down the Little Blue River. On August 14, at Little Blue Station, they combined with Company A of the Seventh Iowa Cavalry and soon fought a large party of Indians at the "Battle of the Little Blue."

Flight from Saline County

From an early pioneer diary: "The Sioux were the most alarming to the settlers. Their hostilities to white settlers were well understood and instances of their atrocities upon them were well known. . . .Settlers soon learned to dread the name 'Sioux'. . . .(Settlers) knew not when they might be made the victims of their savage treachery. So powerfully were they impressed with the feeling of fear, that upon the slightest alarm, they were ready for flight."

In Saline County, scares had been frequent all through the summer of 1864. During mid-year an incident that came to be known as the "Big Scare" or the "Tucker Scare" occurred when a settler by that name mistook a small band of friendly Omahas for a Sioux war party. In the ensuing panic, "the entire county was deserted, not a solitary settler remained."

In August 1864, when the alarm sounded that the Sioux were raiding the settlements, "the people fled for refuge and the county was almost deserted, only one or two families being left, and that happened on account of their living a distance from anyone else and (knowing) nothing of the scare. . . ."

* * *

The Plum Creek Massacre was only the first of several attacks that took place on August 7 and the days immediately following. Wagon trains, stage coaches, ranches, and farms were all ravaged in an onslaught whose fury for a brief but bloody time went unchecked.

August 7: Attack on Wagon Train near Plum Creek

Only a short distance from the site of the Plum Creek Massacre, Cheyennes attacked a second train as it was breaking camp that same morning.

Matt Bowler's "bull train" was corralled two miles west of Plum Creek stage station on the south side of the Platte River when, without warning, Cheyennes rode into the circled wagons. Though wounded, a young "bull whacker" named William Gay fired at the raiders, thus alerting his comrades. Amidst heavy shooting, the teamsters managed to repel the attack, driving the Indians out of the corral and away from the wagons. "After circling a few times, the Cheyennes disappeared, leaving behind two of their own dead and three wounded teamsters."

August 7: Attack on Oak Grove Ranch (Nuckolls County)

On August 8 (the date used on Nebraska State historical markers; many local accounts place it as August 7), the Oak Grove Ranch north of Nelson was assaulted by a war party of forty Indians. Local lore says that the ranch was "the only place in Nuckolls County that held out against the Indians." The well-fortified ranch was defended by members of the Comstock family, aided by an additional five or six men who were positioned in the house and around the stockade.

The struggle began at mid-day when several Indians came to the compound under the pretext of friendship. After receiving a meal, tobacco, and other gifts provided by the Comstock family, the attack began unexpectedly. Among the several immediate casualties was a man named W. R. Kelley (or Kelly) from Beatrice, a guest at the ranch who was killed by a volley of arrows soon after the fighting began. In the ensuing scramble to retrieve Kelley's revolver, the race was won by one of Comstock's young sons who used it to kill three Indians before they could flee through the door. Brisk shooting from behind the barricades kept the Indians at bay through the remainder of the day—"they circled around the premises until after dark, shooting and yelling"—and prevented them from setting fire to the house. Kelley and one other person at the ranch, another guest named M. C. Butler, were killed outright. A third, Nelson Oberstrander (or Ostrander) later died of his injuries. Two other participants recovered from wounds suffered during the fight.

August 7: Attack on Gillette's Ranch

East of Fort McPherson, two brothers were killed during the early stage of the uprising when they ventured away from the ranch buildings. Soon after, their father was killed as he was looking for them.

At about the same time, at least one man was known to have been slain while working in a hay field near the fort. An old settler named Bob Carson was also killed nearby in the initial attacks.

August 7: Attack on Fred Smith's Ranch

Nine miles from Plum Creek, a hired man at Fred Smith's ranch was killed when sixteen Indians attacked the place. Smith's store was burned and his stock was driven off.

The Saga of the Hopeville Ranch

An early pioneer, an eccentric named Moses Sydenham, settled in the area in 1856 and eventually established a ranch, store, and post office at a place on the trail named Hopeville, about eighteen miles west of Ft. Kearny in Phelps County. After the massacre at Plum Creek, fears of further attacks prompted settlers to flee to the east, leaving the Platte Valley nearly deserted. Sydenham, however, remained. He took his family and many of his possessions to islands in the Platte River and concealed people and valuables in the thick brush. He and his brother stayed at the fortified ranch, raising the American flag to leave the impression that soldiers were present there. After a time,

Sydenham took his family to Fort Kearny. During the entire course of the war, the Hopeville ranch was never attacked.

Conditions were not as peaceful through the rest of Phelps County. A pioneer cemetery contains the remains of fourteen people killed in the 1864 uprising. One grave is that of a woman killed during an attack on an emigrant train. Diaries also describe a separate attack near the border of Phelps and Gosper counties against three brothers and a sister from the Fletcher family.

Attack at Martin Ranch

Sometime in early August, a harrowing incident occurred near the ranch of George Martin, about eighteen miles southwest of Grand Island. Two of Martin's small sons, riding a single pony, were away from the ranch house tending a herd of about 100 cattle. From a distance, the boys saw a large band of Indians charging towards them. Quickly jumping on the pony, they attempted to drive the cattle back to the ranch. The Indians gave chase and in the midst of their furious attack, an arrow struck the boys with such force that it pinned them together. Somehow, they managed to cling to the horse and race toward the fortified ranch, reaching the area of the house just moments ahead of Indians who attempted to scalp them. Exhausted and bleeding, they tumbled from their horse and lay stunned and bleeding on the ground. Rapid fire from the ranch buildings wounded one Indian and several of the raiders' ponies, eventually driving off the attackers who took with them many of Martin's horses and cattle. The boys recovered from their wounds.

The Fight at Pawnee Ranch (Clay County)

Early in 1864, a settler named James Bainter took the first homestead in Clay County. Bainter's choice of location, called Spring Ranche, placed his home on the overland stage route, and, as it turned out, in the middle of the massive uprising that began on August 7.

Soon after, Pawnee Indian friends of Bainter came to warn him that Sioux were attacking the ranch nearest west of his and were on the move towards his. Bainter sent his family to the Pawnee Ranch, about a mile east of his own property. Seeking to delay the oncoming Sioux, he then took his fastest horse and rode to meet them. Bainter found the war party about nine miles north along the Platte River. After firing several shots at them at long range, he raced back to his homestead, turned his stock loose and rode to join his family at Pawnee Ranch. From there, he watched the smoke rise from his burning house, stable, and the small store and inn he ran to serve travelers along the trail. Then, Bainter, and others with him—three men, along with several women and children—readied themselves for the Sioux attack.

They did not have long to wait. Soon 150—200 Sioux warriors approached the Pawnee ranch site. Inside the ranch—"a sod building with palisades around it"—Bainter and his companions fought the Indians for three days, keeping them at bay, assisted by the women who loaded weapons and served as lookouts. Finally, Bainter killed a Sioux chief and the Indians withdrew a short distance from the buildings. Not long after, a large band of Pawnee Indians, friendly toward Bainter, arrived at the ranch and assisted in driving the Sioux away.

"The Sioux soon attacked all the ranches along the Little Blue and Bainter and all the settlers were driven out; a large number of settlers and nearly all stage-drivers were killed; also one wagon train of nearly sixty persons was slaughtered." The latter account, from an early frontier history, may refer to the Constable Train discussed in the "Battle of the Little Blue" section. Not all of the material associated with the event, or the numbers cited for it, can be corroborated.

* * *

Captain Murphy's Armed Reconnaissance/Massacres along the Trail/Battle of the Little Blue

Hints of trouble about to come had prompted the military to begin moving some units toward the trail even before the shooting war began. On July 19, Captain Edward B. Murphy received orders to move his unit from its post at Dakota City through Omaha to Fort Kearny. Leaving Omaha on July 24, Murphy began the journey to Fort Kearny that would soon place him and his men in the midst of the biggest battle fought in the early stage of the great uprising.

Shortly after Murphy's company arrived at Fort Kearny, reports came in that "every ranch and stage station between (the fort) and Big Sandy Creek was burned." Murphy was ordered to take his unit east along the Overland stage road to Big Sandy Creek to determine if the reports were correct "and fight Indians if compelled to do so." Company A drew ten days' rations, 100 rounds of ammunition per carbine and pistol, and left immediately. Murphy reports taking two pieces of artillery with him, "to be filled with spherical case grape and canister," but only one cannon is mentioned in reports of the battle that followed a few days later. Murphy left after dinner on August 12 with 125 men. Eight miles to the east his path intersected with a company of soldiers headed towards the fort. Murphy selected twenty of the best men from the west-bound company and added them to his own unit. Murphy's force camped that night at a stage station about fifteen miles down the trail. Immediately, reports began to come in alerting him to atrocities committed nearby along the route, most likely during the attacks on August 7. One of the first accounts spoke of three settlers killed at a ranch five miles away.

The following day, August 13, as they moved east along the trail, the company came upon a place where an eight-wagon train had been ambushed. Apparently taken by surprise as the wagons were being hitched, the teamsters had not had time to form a corral. The soldiers found eight bodies. All had been scalped. All had been dead for several days. The Indians had taken stock, weapons, and ammunition.

After burying those killed in the attack, Company A left for Pawnee Ranch, the next station east along the trail. When they reached the ranch, located at the mouth of Pawnee Creek about fifty-four miles from Fort Kearny in the southwest corner of Clay County, they found it "pierced with bullets" and wagon loads of goods, strewn across the premises. The chaotic scene was the aftermath of the fight at the ranch, where for three days James Bainter and others had held off the Sioux.

Murphy put out strong guards that night, rotating his men, keeping half the company on guard and letting half sleep at nay one time, with "everything arranged in case of a night attack." Throughout the night, the camp drew harassing fire from a large group of Indians, whose actions were obviously intended to keep the main body of hostiles informed regarding the location of the soldiers.

As Murphy and his men rested at the ranch the following day, lookouts spotted several men approaching the compound. Murphy sent a scout party with a guidon to meet the group, who turned out to be a volunteer company of thirty-four men from Beatrice who had come west on their own initiative to help in the struggle. The Beatrice company had left the Big Sandy on August 12. They arrived at Pawnee Ranch on August 14, reporting that "all the principal places between Hackney Ranch (five miles east of Kiowa Station, just west of the present boundary line between Thayer and Nuckolls counties) and Pawnee burned except Little Blue Station. . . ."

Murphy welcomed their assistance and asked the volunteers to clean their weapons and check their ammunition and other gear in preparation for a clash that seemed imminent. Later, somewhere around the ranch, a cache of .36 caliber revolvers and ammunition was found, enabling everyone under Murphy's command to carry three loaded weapons into the fight.

Murphy learned from the Beatrice company that a large train of perhaps 200 wagons mainly out of St. Joseph, Missouri, had been destroyed a short distance away with goods and cattle taken. The wagon master, George Constable, had joined the militia group and reported the presence of a large Indian camp eight miles south of the Little Blue where the goods and cattle stolen from the train were thought to be located.

Soon after, Murphy sent the militia company temporarily ahead, while soldiers scouted and cleared the immediate area around the ranch. After directing the volunteers to stay within a "reasonable distance" and to put two flankers ahead and two on each side, Murphy's men scoured the immediate area, and were delayed for a time when they found three bodies in the weeds near a burned-out ranch. The soldiers halted to bury the remains, which had been scalped and were badly decomposed.

After rejoining the militia company, the combined force continued east, moving past a burned-out stage coach, a stage station in ruins, and four ranches burned to the ground. All through the day, they were tracked by a large party of Indians who sent smoke signals to identify the soldiers' location.

In the afternoon, Murphy's company came to the Little Blue Ranch, about four miles northwest of present-day Oak, Nebraska, in Nuckolls County. Here was where George Constable's large wagon train had been corralled when it came under attack. The troops found a scene of total devastation: boxes, barrels, sacks, boots, shoes, and clothing were scattered across the grounds. Many wagons had been burned. The train carried two hundred barrels of various kinds of liquors, a large amount of which the Indians had sampled and taken. Early arriving members of the militia company imbibed in the substantial quantity that remained. As Captain Murphy reported "some of the militia boys were dry when they got there and took a little too much." Worrying that they would be in no condition to fight, Murphy put a guard over the whiskey. Later, after giving ten gallons to the company doctor for treatment of wounds and sickness, wagon master Constable split the barrels and poured the remaining amount on the ground.

At Little Blue Ranch, Murphy was told that at the next ranch east, three women had been taken captive, and that six people including two children, had been killed. Murphy sent Captain Henry Kuhl with fifty men to investigate and bury the dead. With Indians nearby in large numbers, Murphy told Kuhl "not to bring on a fight. . .only so far as to carry out his instructions to bury the dead, and if he could not to come back and report. . . ."

Kuhl, accompanied by a detail from the Beatrice militia, went to a farm about four miles west of the Oak Grove Ranch, where two generations of the Eubanks (or Eubank or Ubanks in other spellings) were known to reside. Finding Indians there in force, the soldiers drove a war party across the Little Blue and began to search the area. Kuhl's men found several bodies that "were a terrible sight to behold. They were all scalped, their bodies naked, and their bowels cut open." Apparently killed at the time of the initial violence several days earlier, the remains were badly decomposed.

The location of the slain, and their circumstances, vary in the telling, but a credible early account asserts that the elder Eubanks and a twelve-year old son were killed three quarters of a mile southeast of present-day Oak. Eubanks' oldest son, William, and William's little boy were killed at the Eubanks home, located near "the Narrows," one and a half miles northwest of Oak. (The Narrows drew its name from a projection on a bluff on the east side of the Little Blue River that protruded so far that it left only a narrow space for the trail.)

William, his wife, and child were said by a survivor (Laura Roper, a guest at the house who was taken captive and later ransomed by the Indians) to have been gone when the initial raid occurred. A 17-year-old Eubanks daughter was home alone and was accidentally killed by the raiders while attempting to escape. When William Eubanks and his family returned, William was immediately attacked. Badly wounded, he attempted to flee but died on a sand bar in the river where he had sought refuge. By some accounts, William's infant son was killed with

From Massacre Along the Medicine Road

Laura Roper and three children pose for a photo after being released by their Indian captors. Laura is holding Isabella Eubank. The boy on the left probably is Ambrose Asher. The boy on the right is Danny Marble.

a tomahawk as he cried out while his mother was being taken into captivity.

The bodies of two more, the elder Eubanks' sons, Joe and Fred, were located near Kiowa Station. Fred's body was found south of the station across the river. He had been scalped while raking hay. Joe Eubanks had been shot with arrows while looking for a place to mow. His remains were found later, east of the Kiowa dwellings.

As the search continued, information about additional killings was soon forthcoming. News of the two men killed at Oak Grove Ranch, Kelley and Butler, reached Kuhl or Murphy. It is likely that they learned of the death of Theodore Ulich (or Ulig), a boy of about seventeen, who was killed a mile and a half northwest of Kiowa Station. (The station itself was about ten miles northwest of Hebron.) The boy had been sent by his mother to get eggs at the station. About 400 yards from his home, he was halted by four Indians who shot him with arrows and guns.

Further information revealed that a settler named William Bowie had been killed about two miles south of Oak Grove Ranch. George Hunt, another early settler, was known to have been wounded by a rifle ball in one of the first attacks, but had managed to make his way to safety.

Most versions identify the females captured at the Eubanks farm as Mrs. William Eubanks, her infant daughter Isabella, and Laura Roper, aged 15, a guest of the Eubanks at the time of the attack. The captives were later ransomed and exchanged.[3] Ironically, Laura Roper's distraught father was a member of the Beatrice volunteer contingent. Daniel Freeman, known in American history as the first person to receive a homestead claim, was also a member of the Beatrice unit.

Kuhl's report to Murphy confirmed the scope of the attacks. That night, Murphy again posted a guard around the campsite. Once more the Indians maintained a persistent sniping, firing from behind trees and mounds. In the morning, Murphy's lookouts thought they counted about 400 hostiles before the Indians broke away to the south to join the main body of Indians in a major feast of beef, groceries, and liquor taken from looted wagon trains.

Through the morning of August 15, Murphy moved Company A and the Beatrice militia, consisting of a combined total strength of about 175 men, south toward the Republican River. At Elk Creek, finding a bridge down and unable to move their wagon across the stream, they were delayed momentarily until a Beatrice volunteer showed them a dry ford, three or four miles from present-day Nelson. Not long after Murphy's men crossed the creek, they came upon a large party of Indians, thought to be Sioux and Arapahos, "near where the Fort Riley Road crosses Elk Creek about ten miles from Little Blue Station."

Captain Murphy organized his unit for battle, keeping most of his regulars together in a compact group, ready to move in force where the need was greatest. Murphy formed the Beatrice militia into a skirmish line placing two men together with each pair separated from the rest by several yards. When preparations were complete, Murphy ordered an attack. One shot was fired from the cannon as Murphy's men advanced, but—apparently because the weapon had been elevated too much—the timbers were broken and the cannon could not be used again.

The initial attack, made against a force of about 250-300 Indians, drove the hostiles back about six to eight miles. As the advance continued, losses were taken on both sides. George Constable, the wagon master, was wounded during the push. Isolated at the end of the skirmish line, he was cut off and wounded "on the side high up." Heavy firing commenced from nearby militia and soldiers, and Captain Murphy sent the main body of troops to clear the area, forcing the Indians back.

With the cannon disabled and a larger body of Indians visible in the distance moving towards them, Murphy ordered a halt. The command was turned around and a "retreat was made in good order." Several hundred Indians followed, sniping persistently with occasional spasms of heavy fire until the group reached Elk Creek. Militia and regulars formed a rear guard that kept the attackers at bay—"we shot at Indians until it was too dark to see them"—although some horses were wounded as the group fell back. Murphy pushed his men past Elk Creek and on to Little Blue Station where they camped for the night.

Company A and the Beatrice volunteers were joined at the station by one full regiment of the Kansas Militia. The presence of the regiment—the Indians would have seen them on the move from Marshall, Kansas—may be one reason (substantial losses may be another) that the Indians broke off the raid, and "did not bother (the settlements in that area) any more for quite some time."

In a succinct after action report sent to General Curtis, Commander of the District of Kansas, General Robert R. Mitchell, Commander of the Military District of Nebraska, stated:

> "Captain Murphy has just returned from the Blue. Undertook to go from the Blue to the Republican. Got as far as Elk Creek. Met 500 well-armed Indians; had a fight; killed 10 Indians and lost two soldiers. Was compelled to fall back after driving Indians 10 miles. Indians followed him 30 miles in his retreat."

The fight has come to be known as the "Battle of the Little Blue," although, as General Mitchell's report indicates, the heaviest clash occurred nearer Elk Creek. The flow of the battle then took the fighting several miles toward the Republican River, then back again across Elk Creek and beyond as Captain Murphy withdrew his force.

Mitchell's report cites two soldier losses and puts the Indian casualties at ten killed. Some estimates are higher. Mitchell does not mention three lost from the volunteer force, including two from Beatrice who were known casualties.

The next day at Little Blue Station, with the Kansas Militia present and no visible activity on the part of the Indians, Captain Murphy returned to Fort Kearny with Company A and the Beatrice volunteers went home.

Although scattered attacks would continue in the months and years ahead, the effect of the battle was to diminish the immediate threat to the most vulnerable settlements in Jefferson, Thayer, Nuckolls, Clay, and Fillmore counties.

* * *

The government responded quickly to the killings and devastation along hundreds of miles of territory. Supplementing the tiny existing garrisons with local volunteer units and additional forces brought into the region, the army began gearing up for the long, difficult conflict ahead.

The fighting that began at Plum Creek would rage for five more years until a force under the command of General Eugene A. Carr defeated the Indians decisively at Summit Springs, Colorado. In the months ahead, the fighting was persistent and sometimes heavy, but in Nebraska it was seldom more intense than during the bloody August 1864.

* * *

Even today the wisdom of the trailblazers who first moved through the valley of the Platte remains evident. The routes traveled by the transcontinental railroad and Interstate 80 mirror to a remarkable degree the path taken by the frontiersmen who explored and developed the overland trail.

Where in August 1864 embattled ranches, stage and pony express stations faced the onslaught of rampaging Sioux, Cheyennes, and Arapahos, some of Nebraska's most fascinating cities now stand, sparkling along the Platte like pearls on a necklace strung east to west across the state: Grand Island, Kearney, Lexington, Cozad, Gothenburg, North Platte, and then as the river divides, Ogallala to the south

From Massacre Along the Medicine Road
Laura Roper Vance returns to The Narrows in 1929, the site of her capture in 1864.

and Scottsbluff along the North Platte. All are fastened to the river, owing their existence to it and to the commerce brought by travelers along the trail beside it. Some of those travelers made the choice to stay, settling on acres of the world's most fertile soil and, near the sandhills, ranch country made ideal by plentiful grass and water.

Several historical markers along the Great Platte River Road identify key events and locations from the 1864 struggles. Plaques describe the 1864 Indian Raids and The Great Platte River Road itself. Others discuss Fort Kearny, Fort McPherson, Spring Ranche (where James Bainter's home, store, and inn were burned), and the O.K. Store in Grand Island. The assault on the young Martin brothers is commemorated, as is the captive saga of Laura Roper and members of the Eubanks family. The site of the Battle of the Little Blue is not marked.

Some locations, including Kearney, Gothenburg, and Minden ("Pioneer Village") have preserved original stage or Pony Express stations from the 1864 era.

Endnotes

1 www. nebraskahistory.org/publish/markers/texts/1864_indians_raids.htm. Material extracted from website June 12, 2007

2 Unless otherwise indicated, material in this section was assembled from the following sources: www. fortours.com/pages/plumcreekneb.asp (Material extracted June 12, 2007) www. rootsweb.com/ ~neresour/OLLibrary/collections/vol19/v19p001.htm (Material extracted May 17, 2007) www. kancoll.org/books/andreaus_ne. This site links to "Andreas' History of the State of Nebraska." See particularly the entries for the following counties: Adams/Antelope/Blackbird/ Boone/Buffalo/Burt/Butler/Cass/Cedar/Custer/Dakota/Dawson/Dixon/Dodge/Douglas/Dundy/ Fillmore/Franklin/Frontier/Furnas/Gage/Gosper/Greeley/Hall/Hamilton/Harlan/Hayes/Hitchcok/ Holt/Howard/Jefferson/Johnson/Kearney/Keith/Knox/Lancaster/Lincoln/Madison/Merrick/ Nance/Nemaha/Nuckolls/Otoe/Pawnee/Phelps/Pierce/Platte/Polk/Red Willow/Richardson/ Saline/Sarpy/Saunders/Seward/Sherman/Sioux/Stanton/Thayer/Valley/Washington/Wayne/ Webster/Wheeler/York.

3 As related in "Andreas' History of the State of Nebraska," Nuckolls County section, the Eubanks family was new to the area having settled their land only a few months before. The Andreas' acount says they were "Germans from the Eastern States and totally ignorant of Indian warfare . . . ."

In the Nuckolls County version of the tragedy, instead of defending the dwelling, members of the Eubanks family who were at the house when the attack took place fled towards nearby timber and underbrush. Only two—Laura Roper and William Eubanks' wife, who carried her infant child with her—found initial shelter. Later in the day, the cries of the infant revealed the women's hiding place to the raiders. The child was killed with a tomahawk and the women were taken captive.

The Nebraska state historical society marker identifies Laura Roper's age as sixteen and indicates that three Eubanks family members (William's wife Lucinda, their daughter Isabella, aged three, and their infant son William, six months of age) were captured at "The Narrows" that day. According to the historical society, Laura and Isabella were released to the Army at Hackberry Creek, Kansas in September 1864. Lucinda and the infant son, "brutally treated by the Indians," were eventually freed at Fort Laramie, Wyoming, in May 1865. (See www.nebraskahistory.org/publish/markers/texts/indian_captives.htm)

MUD SPRINGS STATION

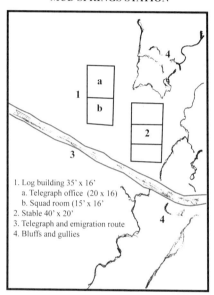

1. Log building 35' x 16'
   a. Telegraph office (20 x 16)
   b. Squad room (15' x 16'
2. Stable 40' x 20'
3. Telegraph and emigration route
4. Bluffs and gullies

The diagram above is a reconstruction based generally on a sketch of the Mud Springs grounds and buildings drawn by Lieutenant Caspar Collins at the time of the battle. The original sketch is at Colorado State University, Archives and Special Collections.

Chapter Five

The Battle of Mud Springs

E ighteen sixty-four was one of the bloodiest of all years on the Nebraska frontier. In the two days after Plum Creek, Cheyennes, Arapahoes, and Brules attacked every stage station and ranch between Julesburg, Colorado, and Fort Kearny, Nebraska.

"The entire Nebraska frontier was thrown into a state of panic, and settlers in the Platte and Little Blue valleys fled eastward. The First Nebraska Cavalry,* recently returned from the South, was recalled from furlough and ordered to Fort Kearny. Major General Samuel R. Curtis. . .came from Fort Leavenworth with a small force and . . . organized an expedition against the Indians. Though Curtis did not have enough men to move against the Indians in force, he provided escorts for stagecoaches and freight wagons traveling west of Fort Kearny. . . . In addition, several companies of the First Nebraska Cavalry were assigned to guard the Union Pacific Railroad at Plum Creek Station between Forts Kearny and McPherson. . . . As one means of combating the Indians, the army in October set the prairie aflame from Fort Kearny to Julesburg and as far south as the Republican River. The Indians were subdued for a while, but (soon) were again launching hit-and-run raids all along the trail."[1]

* * *

Early in 1864, concerned by the possibility of violence after peace talks had failed, General Robert B. Mitchell, commander of the District of Nebraska, placed garrisons at Julesburg, Ficklin's Springs, Scotts Bluff, and Mud Springs. The latter site, twenty-five miles

* Appendix C describes the organization and service histories of Nebraska units formed during the Civil War.

north of Sidney and eight miles northwest of Dalton, was situated on a branch of the emigrant trail. Known as the "Jules Cutoff," for travelers coming up the South Platte the cutoff provided a more direct route to Fort Laramie. Like the other outposts, the purpose of the Mud Springs garrison was to protect the trail and the travelers, as well as the telegraph line that bordered the road. The name of the site was derived from the fact that "buffalo liked to wallow in the waters, churning up sediment and creating a mud flat, later regenerated by soldiers and emigrant wagons and stock."[2] For a long stretch of the trail, Mud Springs provided one of the few fresh water sources. The availability of water made it an attractive location: in 1860, the Pony Express placed a home station on the site. The next year, on July 15, 1861, it became a telegraph outpost, one of the links in the nation's new transcontinental system.

At Sand Creek, Colorado, on November 29, 1864, Colonel John M. Chivington's Third Colorado Volunteers attacked a Cheyenne village and massacred 300 men, women, and children.[3] The actions of Chivington and his men provoked a massive uprising that engulfed the entire region. "All surviving Cheyennes became allies of the Sioux; the Sioux war became the War of the Plains Indians."[4]

The Indians' vengeance for Sand Creek was not long in coming. On January 7, 1865, the town of Julesburg was sacked and four soldiers from the nearby small outpost were killed. A futile twelve-day chase did nothing to dissuade the Indians, who returned on the morning of February 2, further pillaging the town and leaving it in flames. The contraband taken by the Sioux and Cheyenne included thousands of sacks of corn and herds of livestock. The raiding party was extremely large: 1,500—2,500 warriors were estimated to have participated in the second attack.

In the context of the time, the concentration of "hostiles" was almost unprecedented. So ominous was the situation that travel along the trail was limited to large caravans, usually escorted by soldiers. "In 1865 (a traveler's wagon train) was told that it could not start west from (Fort Kearny) 'without permission of the authorities,' who stipulated that before proceeding there would be 'no less than 100 wagons or a like number of armed men.'"[5]

Julesburg would be the Indians southern-most raid. Apprehensive about the approach from Nebraska Territory of Colonel Robert R. Livingston with elements of the First Nebraska Cavalry and the Seventh Iowa Cavalry, the Cheyenne and Sioux turned north toward the Tongue and Powder River regions of Montana. Their route led them over the emigrant road between the North and South Platte Rivers and placed the small outposts along the trail in immediate peril. On February 3, the first, a telegraph station at Lodgepole Creek, was quickly destroyed. The telegraph operator, the sole resident at the time, was away from the station when the attack occurred, saw the flames from a distance, and fled to safety.

Located on the trail in the vicinity of Courthouse Rock, Mud Springs was the next station up the line. The Indians reached it the following day.

The Mud Springs garrison consisted of only nine soldiers and a telegraph operator. Present also when the Indians appeared on February 4 were four stock herders employed by Creighton and Hoel, a nearby cattle operation. The station facilities consisted of two log buildings. One, thirty-five by sixteen feet, was divided almost in half with the telegraph office at one end and a squad room for the soldiers at the other. The second structure was a stable that measured about forty by twenty feet.

The tiny station was about to be set upon by 1,500—2,000 warriors fresh from attacks at Julesburg and the destruction of the station at Lodgepole Creek. In the words of one scholar, "(t)he little compound at Mud Springs was utterly indefensible, being surrounded by hills and knolls full of gullies, allowing attackers to creep up where they could not be seen or reached by cavalry charge."

The Indians wasted no time. Their first assault succeeded in capturing fifteen to twenty horses belonging to the soldiers and cattlemen as well as almost the entire herd of cattle milling on the range close by.

At 4 p.m. that day, the sub district commander, Colonel William O. Collins, based at Fort Laramie, received telegraphed information regarding the attack. Collins immediately wired Lieutenant William Ellsworth, posted at Camp Mitchell, Nebraska, directing him to leave immediately with thirty-six men of Company H, Eleventh Ohio Cavalry. By riding all night, Collins anticipated that Ellsworth and his men would be at Mud Springs, about fifty miles distant, by sunrise the following morning.

Meanwhile, at 7 p.m. that same evening, Collins led 120 men out of Fort Laramie. Stopping only for short breaks through the night, Collins' force, comprised of members of Iowa and Ohio units, arrived at Camp Mitchell late the following morning. There they rested for eight hours, then resumed the march at 7 p.m., with Collins and twenty-five men speeding ahead of the main column.

Lieutenant Ellsworth's forced march brought his reinforcements to Mud Springs before dawn on February 5. Ellsworth ordered a bugle sounded to identify the group to the defenders at the besieged camp. Ellsworth's men were warmly greeted by the members of the small force holding out in the two buildings, but their presence did not prevent another successful raid just before sunrise when warriors captured more horses and mules, including some from Ellsworth's recently arrived party.

Daylight brought immediate action. A bluff at the rear of the buildings provided a vantage point for the Indians. As soon as the sun came up, sixteen of Lieutenant Ellsworth's soldiers advanced up the height to push the raiders back. Firing as they moved forward, Ellsworth's men forced the Indians from one elevation to the next. Suddenly, from a nearby creek bank an enormous number of Indians—estimated at as many as 500—rose up and opened fire in a barrage that one soldier described as like a "shower of hailstones."

The heavy fire, intense and increasingly accurate, caused the soldiers to fall back. As the detachment formed up to retreat, two soldiers (ironically, they were brothers) standing not far apart, were hit almost simultaneously. One received a shoulder wound that knocked him down. Struggling to regain his feet, he was able to stagger back to the station where he was placed in a bunk and eventually treated by a doctor who arrived with Collins' cadre later in the day.

The second casualty was shot in the hip. The shell lodged in his groin and made it difficult for him to move. He fell near a small crevasse and managed to roll over into it while drawing his revolver and preparing to defend himself. Soldiers observing from the station "could see the Indians jumping up, waving their scalping knives and yelling like demons," eager to finish off the trooper.

Watching from the squad building, Sergeant William Hall, a Civil War veteran new to the company, volunteered to try to reach the wounded man and bring him in. Others argued against the attempt, but Hall calmly hung his revolver belt on a nearby peg and stepped through the door. Running through a fusillade, he reached his wounded comrade, hoisted him on his shoulders, and carried him back to safety. Hall's act of heroism cheered his embattled colleagues who were hanging on against long odds, defending the station from firing positions in and around the two small buildings. Unfortunately, despite Sergeant Hall's valor, the wounded man later died of his wounds and was buried on a knoll near the station.

At sundown, the raiders pulled back temporarily, allowing the soldiers some much needed rest.

February 6 dawned cold and wintery. Still, to the defenders of Mud Springs, the daylight hours brought a welcome sight: Colonel Collins and his command from Fort Laramie reached the station. The men were exhausted, having marched two nights and a day with little rest. The long journey through the bitter cold had left several soldiers frostbitten; some had frozen ears and feet. The Indians, some of whom had broken away to steal cattle in the area around the station on February 4 and 5, were taken by surprise by the arrival of additional reinforcements at Mud Springs.[6] As Collins' men moved toward the station, the Indians returned en masse to the nearby heights, swarming over them and laying down a loose fire in an unsuccessful attempt to halt their advance.

Collins estimated that 500 to 1,000 Indians—he was inclined to favor the higher number—fought that day in the vicinity of Mud Springs. His report indicated that in addition to bows and arrows, the hostiles were armed with rifles and revolvers and appeared to have liberal amounts of ammunition. The heavy presence of American horses among the raiders led him to believe that non-Indians may have participated in the attack. The Civil War still raged at the time and rumors of Confederate soldiers or sympathizers aiding the Indians were not uncommon. The battle of Mud Springs yielded a similar story. Some enlisted men of the Eleventh Ohio reported seeing a white man with red hair and whiskers carrying a Texas Lone Star flag. The story has never been corroborated; thus, like other similar tales it must remain a subject for speculation.

When Collins' men fought their way into the Mud Springs compound, they quickly formed an improvised corral out of four overturned wagons and placed the horses and mules inside. The makeshift pen became the focus of several furious attacks throughout the day as the Indians attempted to stampede the cavalry mounts. Although some of the assaults carried up to the compound, none were successful as the now-reinforced garrison met them with heavy fire from their Spencer rifles.

Still, the defenders' situation remained precarious, vulnerable to warriors firing "from sheltered positions in gullies and ravines that encompassed the station." Collins responded by telegraphing Fort Laramie to send an artillery piece which he intended to use to clear the vantage points that allowed the Indians to rake the compound with fire.

The fighting that continued around the station throughout the morning and early afternoon sometimes turned into one on one, hide and seek, pop up and shoot encounters as soldiers attempted to move the Indians away from positions in the rugged terrain near the buildings. This was not an easy task, and at one point during the fighting 200 Indians massed within seventy-five yards of the buildings. Gathering behind a sheltering hill and in sharp ravines that cut through it, they sent floods of high-arching arrows into the corral, wounding several animals.

The losses, which threatened to destroy the soldiers' mobility, could not be tolerated. Collins quickly put one squad of soldiers on horseback and sent another on foot to attack the position. A charge in the face of heavy fire eventually cleared the hillside. After gaining control of the terrain, the soldiers entrenched, dug a rifle pit, and fought off further threats from that portion of the battlefield.

The struggle swirled around the compound and heavy fighting continued for several hours until by mid-afternoon[7] the soldiers' aggressiveness and concentrated fire began to wear on the attackers. Finally, pushed back in all directions, they withdrew.

The fight that day was violent and continuous. Army casualties from the "brisk" action[8] were seven wounded, three seriously. Those were in addition to the two casualties (one killed, one wounded) the day before. Losses in horses and mules were also sustained during the course of repeated attacks. Collins estimated the Indians' losses at about thirty,[9] but acknowledged there was no way of confirming the number since the raiders immediately carried away their casualties. The Indians later asserted that no warriors had been killed.

During the night, the station was further fortified, and Collins, reinforced after dark by the arrival of Lieutenant William Brown— who, in thirty-four hours came all the way from Fort Laramie bringing fifty men and a twelve-pounder mountain howitzer—made plans to take the offensive. The next morning, February 7, as Collins' forces moved to the attack, a scouting party confirmed that the Indians had left the immediate area.

The Battle of Mud Springs was over.

The Battle of Rush Creek was about to begin.

* * *

Although the two buildings that comprised the isolated outpost at Mud Springs have long since disappeared, the surrounding landscape is little changed. The rolling hills from which the Indians launched their attacks remain mostly undisturbed. Fifteen miles southeast of Bridgeport, close to the small spring and sheltered by a grove of trees, a marker identifies the scene of the desperate fight.

71

Endnotes

1 James C. Olson and Ronald C. Naugle, *History of Nebraska*, (Lincoln and London: University of Nebraska Press, 1997) p. 126.

2 John D. McDermott, *The Battles of Mud Springs and Rush Creek*, Nebraska History, Summer 1996, p. 78. Unless otherwise cited, material regarding the Mud Springs battle was drawn primarily from this source.

3 R. Ernest Dupuy and Trevor N. Dupuy, *The Encyclopedia of Military History, Second Revised Edition*, (New York and London: Harper and Row. 1986) p. 868. Other sources cite Indian casualty figures in the range of 200-400.

4 C.M Oehler, *The Great Sioux Uprising*, (New York: Oxford University Press), p. 241

5 Merrill J. Mattes, *The Great Platte River Road*, (Lincoln: The Nebraska State Historical Society, 1969) p. 233

6 Mattes, p. 373

7 R. A. Quelle, *Who's Who in Nebraska, 1940—Garden County*, NEGenWebProject-Garden County Website www.rootsweb.com~neresour/OLLibrary/who1940/co/garden.htm. Material extracted from website May 17, 2005

8 Eugene F. Ware, *The Indian War of 1864*, (Lincoln: University of Nebraska Press, 1960) p. 460

9 The figure of 30 is cited in McDermott's article and comes directly from Colonel Collins' papers. Other sources, such as the website reference in End Note #4, cite estimates of as many as 40 Indians killed.

Chapter Six

The Battle of Rush Creek

L ocated in Morrill County in the valley of the North Platte River, the Rush Creek[1] battle site is near the mouth of Cedar Creek (as Rush Creek is now called), not quite twenty miles northeast of Mud Springs. The series of violent clashes that occurred there on February 8-9, 1865, were a direct extension of the Mud Springs battle.

After scouts confirmed that the Indians had withdrawn from around Mud Springs on the morning of February 7, Colonel William O. Collins rested much of his force through the day and made preparations for pursuit. Leaving one company behind to guard the station, Collins moved out early on February 8, traveling quickly with "scouts in front and rear and on the flanks."[2]

No Indians were immediately sighted but troopers found evidence of the great size of the war party and the general direction of its movement. The converging paths of the various Indian groups appeared to merge and flow toward Rush Creek. Scouts continued to follow the Indian "signs" and within a few miles discovered a recently abandoned village that covered several miles and contained the abandoned spoils of raids on ranches, outposts, and wagon trains. Collins pushed his column forward. Trailing the now concentrated assembly of warriors, Collins followed the traces left "by thousands of travois and tipi poles."[3]

The path led them to the North Platte River, frozen now by the bitter cold, where Indians were sighted grazing stock on the opposite embankment. As the troops tracked toward the river, enormous numbers of Sioux and Cheyenne—Collins thought perhaps as many as 2,000—appeared on the hills behind the opposing bank and began moving in their direction. The immense throng of hostiles advanced towards Collins' soldiers, lapping around the sides of the column. Crossing the river above and below both flanks, the warriors flowed around the entire command, surrounding Collins' force.

An Indian observer watching from a hillside described the scene as follows:

> "Along the road on the south side of the river I could see a train of white-topped wagons moving slowly along, guarded by cavalry, and toward the train the warriors were hurrying, looking like a swarm of black ants crawling across the ice of the Platte. . . I saw that the soldiers had corralled their wagons on the south bank, at the mouth of the little creek on whose upper waters our village had stood the day before. The wagons were corralled on a bit of level ground, but all around the wagons were little knolls and sand ridges, and the soldiers hastily dug rifle pits among these hillocks and ridges and formed a circle of defense all about the wagons. The warriors in strong force, as soon as they had assembled on the south bank of the river, charged at full speed across the knolls and ridges, yelling and shooting as they came."[4]

As the soldiers hurried to corral their wagons and dig in, Lieutenant Brown's mountain howitzer bought them a few minutes of time, scattering the first groups of warriors who had bunched together crossing the frozen river. The respite was only momentary. The Indians quickly returned to the attack as the soldiers jabbed into the loose sandhills soil and built a rudimentary breastwork that they steadily improved as the battle wore on.

Considering the urgency of the situation, the ground chosen for the defensive stand was generally good, although in Collins' words "there were many little sand ridges and hollows under cover of which (the Indians) could approach us."[5]

Collins put sharpshooters on the knolls that overlooked the camp and had rifle pits dug on them. From these vantage points, the troops repulsed several probing attacks and for a time the battle regressed to move, pop up and shoot episodes like those that had occurred at Mud Springs.

Outnumbered and lacking sufficient forces to drive the Indians back en masse, Collins recognized that the struggle would be a defensive fight. As the battle took form, a crisis point soon developed when a large party of warriors penetrated to high ground about 400 yards from the encircled soldiers. Taking cover in a long ravine overgrown by sagebrush and high clumps of fallen grass. "(w)arriors carried one another to the spot, two mounting a single horse, one of them slipping off while the other raced through the gully."[6] The small hill overlooked Collins' position. From their vantage point, the Indians began pouring unrestricted fire into the encampment.

Realizing the threat, Collins ordered Lieutenant Robert Patton to take sixteen men and assault the position. Patton's men, some from Company D, Seventh Iowa Cavalry, the rest from the First Battalion of the Eleventh Ohio, mounted up and revolvers in hand, charged full speed at the Indians' stronghold.

Patton's men raced through the ravine, emptying the two revolvers that each carried and clearing the warriors from the hilltop. With orders to return immediately after scattering the Indians, Patton reformed his men, preparing to lead them back to the compound. As the company began to gather, they were suddenly attacked by an additional 150-200 warriors who came at them from sloping ground in back of the knoll. The Indians' attack carried them into the midst of Patton's men. For a brief time, desperate, hand-to-hand fighting spread across the hillside.

The route of the Indians' counter-attack made them visible to the men at the compound and exposed them to volleys from soldiers in excellent firing positions inside the breastworks. Concentrated fire from the soldier's barricade broke up the Indians' assault and enabled Patton and his men to struggle back to the fortification. Two men were lost during the furious charge. The body of one soldier was recovered before it could be captured and mutilated by the Indians. The other casualty was the victim of an unruly horse. Unable to regain control of the runaway animal, the soldier was surrounded by several warriors and killed; his body was carried away by the Indians before his companions could fight their way to it.

Collins' casualties for February 8 were two killed and nine wounded. Army participants believed that the Indians' losses were heavy, particularly during the course of Patton's charge and its

Fort Collins Museum

Colonel William O. Collins commanded troops at Mud Springs and Rush Creek.

immediate aftermath. Indians denied that claim, asserted that only one brave, a young Cheyenne, was wounded.

At sundown the Indians broke off their attacks and withdrew across the river. Collins took advantage of the respite, sending work details to Rush Creek to water horses and mules. One group mistakenly headed for the North Platte where they reported seeing the body of a warrior, apparently a casualty of the battle, laying on the ice. As the soldiers approached the river, they were placed under threat by a large party of Cheyennes and Sioux who moved toward them with apparent intent to resume their attack. Aware of the situation, Collins sounded recall, hurrying the soldiers back to the fortification.

During the night and early morning hours, soldiers labored to improve the breastworks, expecting a resumption of full-scale fighting when the sun came up. Sunrise instead brought 400 warriors to some nearby bluffs. Some at first crossed the river provoking an initial short-lived exchange of fire. After a few minutes, the shooting terminated when the Indians withdrew and began moving away in a northerly direction.

Soon after, another group of warriors was sighted on high ground about a quarter-mile away, absorbed in some activity. Lieutenant Brown double-loaded the howitzer and the blast scattered the last group of Indians on the battlefield.

Eventually, a group of twenty soldiers scouted the location where the Indians had last been seen. There they discovered the horrifically mutilated body of the soldier killed in the previous day's charge.

By early morning, it was apparent that the Indians were gone. With his men exhausted and lacking sufficient supplies to fight a conclusive battle, Collins chose not to pursue. His men had "marched nearly

400 miles in ten days, suffering greatly from the cold, and the men had been two days and nights on a diet of hardtack and raw flesh. They had also lost significant numbers of horses and mules to their adversaries."[7]

Collins' summary report for the combined Mud Springs-Rush Creek fights cited his total casualties at three killed, sixteen wounded and seven disabled by frostbite. Collins estimated Indian losses from both engagements at 100-150. Contemporary Cheyenne and Sioux sources assert far fewer losses.

* * *

The encounters at Mud Springs and Rush Creek are significant in several ways. More than a decade ahead of the Little Bighorn, the size of the Indian assemblage—2,000-2,500 warriors, predominately Cheyennes, Arapahos, Ogallalas and Brule Sioux, but perhaps, as Collins believed, also including some Kiowa, Apaches, and Comanches—was unprecedented for its time. The Indians' tactic of returning within days to launch a second large scale attack on Julesburg was not typical of the warfare usually waged by the Plains Indians. The intensity of the combat itself, both at Mud Springs and at Rush Creek, was marked by sustained ferocity. Certainly, the charge of Lieutenant Patton and his sixteen men at Rush Creek equaled more noted episodes in terms of risk and gallantry.

The long-term results of the two encounters were "inconclusive."[8] The Indians did not prevent the military from defending the trail or the telegraph, but neither did the military restrain the Indians from moving to Powder River, as was their goal all along. For the territorial and national governments, the twin battles were important because in combination they helped keep—although just—the trail and the telegraph lines open during a difficult time.

For the military, the campaign—and the possibly exaggerated reports of Indian losses—had the short-term effect of boosting morale after the devastating attacks at Julesburg. It did not, however, deter future raids that resumed rather quickly. Diaries as well as official reports indicate that both regular army and militia forces gained a new—albeit sometimes grudging—respect for the skill and toughness of their Indian opponents.

The massive Sioux outbreak along the Nebraska frontier caused the government to reorganize the command structure for the Plains.

Ironically, among the first troops ordered to the area were regiments of former Confederate prisoners. Called "Galvanized Yankees," they were freed from prison camps in return for their promise to fight Indians on the Plains. A major Indian war had begun and important parts of its opening chapter had been fought on Nebraska soil.

* * *

The landscape around the Rush Creek battle site remains generally unchanged. On the rolling hills near the head of the creek where the heavy fighting occurred, scattered trees now dot ground used mostly for pasture and cropland.

Endnotes

1 John D. McDermott, *The Battles of Mud Springs & Rush Creek,* Nebraska History Summer 1996. Material for the Rush Creek chapter was drawn primarily from this source. References for specifics and direct quotations are provided below.
2 McDermott p. 82.
3 Ibid.
4 McDermott P. 83.
5 Ibid.
6 Ibid.
7 McDermott p. 84.
8 Eugene F. Ware, *The Indian War of 1864,* (Lincoln: University of Nebraska Press, 1960) p. 460.

REPUBLICAN RIVER EXPEDITION

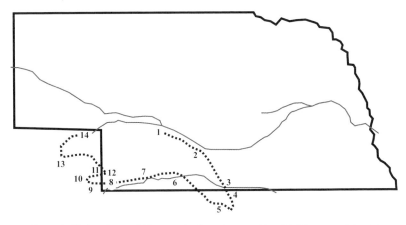

1. **June 9**: Major General Eugene A. Carr departs Fort Mcpherson with eight companies of the U.S. Fifth Cavalry and two companies of Pawnee Scouts. Later, a cavalry company would be withdrawn for duty elsewhere and replaced by a third company of Pawnee Scouts.
2. **June 12**: First contact. A patrol scouting along Deer Creek stumbles across and chases a hunting party of twenty Indians.
3. **June 13**: Carr's force reaches the Republican River about five miles below the mouth of Medicine Creek.
4. **June 15**: Along the Republican River, four miles from the mouth of Prairie Dog Creek, Carr's force is ambushed while camped for supper. One teamster is wounded and two attackers are killed in the chase that follows.
5. **June 16**: North Fork, Solomon River. Carr's scouts lose the Indians' trail.
6. **June 19**: Carr moves back to the Republican River.
7. **June 19–29**: Long daily marches (25–30 miles) east to west through the Republican River Valley.
8. **June 29 – July 2**: "Thickwood" rendezvous area. Carr's troops are re-supplied from Fort McPherson.
9. **July 4**: A patrol detached from Carr's main body of troops chases a twelve-person war party.
10. **July 7**: Carr momentarily backtracks to find a better wagon route. The change of direction may have been (mis)interpreted by Tall Bull as a retreat by some or all of Carr's force.
11. **July 8**: A three-person soldier detail looking for a stray horse is attacked by a small war party. Two Cheyenne are wounded.
12. **July 8**: Night attack by the Cheyenne on Carr's camp. One Pawnee Scout is wounded.
13. **July 11**: Battle of Summit Springs. Tall Bull and 51 other Cheyennes are killed and large amounts of weapons and provisions are captured. One cavalry trooper is wounded.
14. **Mid-July**: Expedition ends at Fort Sedgwick, Colorado.

Chapter Seven

The Republican River Campaign

T he strategic value of the Republican River Valley was obvious long before military campaigns brought notoriety to the region. From time immemorial, the Indians had used the valley as fortress, shelter, and hunting ground.

It was a citadel: the Gibraltar of the Plains Indians.

The strategic importance of the area, recognized from the earliest days, increased with each passing year as the frontier moved westward. Beginning in the 1850s, U.S. forces in considerable strength scouted the region in forays that inevitably provoked clashes as the military units moved through the valley. By the end of the next decade, the isolated reconnaissances had escalated into a series of campaigns. Conducted each year, the separate expeditions were part of a larger whole, linked together by the military's overall strategic objective of subduing the tribes in the valley or driving them from it.

* * *

1858

In 1858, Colonel Edwin V. Sumner led dragoons from Fort Leavenworth, Kansas, on a scout through the valley, patrolling as far north as Fort Kearny. Sumner's reconnaissance in force was the first of the many expeditions through the area that would grow ever larger and more eventful over the years.

1860

Two years after Sumner's scout, one of the first recorded instances of significant combat in the region between army and Indians occurred as a column of the First United States Cavalry led by Captain Samuel Sturgis moved through the valley. In the vicinity of present-day Cambridge, "a determined but inconclusive fifteen-mile running skirmish" broke out as the presence of Sturgis's cavalry drew the wrath of local tribesmen. The Indians' belligerence, made obvious by this episode and by the tribes' continued harassment of overland traffic and the Pony Express, was a prelude to the major Indian war that broke out in 1864.[1]

1867: Custer in Nebraska

In the late 1860s, the Republican River Valley became a cauldron of military activity. Indians across the southern tier of Nebraska were increasingly active at a time when the army was withdrawing forces from posts along the Bozeman Trail in Montana. The combination of the Sioux's heightened aggressiveness and the availability of additional troops made the Republican River region a focal point for military operations on the Plains.[2]

The first of a series of expeditions through the area began in the summer of 1867 when Lieutenant Colonel George Armstrong Custer, nine years away from his rendezvous with destiny at the Little Bighorn, led a detachment of the Seventh Cavalry from Fort Hays, Kansas, across the border into Nebraska. Initially conceived as an enormous semi-circle reconnaissance, the plan was to scout the hundreds of miles along a route that would take the troopers of the Seventh to Fort McPherson (near North Platte), Fort Sedgwick (near Julesburg, Colorado), and Fort Wallace (near present-day Wallace, Kansas) before returning to Fort Hays.[3]

Custer's move through the Republican Valley to Fort McPherson was generally uneventful. No major encounters took place although Indian "signs" were seen along the way and just after crossing the Republican, troopers chased for a time a band of about 100 warriors.[4]

At Fort McPherson, Custer met with General William T. Sherman, another famous personage from American history whose name graces Nebraska's past. Plans were modified at the meeting, and Custer was directed to proceed southwest to the Republican River where Cheyenne and Sioux were thought to be assembling.[5]

Four days later, after moving through rugged, broken country, Custer's troops reached the forks of the Republican just south of present-day Benkelman. There, with six companies of the Seventh Cavalry, the major portion of his force, he camped from June 22— June 30.[6]

After dispatching an eleven-person courier detachment to Fort Sedgwick and a guarded wagon train to Fort Wallace to replenish his supplies on the morning of June 23, Custer and his men settled into their camp.[7] Their anticipated sojourn was quickly interrupted.

The stillness of the pre-dawn hours the following morning, June 24, was broken by a shot from a sentry followed by heavy shooting from around the camp's perimeter. During the night, a large Sioux party led by chief Pawnee Killer[8] and thought to number in the hundreds, had surrounded the Seventh Cavalry's bivouac. Custer's account indicates that a party of about fifty warriors on horseback, their approach concealed by a deep ravine, made a dash toward the encampment. The picket's timely shot disrupted their attempt to race through the camp and stampede the cavalry's horses, which would then be caught by the warriors encircling the encampment. That outcome, Custer noted, might have allowed the Sioux to "finish us at their leisure." [9]

The "particularly sharp conflict"[10] was not of long duration. The Sioux, under brisk fire and seeing their plans foiled, withdrew to a safe location about a mile away. Custer's only casualty was the sentry, who was badly wounded and ridden over by the fleeing Indians. The war party's attempt to scalp him was thwarted by heavy fire from troopers who rushed out of the camp to retrieve him.[11]

Then followed one of those unusual episodes that occurred with some frequency during Plains warfare: a parley. Seeking to determine the identity, number, and intent of the hostiles, Custer had his interpreter arrange a meeting. After a time, along the bank of the stream, Custer and six officers met initially with seven Sioux chiefs led by Pawnee Killer. The Indians were joined at random intervals by successive numbers of warriors who came to the council ground. The increasing size of the warrior contingent aroused the suspicion of Custer and his cadre. Worried that any additional interventions could lead to an attack directly upon the negotiators or cause the nearby cavalry to strike in the face of the increasing threat, the talks were broken off. The Indians eventually rode away having revealed little meaningful information. A cavalry detail attempted to follow but was not successful in finding the location of the main Sioux camp.[12]

Later that day, Indians were again sighted near the cavalry's camp. Captain Louis Hamilton, a grandson of Alexander Hamilton, took forty troopers in pursuit. The small group of Indians—a decoy—moved

Wikipedia
Lt. Colonel George Armstrong Custer

gradually away, drawing the troopers ever farther from their base. Eventually the Indians split up and Hamilton divided his force into two detachments. Hamilton, with twenty-five troopers, followed the largest group. At a location about seven miles northwest of the campground, in the direction of present-day Haigler,[13] with the two cavalry detachments now far apart, the Sioux sprang an ambush. A party of forty to fifty warriors hidden in a ravine surrounded the soldiers "circling about the troops, throwing themselves on the sides of their ponies and aiming their carbines and arrows over the necks of their well-trained steeds."[14]

Hamilton, held by Custer to be an officer of "presence" and "unquestioned courage,"[15] defended quickly and well, dismounting his cavalry and forming them to repel several attacks. In the meantime, the party's doctor, who had somehow become separated from both detachments, heard the sound of the fighting. Chased by a party of Indians, he made a narrow escape as he raced back to the main camp to report Hamilton's plight.[16] Assistance was immediately sent, led by Custer, but the relief party found that Hamilton's detachment had beaten back the attacks, killing two Indians and wounding others. Hamilton's only casualty was a wounded cavalry horse.[17]

In the following days, the small courier party sent to Fort Sedgwick returned safely from their mission through exceptionally hazardous territory. The sixteen-wagon train sent to Fort Wallace for provisions was heavily attacked by 600–700 warriors near Butte Creek, Kansas, on the return journey. The three-hour assault was eventually broken off when a relief force sent earlier as a precaution by Custer appeared on the horizon.[18]

Photo by Nita Phillips
Custer battlefield near the forks of the Republican River.

The most horrific episode associated with the expedition occurred after the other major events—the confrontation between Custer's cavalry and Pawnee Killer's Sioux, the safe return of the courier detachment, and the attack on the wagon train—had concluded. The victims were not part of Custer's party.

Replenished with supplies brought by the wagon train to the Republican River campground, Custer, acting on new instructions from General Sherman, struck west up the north fork of the Republican—a route that took the cavalry from their bivouac location near Benkelman, past present-day Parks and Haigler and into Colorado. Several miles inside eastern Colorado, the force turned north and made a grueling march that eventually brought them to the Platte River fifty miles west of Fort Sedgwick.[19]

At this point Custer received disturbing news that a courier detachment composed of an officer, ten enlisted men and a scout, had left Fort Sedgwick with dispatches for him several days before. The young lieutenant in charge was directed to proceed to the forks of the Republican where Custer was still presumed to be camped. In reality, Custer and his entire command were by that juncture far away—100 miles or more—to the north and west.

Finding the camp at the forks of the Republican vacated, the courier party apparently misread Custer's trail, believing him to be headed south toward Fort Wallace. The path took the small command deep into the same territory where several hundred warriors had so recently attacked Custer's wagon train. Custer realized the danger to the courier party and hurried his force back, first to the forks of the Republican and then, correctly surmising what must have happened, immediately put the entire command on the march toward Fort Wallace, eighty desperate miles to the south. On July 12, several miles down the road near a small rivulet called Beaver Creek,[20] the fate of the courier party was determined. In Custer's words "Lying in irregular order, and within a very limited circle, were the mangled bodies of the poor (party), so brutally hacked and disfigured as to be beyond recognition as human beings. Every individual in the party had been scalped and his skull broken. . .Even the clothes of all the party had been carried away; some of the bodies were lying in beds of ashes, with partly burned fragments of wood near them, showing that the savages had put some of them to death by the terrible tortures of fire. The sinews of the arms and legs had been cut away, the nose of every man hacked off, and the features otherwise so defaced that it would have been scarcely possible for even a relative to recognize a single one of the unfortunate victims . . .Each body was pierced by from twenty to fifty arrows. . ."[21]

While one source places the site of the courier party's fight to the death ten miles west of Custer's camp at the forks of the Republican[22] —which would place it between Benkelman and Haigler—it seems clear from Custer's personal account and his reference to Beaver Creek (located about halfway between the forks and Fort Wallace) that the action occurred in western Kansas.[23]

The episode concluded the inconclusive Republican River campaign of 1867. A more successful venture followed the next year. Two years later, in 1869, would come the notable expedition that forever broke the Indians' power in the Republican River Valley.

1868: Carr's First Expedition

The loss of the courier party punctuated the somber aftermath of Custer's inconclusive 1867 campaign. The following year's expedition, while not yet decisive, would prove to be more notable and successful.

Despite attempts by a congressional committee to reach agreement with warring tribes, in 1868[24] large bands of Indians resumed hostilities along and below the Republican River. To oppose them, as part of a plan designed by Lieutenant General Philip H. Sheridan, Brevet Major General Eugene A. Carr took the field with a contingent of the Fifth United States Cavalry.

In early October Carr, posted in Washington D.C., received orders to join "the Dandy Fifth" on the Kansas plains.[25] On October 18, with an escort of 100 troopers, Carr was hurrying to locate and join his command, already in the field, when his force was attacked by a large Sioux and Cheyenne war party near Beaver Creek, Kansas. Carr formed his supply wagons in an oval, placed his horses and mules inside, and for the next eight hours fought off repeated attacks by the 700 or more warriors who rode in constricting circles around his makeshift stockade. After a struggle through the heat of the day, the Indians withdrew in the face of increasing losses. Three of Carr's troopers were wounded.[26]

Carr caught up with his command, seven cavalry companies and a contingent of scouts, on October 22 at Buffalo Tank, a railroad stop on the Kansas Pacific Railroad. The general immediately set the force in motion towards Nebraska and the Republican River Valley. On October 27, near the Solomon River[27] in northern Kansas, the cavalry's advance guard ran into a substantial force of Sioux and Cheyennes. The initial skirmish grew quickly into a full-fledged battle as 500 Indians joined the fray and Carr poured his entire command into the fight. A large, confused, running melee then resulted that continued for about six miles. At nightfall the Indians broke off the action after having lost about thirty warriors killed and wounded.[28]

Unlike most battles on the Plains, which were intense, spasm exchanges that were seldom of long duration, the first day's encounter was only the beginning of a prolonged period of violent, near-continuous action that followed. For the next four days a furious running battle raged, tracing a long northward crescent across the Republican into Nebraska, west through the valley and then back again south to Beaver Creek.

The Sioux and Cheyenne losses were thought to be significant, and when the cavalry prepared to resume the attack at dawn on October 31, they found that "the enemy had suddenly disappeared like mist before a morning sun."[29]

Used with permission of the Military Order of the Loyal Legion of the United States

General Eugene A. Carr

Carr's efforts scattered the Indians, pushing many of them south, driving them against Sheridan's forces that waited there in Indian Territory. At Washita, in a battle led by George Armstrong Custer and forever engulfed in controversy, the Indians suffered heavy losses in a decisive defeat.[30]

The 1868 campaign ended with the battle at Washita. From the government's perspective, the expedition had been more successful than the one that preceded it the year before. Still, while the Indians had suffered substantial losses and had been temporarily dispersed, the danger along the Republican River Valley had not been removed.

Indeed, as events would show, the threat would soon reappear larger and more ominous than before.

1869: Sappa Creek

A short distance south of present-day Orleans, the Sioux massacred a party of United States surveyors near where Sappa Creek flows into the Republican River. Every member of the survey party was killed.[31] At about the same time, Cheyenne Dog Soldiers, members of the tribe's elite warrior society, and large Sioux war parties moved back into the area. The resulting outrage from the massacre of the survey party combined with the alarm over the presence of the Indians' most fearsome fighters influenced the eventual decision to launch a campaign aimed at clearing the valley once and for all.

1869: Republican River Expedition

A command of cavalry will leave Ft. McPherson on the 9th inst, against all Indians in the Republican country. The only permanent safety to (Nebraska's) frontier settlements is

to drive the Indians entirely out of the Republican country.
That is what I hope to do this summer.
Letter from General C.C. Auger to Nebraska Governor
David Butler, June 1, 1869[32]

During the early spring of 1869, Cheyenne Dog Soldiers led by Chief Tall Bull and accompanied by large Sioux war parties moved aggressively into the Republican valley. Beginning on May 21, they launched a campaign of terror that cut a swath of destruction "from the Saline River in Kansas to the Big Sandy in Nebraska,"[33] Moving swiftly, the Indians struck hunting parties, burned homesteads, derailed and nearly wiped out the crew of a Kansas Pacific train, and killed thirteen persons in raids up and down the river. On May 30, war parties destroyed a Kansas settlement, killing an additional thirteen settlers and kidnapping two women.[34]

David Butler, the governor of the two-year old state of Nebraska, wrote to General C. C. Auger, commanding officer of the military district of the Platte, imploring the army to provide immediate assistance.

General Auger replied the following day, assuring Governor Butler that help would be quickly forthcoming from Fort McPherson. Eight days later, Auger made good his promise. On June 9, a force under the command of General Carr left the post, moving first south and east along the Platte, then south to Medicine Creek, and then into the valley of the Republican River.

Carr's troopers reached the Republican on June 13 and camped at a point about four miles below the junction of the river and the mouth of Beaver Creek. These steps were the first in a series of moves that eventually formed a horseshoe-shaped track that extended over 150 miles[35] and ranged over parts of Kansas, Colorado, and Nebraska. The campaign became known as the Republican River Expedition.

"The object of your expedition is to drive the Indians out of the Republican country, and to follow them as far as possible. . ." Carr's orders read.[36] First alerted by General Auger on June 7 for deployment on June 9, Carr had his troops provisioned and on the march two days later. The frontier army was small, impoverished, and desperately undermanned at the time—the demobilization following the Civil War had been massive in scope and size—and throughout the five-week campaign Carr sent repeated requests for additional weapons, ambulances, and assorted provisions. Still, in the context of the times it was a sizable force that Carr took with him from Fort McPherson: eight companies of the Fifth Cavalry (although none of the companies was at more than half of its authorized strength), two companies of Pawnee Scouts, fifty-four over-loaded wagons pulled by mule teams, and a complement of teamsters, wagoneers, and herders, many of whom were deemed by Carr to be "unruly" and "unreliable."[37]

Midway through the expedition—an indication of how thinly stretched was the army at the time—one veteran cavalry company was withdrawn from Carr's force and sent for duty along the Little Blue. That unit was replaced by a third company of Pawnee Scouts.[38] Initially, General Carr had misgivings about the quality and competence of the Pawnee contingent. As the campaign progressed, and the caliber of the Pawnees' service became more evident, Carr's concerns were considerably reduced.[39]

General Carr was well-chosen to lead the expedition. A highly experienced veteran of Plains warfare, during the previous year he had defeated large parties of Cheyennes at Beaver Creek and Solomon River in Kansas, and had commanded a winter expedition to the Canadian River.[40]

By far the most famous personage on the expedition, however, was William F. Cody, Chief of Scouts of the Fifth Cavalry. Carr and "Buffalo Bill" had served together previously and the general had been so impressed with Cody's "skill, fighting, and marksmanship," that Carr had expressly requested that Cody serve with the Fifth Cavalry for "as long as I am employed in this duty." High praise, indeed, following as it did public compliments from General Philip H. Sheridan for Cody's "endurance and courage."[41]

Obvious to all was that "endurance and courage" would be required in the days ahead, for Carr, Cody, and the Fifth Cavalry were unquestionably moving in harm's way. "The lush Republican Valley had long been a refuge for the Plains Indians. It sheltered them from prairie blizzards in winter and provided game and comfort in its soft coolness in the summer. Now, in the spring of 1869, it was their last stronghold in the central plains."[42]

They would not relinquish it easily.

Carr's force moved across terrain that was alternately rugged and sandy and, at the time, not well charted. The harsh landscape and the absence of roads and trails made it difficult for the wagons to keep up with the main body of troops. Breakdowns were frequent and the mules often played out from dragging wagons through the sand. To maintain the momentum of the pursuit, on two occasions Carr left a cavalry company and the wagon trains behind with orders to catch up later.

The journey to the south provided evidence of the Cheyennes' presence in the area. On the morning of June 12 a cavalry patrol was scouting along Deer Creek when it ran into a hunting party of about twenty Indians who fled before an attack could be organized. The trail was soon lost as the Cheyennes dispersed and little of consequence resulted from the campaign's first, fleeting contact.[43]

For two days after entering the valley, Carr moved mostly west, crossing over Deer Creek before stopping early on June 15 to rest his troops at a campsite along the banks of Prairie Dog Creek. The troops bivouacked along the creek side with the Pawnee Scouts camped about a half mile from the cavalry. The wagon train was positioned between the two camps. Apparently hidden in the tall grass throughout the day, in late afternoon Indians attacked the wagon train area as Carr's men settled down for supper. In the shooting and melee of the first few minutes, a teamster was wounded and Carr's troopers struggled to respond. The sudden attack was aimed at driving off the mule herd and thus immobilizing the wagon train carrying Carr's supplies. Quick reaction by the Pawnee Scouts foiled the Cheyennes' plan. Before the cavalry could react, the Pawnees raced to their ponies and went after the attackers. Along with Bill Cody—who had left his horse saddled— and the scout's commander, Major Frank North, the Pawnees engaged the Cheyennes in a running battle that extended over several miles as the raiders raced away to the south. As the chase continued, Cody and the Pawnees were joined by several companies of cavalry before darkness fell and the chase was broken off. The Pawnees killed two of the marauders before night obscured the trail.[44]

At 3 a.m. the next morning, the main force turned south, toward Kansas, tracking Indian "sign" to the north fork of the Solomon River. After trailing the Indians for twenty-five miles, the trail was eventually lost as the Indians scattered and blurred their path.[45]

Three days later, after scouring the area, Carr turned back north, crossing again into Nebraska and returning to the Republican River with the intention of scouting along it and clearing it to the extent that his manpower and supplies allowed.

For the next several days, Carr's troops moved in a series of long marches—twenty-five to thirty miles a day—tracking generally west along the river. Patrols were dispatched daily, scouting ahead and to the north and south of the main body. At the end of the month, Carr brought his force to a pre-arranged rendezvous at a location called "Thickwood" in southwestern Nebraska. There, he was reprovisioned by a wagon train sent from Fort McPherson. Carr sent his sick and injured back to the fort with the return train and rested his men in the timbered area for most of two days.[46]

On July 2, the troops resumed the march, moving westward toward the Colorado border. The following day a large, promising trail was discovered. "Signs" indicated that the tracks might have been made by the Dog Soldiers who had raided the settlements. Although the party was obviously large, the Cheyennes again did a masterful job of disguising their path: scattering, driving livestock over the trail and traveling on hard ground before reassembling at night.[47]

Nonetheless, the evidence indicated that Carr's men were narrowing the gap. Carr again stripped a group free of the main body and wagon train and sent three companies of cavalry and one company of Pawnee Scouts with three days of packs in pursuit of the Cheyennes. On July 4, the detached force came across a twelve-person war party carrying a wounded brave on a litter. The Pawnee Scouts ran the Cheyennes down, scalped three of them and captured eight horses, two with army brands.[48]

Although skeptical of catching up with the main body of Cheyennes, who probably would have been warned by the surviving members of the hunting party, Carr put his entire force on the march. After backtracking momentarily to find a better route for his wagons,[49] Carr then led his main body back west through difficult, sandy, inhospitable terrain.

Clashes were soon forthcoming. On July 8, four men were detailed from the column to retrieve a horse that had strayed. Several miles from the main body, they were jumped by eight Indians. The small detail sought refuge in a rock outcropping and killed the horse they had only recently recovered, using the carcass for shelter. The Cheyennes eventually left the sharp fight that followed after two warriors were wounded.[50]

Late that night, Carr's main camp again came under attack. In an unusual night foray, a group of Indians—by most accounts five to seven, by one version as many as thirty—rode from east to west sweeping through the entire camp. Hollering and shooting as they raced among the tents and wagons, they attempted to stampede the horses and cause casualties in the resulting confusion. The attack was over as quickly as it began as the raiders disappeared into the night.[51]

Other than for one Pawnee Scout wounded by "friendly fire" from a cavalryman, the attack did little material damage.[52] The brazenness of the raid, however, signaled that the Cheyennes were nearby in substantial numbers.

Determined to maintain the pursuit, Carr moved at dawn the next day. Turning north, he began a series of forced marches through the desolate country of northeastern Colorado that each day brought him closer to Tall Bull's Dog Soldiers. Signs of recently abandoned campsites were discovered. The prints of a white woman's shoe were found, reaffirming the possibility that Carr was on the track of the Dog Soldiers who had raided, killed, and kidnapped in Kansas and Nebraska. Carr's fast-moving soldiers continued their relentless pursuit, "covering in one day the territory the Indians had traveled in three."[53]

On July 10 troopers found a camp that the Indians had apparently abandoned earlier the same day. Carr halted at the encampment and readied his command for action.[54]

Meanwhile, in recent days Tall Bull had first taken his band east toward Nebraska and the South Platte. Finding the Platte and other streams running too full for safe crossing, and worried that the route would take him in the direction of known military presence, he changed course. Lulled possibly by Carr's momentary backtracking in the past week into thinking that at least some of the force was being withdrawn, Tall Bull went into camp at White Butte Creek, near Summit Springs, Colorado.

Carr was now twenty miles away.[55]

Carr's provisions were running low and his men were tired. More critically, the cavalry's horses were by now ill-fed and exhausted. Carr formed his command, sorted it by the physical condition of troopers and their animals and chose to take to battle with him "those whose horses were fit for service."[56] There were not nearly as many as he would have liked: only 244 out of 400 men from his seven cavalry companies and only fifty of 150 warriors in three companies of Pawnee Scouts[57] would accompany him when the small force left at dawn on July 11.

By evening, they were victorious.

At Summit Springs, Carr and his men surprised, out-fought, and out-generaled their Indian adversaries. About fourteen miles southwest of Sterling, Colorado, Carr's outnumbered force of less than 300 cavalry and Pawnee Scouts slammed into Tall Bull's 500 Dog Soldiers, thoroughly routing them. Tall Bull and fifty-one other Cheyennes were killed; the remainder fled or were taken prisoner. Carr's after action report also listed "274 horses, 144 mules, 9,300 pounds of dried meat, 84 complete lodges, 56 rifles, 22 revolvers, 40 bows and arrows, 50 pounds of gunpowder, 20 boxes of percussion caps, 17 sabres, 9 lances, 20 tomahawks, and much more."[58]

Troopers freed one of the women captured in Kansas. She was found wounded but alive near Tall Bull's lodge where, by some testimony, the chief had shot her during the attack. According to some participants, a second woman prisoner was tomahawked by one of Tall Bull's wives and died soon after the battle. Carr's cavalrymen sustained only one casualty, a minor wound inflicted by an arrow.[59]

Initiated by a classic cavalry charge, the battle was "one of the few in the history of the frontier that would measure up to all the requirements of writers of western fiction."[60]

The expedition—the campaign itself and the results of it—forms a significant chapter in the state's history. Although the climactic battle occurred elsewhere, the campaign covered large portions of the south central and southwestern parts of the state, and several engagements were fought on Nebraska soil.

For years a bastion of the Plains Indians, the Republican River Valley was finally cleared for settlement.[61] The expedition eliminated the last Indian stronghold in the Central Plains region.

For the army and the nation, the campaign had a secondary benefit: the expedition added considerably to the information about the valley; it filled in blank spots on some maps and corrected inaccuracies in others. Many of the place names first assigned during the expedition—Driftwood Creek, for example, was named by Carr himself—remain with us.[62]

* * *

With the exception of Custer's battlefield, the sites of most other clashes that took place along the Republican River are unmarked. The forks of the Republican where Custer was attacked remain generally free of habitation or commercial growth. The trees scattered along the river bank—thick in some places, sparse in others—probably present much the same picture that Custer saw in late June, 1867. The grass in the flat, even meadow where he camped is shorter now due to the grazing of livestock. Portions of the area are now fenced, enclosing pastures and fields. A marker just south of Benkelman on U.S. Highway 34 identifies the location.

Endnotes
1858 and 1860

1 R.Eli Paul, editor, *The Nebraska Indian Wars Reader 1865-1877*, (Lincoln and London: University of Nebraska Press, 1998) p.3.

1867: Custer in Nebraska

2 Paul p. 5.
3 George Armstrong Custer, *My Life on the Plains*, (Lincoln: University of Nebraska Press, 1952) p. 114.
4 Custer p. 121.
5 Custer p. 126.
6 General Custer in Nebraska Historical Marker, History of Benkelman website www. Benkelman. org/history.htm. Material extracted from website November 1, 2005.
7 Custer p. 132.
8 General Custer in Nebraska Historical Marker, History of Benkelman website.
9 Custer p. 135-137.
10 Paul p. 5.
11 Custer p. 137.
12 Custer p. 140-144.
13 Alan Boye, *The Complete Roadside Guide to Nebraska* , (St. Johnsbury, Vermont: Saltillo Press, 1993) p. 287.
14 Custer p. 146.
15 Custer p. 145.
16 Custer p. 146.
17 Custer p. 150.
18 Custer p. 166-171.
19 Custer p. 177.
20 General Custer in Nebraska, Nebraska State Historical Society, Website www.nebraskahistory. org/publish/markers/texts/general_custer_in_nebraska.htm. Material Extracted from website November 9, 2005.
21 Custer p. 188-200.
22 Boye p. 287.
23 Custer p. 188-200.

1868: Carr's First Expedition

24 Paul p. 5.
25 James T. King, *War Eagle: A Life of General Eugene A. Carr*, (Lincoln: University of Nebraska Press, 1963) p. 81.
26 King p. 82-84.
27 Eugene A. Carr , NNDB website www.nndb.com/people/699/000050549/ Material extracted from website November 2, 2005.
28 King p. 86.
29 Ibid.
30 Paul p. 5.

1869: Sappa Creek

31 Boye p. 224.

1869: Republican River Expedition

32 James T. King, *The Republican River Expedition June-July* 1869, Nebraska History September 1960 p. 168.
33 King, The Republican River Expedition June-July 1869, p. 167.
34 King, *War Eagle: A Life of General Eugene A. Carr*, p. 99.
35 Kevin Moeller, Fort Kearny's Unconventional Army Units, Buffalo County Historical Society – Buffalo Tales March-April 2005, website bchs.kearney.net/BTales_200502.htm. Material extracted from website October 19, 2005.
36 King, *The Republican River Expedition June-July* 1869, p. 172.
37 King, *The Republican River Expedition June-July* 1869, p. 169-171.
38 King, *War Eagle: A Life of General Eugene A. Carr*, p. 105.

39 Carr's comfort with the Scouts eventually increased to the point that on a later campaign—the Big Horn and Yellowstone Expedition of 1876—he explicitly asked for Pawnee Scouts to be assigned to him. King, War Eagle: A life of General Eugene A. Carr, p. 154.
40 Eugene Asa Carr, NNDB website.
41 King, The Republican River Expedition June-July 1869, p. 170.
42 King, *War Eagle: A Life of General Eugene A. Carr*, p. 94.
43 King, *The Republican River Expedition June-July* 1869, p.177.
44 King, *The Republican River Expedition June-July* 1869, p. 178,179.
45 King, *The Republican River Expedition June-July* 1869, p. 181.
46 King, *The Republican River Expedition June-July* 1869, p. 189.
47 King, *The Republican River Expedition June-July* 1869, p. 191.
48 King, *The Republican River Expedition June-July* 1869, p. 193.
49 King, *War Eagle: A Life of General Eugene A. Carr*, p. 110.
50 Ibid.
51 King, *The Republican River Expedition June-July* 1869, p. 195,196.
52 Ibid.
53 Ibid.
54 King, *The Republican River Expedition June-July* 1869, P. 197.
55 King, *The Republican River Expedition June-July* 1869, p. 198.
56 Ibid.
57 King, *The Republican River Expedition June-July* 1869, p. 199.
58 King, *War Eagle: A Life of General Eugene A. Carr*, p. 116.
59 In 1869 the US Army and Cheyenne & Sioux Warriors fought the Battle of Summit Springs, Logan County website www.logancountychamber.com/tourismsummitsprings.html. Material extracted from website October 19, 2005.
60 King, *War Eagle: A Life of General Eugene A. Carr*, p. 112.
61 Franklin County, Nebraska State Historical Society website www.nebraskahistory.org/publish/markers/texts/franklin_county.htm Material extracted from website October 19, 2005.
62 King, *War Eagle: A Life of General Eugene A. Carr*, p. 107.

Chapter Eight

Massacre Canyon

“ “**M**uch has been written and filmed about the Indian wars in the trans-Missouri West, conjuring up the image of the United States Cavalry fighting and defeating some band or tribe of Indians. But there is another image of which the term “Indian wars” could and should remind us: long before Europeans came to the Americas, long before Nebraska was settled, Indians were engaging in intertribal warfare. These wars, ranging from minor raids to major battles, continued in varying degrees almost to the turn of the century.”[1]

* * *

On Tuesday morning, August 5, 1873, near Trenton, one of the most significant of all battles between Native tribes was fought on Nebraska soil.

The Battle of Massacre Canyon, as it almost immediately came to be known, far exceeded the usual dimensions of Plains warfare. Encounters between Plains Indians often involved small raiding parties: at Massacre Canyon a thousand or more warriors partici-pated in the fight. Combat between tribal groups typically ended with horses stolen and, occasionally, a few braves killed or captives taken: at Massacre Canyon dozens of lives were lost. The consequences of most tribal battles have long since been forgotten: the significance of Massacre Canyon is engrained in our nation’s history—it was the last major battle between Indian tribes in the United States.[2]

Even by prevailing standards, which were savage in the extreme, the fight was notable for its brutality. A medical officer accompanying a U.S. Cavalry company saw the battlefield on the afternoon of the August 5 and described it as follows:

"It was a horrible sight. Dead braves with bows still tightly grasped in dead and stiffened fingers; sucking infants pinned to their mothers' breasts by arrows; bowels protruding from openings made by fiendish knives; heads scalped with red blood glazed upon them—a stinking mass, many already fly-blown and scorched with heat."[3]

* * *

There was a history of "bad blood" between the Pawnee and the Sioux. Long before the first white men arrived on the Great Plains, these hereditary enemies had waged warfare on one another.[4] Occasional large battles like the one at Ash Hollow in 1835[5] were interrupted by persistent raids, horse stealing, and conflicts over hunting grounds.

The Pawnee were the first to arrive in Nebraska, migrating from the south at least 300 years before destiny took large numbers of them to the canyon near Trenton.[6] They were semi-sedentary, living in permanent, circular earth lodges and planting corn, beans, and squash. The Pawnees' year was built around two large buffalo hunts on which they depended for their meat supply. The summer hunt began after the crops were planted, usually in early July, and ended when the hunters returned for the harvest. There was a long winter hunt also, commencing typically in November and lasting until January.[7] By 1700, the Pawnees began to acquire horses by raiding tribes far to the southwest who had, in turn, gotten their animals through trade, warfare, or theft from Spanish inhabitants of the region.[8]

Once the largest and strongest tribe in the state, the Pawnees' numbers and strength were declining at the time of the battle. When Zebulon Pike visited the tribe in 1806, their population was thought to be about 6,500.[9] By the time the battle at Massacre Canyon occurred sixty-seven years later, their numbers had dwindled to about 2,400 of which 600 or so were warriors.[10] The sharp fall was caused mainly by diseases: small pox, cholera, and tuberculosis. The Pawnees had no immunity for these illnesses which ravaged the dark, damp earth lodges where they lived.

Over the years, the Pawnees' territory was reduced as well. By 1873, a series of treaties had left them with only a small reservation on the Loup River in what is now Nance County.[11] There, they were increasingly encroached upon by white settlers migrating west and subjected to pony raids by the aggressive, nomadic Sioux.

Even with their shrinking territory, the Pawnees retained hunting rights in the Republican River Valley. However, as white settlements spread up the river—a migration that grew steadily after 1870—they were forced further west in search of buffalo herds. With each hunt their peril increased, because traveling west took them into territory along the upper Republican River that was also a hunting ground of the Oglala and Brule Sioux.[12]

The Sioux presence in Nebraska began later than the Pawnees'. From their original homeland near the headwaters of the Mississippi, beginning in about the mid-1600s the Lakota people began to migrate westward, eventually evolving into buffalo hunting nomads. By the middle 1700s, they were at the Missouri River in present-day South Dakota, where they violently displaced the Arikara inhabitants.[13] From the Arikara they acquired horses, an event of enormous consequence to the history of the Great Plains. Superb horsemen, they became some of the world's best light cavalry.

The Sioux's feud with the Pawnees began in the 1830s, when the Lakota began raiding Pawnee villages in central Nebraska.[14] As Pawnee strength declined, Sioux raids increased in number. The countless clashes fought over the years—persistent and bloody—added to the animosity between the tribes.

In 1872, a Pawnee band on a buffalo hunt left their horses in camp while they attempted a buffalo "surround" on foot. Sioux raiders pillaged the mostly unprotected camp and made off with more than 100 horses. At some point following the raid, four Pawnee youths gave chase; led into a trap, one of the young men was killed. The loss of so many horses was devastating to the Pawnees, who were "forced to cache their buffalo meat as well as their tents and other equipment and return to the reservation on foot, most of them arriving in terrible condition."[15] The Pawnees had forgotten neither the harm to their economy nor the blow to their prestige.

The Sioux also had a score to settle with their ancient enemy. In 1864, groups of Pawnees began serving as scouts with the U.S. Army. The resulting organization—the Pawnee Scouts—became legendary on the Plains. The Scouts accompanied major expeditions and won repeated victories over the Sioux and Cheyenne.[16] "Their determined zeal in seeking out their traditional enemies. . .did nothing to lessen old antagonisms."[17]

The Sioux were also smarting over two recent events. Neither had anything to do with the Pawnees, but both combined to leave them angry and predisposed to fight. In early July, a "Cut Off" Sioux camp (the name comes from the group's separating from Red Cloud's Oglalas after an internal tribal feud), was raided on consecutive nights by Ute braves, who stole ten horses the first night and fourteen the second. Assuming that the missing horses from the first episode had only wandered off, the Sioux, under Chief Pawnee Killer, took no extra precautions. After the second raid, however, 100 warriors joined the chase.[18]

"The pursuit was hotly pushed and thirty-nine horses died on the road from exhaustion. The advance (party) of the Sioux, seven warriors, got up with the rear guard of the Utes, numbering eleven warriors about 3 p.m.; fighting immediately ensued, resulting in the defeat of the Sioux, with the loss of one man and three horses killed, and six men wounded. Other (groups of) Sioux arrived and the Utes left. The exhaustion of their horses precluded further pursuit on the part of the Sioux."[19]

The Ute raids had an unintended, but important, side effect. Perhaps as a precautionary measure, Pawnee Killer moved the Cut-Off camp south and west.[20] The move was probably aimed at distancing his group from the Utes, but the result was to place the band closer to the track the Pawnees would take in the following days as they turned for home from their summer hunt.

The Cut-Offs were not the only Sioux in proximity to the Pawnees' path. Chance had also placed a large group of Brules—probably 700 or more—in the area. Like the Cut-Offs, they were historic enemies of the Pawnees. Like the Cut-Offs also, they had been angered by a recent event. On their journey to the buffalo hunting grounds, the government sub-agent traveling with the Brule band, Stephen F. Estes, had asked the commandant of Sidney Barracks, an army post at present-day Sidney, Nebraska, to provide rations for the Indians. Estes hoped the rations would keep the Brules, already restless, "satisfied and contented."[21] Estes's request, made on July 21, was initially disapproved by the Secretary of War, William H. Belknap. Belknap stated that even if reimbursed by the Bureau of Indian Affairs, the army could not replace the rations. Two weeks later, on August 4, Belknap reversed his decision and authorized the distribution of coffee and sugar.[22] By then it was too late: the Brules were far to the south near the Republican Valley hunting grounds, close to the Pawnees and spoiling for a fight.

Like the Brule band, the Pawnees and Cut-Offs were also accompanied by government sub-agents. John Williamson was assigned to the Pawnees; Antoine "Nick" Janis rode with the Cut-Offs. The actions of both men were later subjected to criticism. Williamson, twenty-three years old, was likeable but inexperienced—this was his first hunt.[23] Perhaps thinking he could be manipulated, the Pawnees had requested his appointment as sub-agent. Throughout the hunt, the Pawnee leaders, probably relishing the opportunity to be away from the reservation and free from the stifling supervision of the Quaker agent there, had tested the limits of the young sub-agent's tolerance.

The later accusations against the Cut-Off's sub-agent, Janis, were of a different nature. Among others, Estes denounced Janis for not doing enough to prevent the Cut-Offs from attacking the Pawnees. Janis interpreted his role narrowly. The day after the battle he wrote: "Little Wound (a chief) came to see me and asked if I had any orders to keep him from going to fight (the Pawnee). I told him I had not. He said he had orders not to go to their reservation or among the whites to fight them but none in regard to this part of the country."[24] Estes later stated that Janis's lack of reaction left Little Wound "impressed with the idea that he had a perfect right to make war on the Pawnees." Both Estes and Janis acknowledged that by this point it was impossible to control the war fever among the young men, who would "listen to nothing" about making peace with the Pawnee.[25] Thus, the stage was set for conflict even as the various groups set out on trails that would, by early August, bring all of them to the vicinity of Massacre Canyon.

When the Pawnees left their reservation on July 3, they first traveled west along the Platte to Plum Creek Station (near Lexington) and then turned south to the Republican River. There they were in prime buffalo country and the hunt soon began.[26] The Cut-Off band was already near the area, about twenty-five miles to the northwest, having moved there as a result of their run-in with the Utes. The Brules were the most recent arrivals, having passed by Sidney Barracks and Julesburg, Colorado, moving south and east toward the buffalo range.

All three groups were large in size, although the exact numbers in each cannot be determined precisely. Estimates of the Pawnee party range from 350 to as many as 700.[27] The most often cited figure—which was also apparently sub-agent Williamson's estimate—is about 400 total, comprising 250 warriors, 100 women, and fifty children.[28] Figures for the combined Cut-Off and Brule warriors vary between 600 and 1,000 or more warriors,[29] although most accounts favor the higher number.[30] Never again would there be so many Indians in the Republican Valley.

When the Pawnees found the buffalo, they hunted with great success—1873 would be the last good year for major hunting in the region—in southwestern Nebraska and northwestern Kansas. On about August 2, they began their journey home, turning north, back towards the Republican River. That track led them to a campsite near present-day Trenton, where they spent the night of August 4.[31]

That night, the camp was visited by three white buffalo hunters who warned that a great number of Sioux were close by,[32] a few miles to the northwest. The hunters insisted that the Sioux had been spying on the Pawnees and knew their location.[33] The Pawnee leader, Sky Chief, disagreed. He had heard similar rumors in the past and believed the story was a made up attempt to get the Pawnees to leave the area. With the Pawnees out of the way, the buffalo hunters would have the hunting ground to themselves.[34]

Sub-agent Williamson, however, believed the report. He urged the Pawnees to take precautions, advising them to move east and stay on the south side of the Republican River on the way back to the reservation. A heated argument broke out between Williamson and Sky Chief, who insisted on continuing the present route. Williamson did not order him to do otherwise and the next morning, August 5, the Pawnee crossed north of the Republican River, moving first through an area walled by bluffs and then on to the more open plains west of Frenchman's Forks.[35] The Pawnees' route that morning first took them downstream about two miles. The band then turned northwest, following mostly along the west bank of a canyon that cut through the higher ground between the valleys of the Republican and Frenchman Rivers. They rode at first between steep canyon walls that enclosed

Photo by Nita Phillips
The tiny runnel mentioned by battle participants, zigzags across the canyon floor.

a small stream lined in places by ash and cottonwood trees. As they moved south to north, the canyon walls flattened out until at one point, about three miles from the mouth of the canyon, they blended almost entirely into the landscape. Further north, not far past this area, was the entrance to another canyon which led into the valley of the Frenchman River.[36] It was toward this defile that the Pawnees traveled.

During the early morning, Sky Chief attempted to make amends for his argument with young Williamson. However, the chief remained unimpressed with the potential threat and saw no reason to scout the area where the Sioux were reported to be.[37]

True to the account of the three buffalo hunters, the Sioux had indeed sighted the Pawnees. Two days earlier, on August 3, six warriors reported the Pawnees' location to the Cut-Off camp. Representatives hurried to the nearby Brule camp inviting them to join in an attack on the Pawnees. Despite strong efforts, Estes, the sub-agent to the Brules, was unable to talk them out of taking part. Later that same day a combined Sioux force thought to number more than a thousand braves set out down Frenchman's Fork to the point it merged with the Republican River just east of Culbertson.[38]

The Pawnees crossed the flat area where the walls of the canyon they had been following dwindled away. Staying mainly along the higher ground on to the west, they moved toward another small canyon that opened in an almost northerly direction. "Canyon" does not best describe the landscape the Pawnees entered and where the battle would be fought. In most western literature, the place would be called a "draw." There are indeed distinct sides to a soft, rolling "u"-shaped depression, but they are for the most part not steep; they rise gradually to form small bluffs whose flat tops match the elevation of the surrounding landscape. Inside the "u," generally in the middle but sometimes wandering nearer each side, there is occasionally a sharper gash, a small slice in the soil caused by a tiny runnel who path has carved a niche in the otherwise gentle terrain.

The canyon is not straight. It curves randomly in a series of gradual turns both east and west. The turns serve to periodically narrow or widen the base of the canyon, expanding the space between the walls in some places and greatly constricting it in others.

When the Pawnees moved into the draw, all were mounted and they had with them several hundred extra ponies to carry gear, buffalo meat, and skins. Their armament consisted of bows or "old-fashioned muzzle loading rifles, though a few had modern Spencer carbines."[39]

Unknown to the Pawnees, the Sioux were now only a short distance away. They were better armed than the Pawnees, possessing more and newer rifles. Over time, the aggressive Sioux had received payments of food, guns, and other goods, distributed by the Bureau of Indian Affairs[40] in efforts to pacify them. These attempts to "buy off" the Sioux were mostly futile and had the ironic effect of increasing the lethality of what was already the most warlike tribe on the Plains.

Sometime during the morning, the Pawnees came upon buffalo feeding. After pursuing and killing several, part of the Pawnee band was left to skin the carcasses and cut up the meat while the main group continued up the canyon.[41] Soon, additional numbers of feeding buffalo—the story persists that at least some may have been camouflaged Sioux horses and riders—were sighted in the distance.[42] After continuing ahead for a mile or so,[43] the Pawnees were suddenly attacked by a large Sioux war party that raced toward them over a bluff.[44]

By most accounts, this initial attack by almost 100 Sioux warriors killed Sky Chief, the Pawnee leader, and some others.[45] Startled by

Photo by Nita Phillips

Retreating Pawnees may have used this small copse of trees to make a defensive stand during the battle.

the assault, the Pawnees hurried women, children, and pack animals into the canyon.

At some point early in the attack, sub-agent Williamson and either an interpreter or Lester Platt, a young white man accompanying the expedition, attempted to parley with the attacking Sioux.[46] They advanced using a white handkerchief, but were fired upon and forced back.[47] As they raced away, Williamson's horse was shot from under him near the rim of the canyon and at that point, or soon after, Platt was momentarily captured but released not long after by the Sioux.

At the outset, Williamson advised the remaining Pawnee chiefs to fall back down the canyon and take up a defensive position in a copse of trees—possibly the ash and cottonwood timber they had passed earlier—about two miles away. Some agreed, but were quickly overruled by others who insisted on forming a defense and fighting where they stood.[48] It is uncertain how many of the 250 or so Pawnee warriors were engaged at this point. Platt contends that many were elsewhere hunting.[49]

The Pawnee at first held their own against the initial wave of attacking Sioux.[50] After the struggle had gone on for about an hour, a huge band of 700 to a thousand Sioux—the main body of the combined

Cut-Off and Brule groups—swarmed into the canyon area.[51] As the Pawnee women chanted their war song,[52] Pawnee warriors attempted to repulse the massive new assault by the Sioux. The numbers were too great for the Pawnees to handle; the Sioux reinforcements charged the Pawnees from three sides, threatening to engulf them. Overwhelmed and facing annihilation, the Pawnees fell back on their pony herd, tearing off packs, skins, meats, and camp paraphernalia, desperately attempting to put women and children on the ponies for a flight to safety. A mass of Sioux warriors surged around the Pawnees on the canyon floor while others in the large group split apart and raced along the walls of the canyon, firing into the melee. Fearing that the mouth of the canyon was about to be closed by enemy enveloping them from both sides, the Pawnee began a retreat that almost immediately turned into a panic-stricken rush through the canyon.[53] At places where the defile narrowed, the terrorized throng of warriors, women, children, and horses was forced together in a constricted flood of animals and people. At times slowed or almost stopped by the crush, the Pawnees were fired upon by Sioux shooting down at them from canyon walls on each side.

Several participants, including Williamson, left recollections of the furious dash for safety. Williamson, now on a fresh mount, recalled racing down the draw, one small part of the stream of Pawnee humanity trying desperately to flee the killing field on the canyon floor:

"I have often thought of a little Indian girl, who evidently had fallen from her mother's back, in our retreat down the canyon. She was sitting on the ground with her little arms raised as if pleading for someone to pick her up. As I passed I tried to pick her up but only succeeded in touching one of her hands."[54]

Pressed by the swarming mass around and behind him, Williamson could not change his course to retrieve her.

The little girl was found later, lying in her own blood, the top of her head hacked away.[55]

At one point during the flight, there was apparently an attempt to make a stand, perhaps only to buy time for others to escape. A visitor to the scene a few days later wrote:

(A)bout a mile and a half from the commencement of the retreat
. . .eight warriors took shelter behind a sort of bank or opening on one
side of the canyon, and all of them are lying there in death, a squaw
and papoose with them.[56]

Pawnee lore says these warriors held off repeated charges after
vowing they were "through living" and "(t)his is where I shall remain.
I do not wish to see the sun come up."[57]

The terrorized survivors fled through the canyon and managed
to get south of the river to relative safety[58] before moving down the
valley to the east.[59] Eventually, the Sioux gave up the chase.[60]

The full length of the canyon from the point of the first encounter
through its opening onto the plains, was strewn with supplies and
equipment abandoned during the Pawnee's flight.[61] A settler who saw
the canyon a few days later said

> "The first thing we met (at) the head of the canyon was the
> loading thrown off their ponies, and this was done in a space
> of fifty yards, and over this space the ground was literally piled
> up with packed meat, robes, hides, tents, camp kettles, and in
> fact everything they carry on their hunting expeditions. . .In
> one place is a pond hole two or three rods long, where, I should
> judge, near twenty bodies were lying in a most sickening state
> of decomposition."[62]

As chance would have it, there was a cavalry unit in the vicinity of
the canyon that day. Company B, U.S. Third Cavalry, commanded by
Captain Charles Meinhold, accompanied by another officer, a surgeon,
a civilian scout, and forty-seven enlisted men, had left Fort McPherson
on July 30.[63] A story soon surfaced that they came upon the massacre
scene and prevented further bloodshed.[64] However, it is certain that
the unit reached the canyon later in the day, having been informed of
the massacre by Pawnee refugees who came upon them during their
eastward flight[65] or—the sources vary—by Lester Platt subsequent to
his release by the Sioux.[66] Conceivably, both may have intersected the
cavalry at some point as the troops moved west into the area.

After first directing the Pawnee to proceed east down the valley to
Red Willow, Captain Meinhold led his troop to the battlefield.[67] When
the cavalry entered the canyon, the "evidence of savage brutality" on

the killing field was everywhere apparent. "Dead Pawnee women and children were lying among the dead horses. The Sioux had stripped, scalped and mutilated the dead. They had gathered lodge poles and piled bodies on the poles and burned the dead and dying Pawnees."[68]

According to military reports, Pawnee women who fell behind were raped and in some cases killed and mutilated.[69] "Pawnee possessions were piled and put to the torch. Bodies, sometimes still breathing were thrown into the flames. . . . (w)ounded squaws were raped, children were brutally killed."[70]

Meinhold's cavalrymen immediately scouted the battle area. Finding no sign of the Sioux, they returned to the mouth of the Frenchman River, where they camped that night. Although the Sioux remained in the area for several days, a cavalry reconnaissance the following morning again failed to locate them[71] and the episode drew to its bloody close without further incident.

When Captain Meinhold's troops scoured the battlefield on the afternoon of August 5, they counted fifty-seven Pawnee bodies. Some were apparently missed and others likely died afterward of their wounds. A census taken at the Pawnee Agency the following month showed that a total of sixty-nine Pawnee—twenty men, thirty-nine women, and ten children—had been killed.[72] It is possible that two additional children died later. By another account, the census showed twelve children's death, bringing the total to seventy-one killed.[73] Through sub-agent Estes' efforts, eleven Pawnee prisoners, four taken by the Brules and seven by the Cut-Offs, were later returned.[74]

Sioux casualties are more difficult to determine and the sub-agents' accounts are somewhat contradictory. However, a few weeks after the battle, a local settler found six recent Sioux burials and historians have assumed them to be casualties from the battle.[75]

Sky Chief, the Pawnee leader killed in Massacre Canyon, was one of the most respected of all Pawnee chiefs. Like several aspects of the battle—the timing of Williamson's attempted parley, the existence of Sioux horses camouflaged as buffalo, the reasons the Sioux broke off the pursuit, the exact number of casualties—uncertainties remain regarding his death. Many contemporary accounts indicated that he was killed in the first assault while skinning a buffalo and was quickly scalped.[76] Williamson was informed that Sky Chief was wounded by the first wave of Sioux and that he died fighting, surrounded as he struggled to reach his horse.[77]

Pawnee lore carries Sky Chief's story farther. Pawnees say he survived long enough to rally some of his men and to make a final gesture of defiance. By the tribe's account, the chief's three-year-old son was with him on his horse when they were attacked by an overwhelming number of Sioux. Sky Chief slew the boy with his knife rather than having him captured and tortured by his enemies.[78]

* * *

The Pawnees' power was on the wane long before catastrophe struck them at Massacre Canyon. Never again would they regain it. A drought that same year, 1873, and the following year left the tribe further destitute. Meanwhile, settlers continued to encroach upon their land and lobby for the tribe's removal.[79]

For a considerable time, some tribesmen had advocated a move to Indian Territory (Oklahoma). The proposal was initially resisted by a majority of the tribe, despite Sioux raids and increasing white incursions. Massacre Canyon devastated the tribe and influenced the decision to move. A group of Pawnees spent the winter of 1873 in Oklahoma and returned the following year to press the case for moving. In the meantime, the tribe had not been able to make their annual winter buffalo hunt and the Sioux continued to raid their horse herds.[80]

Demoralized by the battle and by the combination of misfortunes that had befallen them, after considerable debate the tribe ceded its reservation in Nebraska to the United States government. In return, the Pawnees received lands in Indian Territory. Some left for Oklahoma in 1874; the remainder followed the next year.[81] Two years after Massacre Canyon, the entire Pawnee nation—Nebraska's oldest and once its largest tribe, whose legendary Scouts served the United States Army with valor and loyalty—was gone from the state forever.

* * *

Three and a half miles east of Trenton an impressive monument marks a site where the southern end of the canyon cuts across U.S. Highway 34. A few hundred yards further west, a small copse of trees – possibly the one suggested by Williamson as a place for the Pawnees to make a stand—fills the small ravine. The entrance lies two to three miles north of the monument, where the canyon begins its north to south flow, running almost its entire length on private property. Portions of it are used for grazing. Although at widely dispersed intervals the canyon is cut through by fences, for the most, it is undisturbed. The small runnel that was so often noted by participants still cuts its zigzag course along the canyon floor.

Endnotes

1 R. Eli Paul, Editor, *The Nebraska Indian Wars Reader 1867-1877*, (Lincoln and London: The University of Nebraska Press, 1998) p. 88.
2 Paul, p. 89.
3 Paul p. 88.
4 B. W. Allred, Editor, *Great Western Indian Fights*, (Lincoln: The University of Nebraska Press, 1960) p. 183.
5 Merrill J. Mattes, *The Great Platte River Road*, (Lincoln: The Nebraska State Historical Society, 1969) p. 287.
6 *Nebraska Trailblazer #1: American Indians*, Nebraska State Historical Society p. 1 website www.nebraskahistory.org/museum/teachers/material/trail/indians/backgroun.htm. Material extracted from website November 11, 2004.
7 Paul p. 91.
8 *Nebraska Trailblazer #1*, p. 1.
9 Allred p. 183.
10 David L. Bristow, The Battle of Massacre Canyon, *Nebraska Life*, July/August 2004: p. 48. See also Walt Sehnert, The Pawnee's Brave Fight at Massacre Canyon, *McCook Daily Gazette*, January 5, 2004:p. 1.
11 Allred p. 183.
12 Paul Riley, Massacre Canyon, Hitchcock County, NE, *McCook Gazette Centennial Edition 1867-1967*: p. 3.
13 *Nebraska Trailblazer #1*, p. 4.
14 Ibid.
15 Paul p. 94.
16 Allred p. 185.
17 Paul p. 89.
18 Paul p. 97.
19 Ibid.
20 Ibid.
21 Riley p. 6.
22 Paul p. 98.
23 Riley p. 5.
24 Riley p. 6.
25 Riley p. 6,7.
26 Bristow p. 50.
27 Paul p. 89 and Bristow p. 48 put the number at 350. Among others, Sehnert (p. 2) and Nebraska State Historical Society Marker 8 estimate 700.
28 Allred p. 186.
29 Bristow p. 49.
30 Allred p. 187. Paul (p. 96) says the "total number (was) over a thousand warriors. By another account, more than 1,500 Sioux warriors participated in the battle (Sehnert p.3).
31 Paul p. 96.
32 Ibid.
33 Riley p. 4.
34 Sehnert p. 3.
35 Allred p. 187.
36 Paul p. 100.
37 Sehnert p.3.
38 Paul p. 98.
39 Bristow p. 49.
40 *Nebraska Trailblazer #1*, p. 5.
41 Allred, p. 187.
42 Riley p. 5. See also Alan Boye, *The Complete Roadside Guide to Nebraska*, (St. Johnsbury, Vermont: Saltillo Press, 1993) p. 283.
43 Sehnert p.3.
44 Allred p. 187.
45 Ibid.
46 Paul (p. 100), places Williamson's attempt after the main body of Sioux arrived, and indicates that the Pawnees suggested the attempt. Bristow (p. 52) asserts that Williamson tried while the larger Sioux party was still a mile and a half away. Both agree that his horse was shot as

he raced away from the scene. Riley's account (p. 5) has Williamson's effort occurring earliest, right after the first wave of Sioux was sighted.

47 Allred p. 187.
48 Paul p. 100.
49 Bristow p. 52.
50 Allred p. 187.
51 Allred p. 187.
52 Paul p. 100.
53 Allred p. 187.
54 Paul p. 101.
55 Bristow p. 52
56 Paul p. 101.
57 Bristow p. 53.
58 Allred p. 187.
59 Allred p. 187.
60 Riley (p. 5) states that so amazed were the Sioux by their great success – Plains Indians seldom fought all out battles – that they gave up the chase before most of the Pawnee reached the head of the canyon and began to vent their fury on the dead and wounded Pawnees. Allred (p. 187) indicates the pursuit lasted for about ten miles. Paul (p. 100) suggests the possibility that the Sioux heard rumors of the cavalry unit's presence in the area and ended the chase for that reason.
61 Riley p. 5.
62 Paul p. 101. The settler's name was Royal Buck. Buck was the first to use the name "Massacre Canyon."
63 Riley p. 6.
64 Allred p. 187.
65 Ibid.
66 Allred p. 187.
67 Riley p. 6.
68 Allred p. 187.
69 Bristow p. 53.
70 Riley p. 5.
71 Riley p. 6.
72 Riley (p. 6), Allred (p. 188), Sehnert (p. 4) say "between 60 and 80" were killed. The Nebraska State Historical Society indicates there were "between 70 and 100 Pawnee killed or wounded." *Trailblazer* puts the number at "about 100."
73 Bristow p. 53.
74 Riley p. 6.
75 Riley (p. 7) and Sehnert (p. 4) say the Sioux lost three warriors, but acknowledge reports indicating six fatalities.
76 Allred p. 187.
77 Bristow p. 53.
78 Ibid.
79 *Nebraska Trailblazer #1*, p. 2.
80 Riley p. 9,10.
81 *Nebraska Trailblazer #*, p. 2 .

114

Chapter Nine

The Battle of the Blowout

B y one tally, the Great Sioux War of 1876-1877 was fought on twenty-nine different battlefields over an enormous landscape that covered much of the north central region of the continental United States.[1] The clashes that began at Fort Pease, Montana, in February 1876 and ended nineteen months later at Fort Robinson, Nebraska, were the climactic phase of the long, bitter conflict with the Plains Indians.

* * *

"At the beginning of 1876, the government estimated the war would involve no more than 3,000 non-treaty Lakotas, of which only 600 to 800 were warriors."[2] As is so often the case even today, intelligence indicators were wrong. In fact, the Sioux War involved thousands of warriors from several tribes.

What came to be known as the Battle of the Blowout was the first of three encounters from that conflict (along with the fight at Warbonnet Creek and the confused melee that led to the death of Crazy Horse) that occurred in Nebraska.[3]

War came to the state in April, 1876, when soldiers of the Twenty-third Infantry fought a group of Lakota Sioux a few miles northwest of present-day Burwell. Trouble had previously visited the area and the memories of recent skirmishes at nearby Sioux Creek (1873) and Pebble Creek (1874),[4] increased tensions at a time when the Sioux were known to be on the warpath.

The clash and the resulting loss of life at Pebble Creek led to the construction of Fort Hartsuff,[5] near present-day Elyria. For settlers in the North Loup Valley, the timing was fortunate: on April 28, soldiers from the new outpost were called upon to confront a party of Indians holed up in a large hillside "blowout" after skirmishing with settlers, local trappers, and gold seekers in a day-long running fight.

The fighting at the blowout location came late, after a long series of "pop up and shoot" exchanges—sometimes heavy—that extended over several miles. The incidents began early in the morning when a band of Indians, thought to be about six in number, was spotted near the Jones Canyon region a few miles from Burwell. A collection of settlers, trappers from the local area, and gold seekers traveling toward the Black Hills quickly formed and moved against the Sioux. Loosely led by a settler named C. H. Jones, the group would eventually total twelve to thirteen as nearby settlers joined the fray.[6]

On occasion, the Indians' trail was momentarily lost as pursued and pursuer moved through the rugged canyons and windblown hollows that form the region's landscape. As the chase tightened, the Indians discarded all of their packs except weapons and ammunition as they moved in the general direction of Calamus Valley.

As the fighting persisted through the morning, one of the settlers rode to Fort Hartsuff, about fifteen miles to the southeast, to alert the garrison.[7] Within minutes, Lieutenant Charles Heyl and eight soldiers from Company A, Twenty-third Infantry[8] were in the saddle and on the way to the scene of the fighting.

Heyl's men came on the scene slightly north of where the Indians were holed up in a large blowout, perhaps originally a buffalo wallow, now wind-eroded into a deep scoop-shaped crevasse in a hillside above a small creek. Cone-shaped, the blowout opened to the south/southeast and sat at the top of a sandhill higher than the others nearest it. Settlers pointed out the location to the approaching soldiers and attempted to keep the Indians pinned down until the troops arrived. As the soldiers moved toward the hillside, some of the Sioux left the blowout to pursue a settler who had ventured close to the edge. Shot by another settler, an Indian fell back into the hollow as the rest of the Sioux, now under additional fire, raced back to the shelter of the blowout.

It was by now late in the afternoon. With daylight beginning to fade, Heyl was concerned that the Indians would take advantage of the broken terrain and escape after nightfall.[9] Heyl had his men dismount and after some discussion, decided to attack straight up the hill towards the blowout. Several settlers were posted on a small promontory from

Photo by Nita Phillips
Troops from the 23rd Infantry left Fort Hartsuff to fight the Battle of the Blowout. The fort has been beautifully restored.

where they could fire into the hollow[10] and keep the Indians pinned down while the troops advanced. Splitting his small force, Heyl sent four men to block the Indians' most likely escape route, and then led three soldiers—Sergeant William Dougherty and Corporals Patrick Leonard and Jeptha Lytton—in a charge against the well positioned Sioux.[11]

Heyl moved up the hillside with his troops in a line with himself on one end on the right and Sergeant Dougherty on the opposite side at the left. By one account, Dougherty was the first to reach the rim of the depression. Locating the Indians—and being seen by them—he stepped back, motioning the specific location of the Sioux to Heyl, then returned to the edge of the cavity preparing to fire. As he moved toward the blowout, he was killed instantly, struck through the heart by a shot fired from a warrior inside the hollow.[12] A spasm of heavy fire then ensued before the soldiers, recognizing the futility of assaulting an excellent defensive position with only a handful of men,[13] retreated back down the hillside. Sergeant Dougherty's body was recovered later in the day by a party led by Lieutenant Heyl.[14]

After the initial attack failed, Heyl sent one of his soldiers to the fort, requesting reinforcements and an ambulance. At sundown, pickets were placed near the hole, ringing it in an attempt to keep the

Courtesy Fort Hartsuff State Historical Park
Painting of the Battle of the Blowout, by John Russell Cole. The painting now hangs at Fort Hartsuff.

Indians trapped inside. Additional troops from Fort Hartsuff arrived at about midnight. At daybreak another assault with heavier numbers was made against the blowout. The attacking force found the hollow empty: the Sioux had slipped away during the night.[15]

There was no attempt at pursuit. The troopers returned to Fort Hartsuff with Sergeant Dougherty's body. By a settler's account, about three weeks later the remnants of the Sioux war party struggled into the Rosebud Agency.[16] Dougherty was the only casualty among the soldiers. Most sources also put the Indian losses at one.[17]

Though the portion of the fight that occurred in and around the blowout was relatively brief, its fury was such that three Medals of Honor were awarded to soldiers (Lieutenant Heyl and Corporals Leonard and Lytton) who participated in the dash up the hillside.[18]

It is a reflection of the times that the battle was fought when and where it was. The Sioux were outraged by incursions of gold seekers into the Black Hills. The Army, confronted by the reality that the entire Sioux nation was on the warpath, adopted a policy that Indians who roamed off a reservation "were presumed to be a war party."[19] Thus, with tensions already high after Sioux Creek and Pebble Creek, the presence of a group of well armed Lakotas triggered the day-long clashes that culminated at the blowout.

The Battle of the Blowout was a precursor to other, often bloodier clashes that would follow in the months ahead. In the short run, the battle caused some pioneer families to leave the area, unsettled by an episode that showed yet again how insecure life was on the frontier. Others resolved to stay but constructed almost fortress-like homes as protection against raids that seemed likely to continue.

Over the long-term, events unfolded differently. Hostile Sioux vanished from the area. Initially, many joined Sitting Bull, Crazy Horse, and other chiefs in the great struggle against the army forces sent against them. Later, after the victory at the Little Bighorn, a series of setbacks culminating in the death of Crazy Horse all but ended the uprising. Grudgingly, most Sioux entered reservations.

Although the number of combatants was small, the Battle of the Blowout was, in fact, a watershed. It was the last significant encounter between soldiers and Sioux warriors in north central Nebraska. Indeed, the situation in the region quickly became so peaceful that by 1880 the Army decided to abandon Fort Hartsuff. Orders for doing so were issued the following year.[20]

* * *

The presumed battle site, described in at least one pioneer diary and researched extensively in the 1970s, is near the Loup-Garfield County line, north of the Calumus Reservoir. The battle area is located on private property on land presently used for pasture grazing. The scene is little changed from April, 1876; the native grass around the blowout site has never been disturbed. Except for its higher elevation and the existence of the blowout feature near the top, the general appearance of the sandhill is typical of the terrain around it.

Today, Fort Hartsuff is one of the most remarkably restored of all frontier outposts. Located near Elyria, the outpost's nine original buildings and three reconstructions are fully equipped and furnished. The fort provides an extraordinary look at military life on the Plains in the 1870s.

Endnotes

1 Paul Hedron, "Battlefields as Material Culture: A Case Study from the Great Sioux War," *Nebraska History* Summer 1996, p. 99.

2 Charles M. Robinson III, *A Good Year to Die: The Story of the Great Sioux War*, (Norman and London: University of Oklahoma Press, 1996) p. 51.

3 A full list of the battles and skirmishes of the Great Sioux War of 1876-1877 is shown in *Nebraska History* Summer 1996, p. 106-107.

4 *Fort Hartsuff 1874-1881*, Nebraska State Game and Parks Commission, 1999.

5 Harold Foght, *The Trail of the Loup*, (Ord, Nebraska, 1906) p. 130-135.

6 Foght p. 157,158.

7 Foght p. 159.

8 R. Eli Paul, Editor, *The Nebraska Indian Wars Reader 1865-1877*, (Lincoln and London: The University of Nebraska Press, 1998) p. 222.

9 Ibid.

10 Foght p. 160.

11 Paul p. 222.

12 Foght p. 161.

13 Paul p. 222.

14 Foght p. 161.

15 Ibid.

16 Ibid.

17 Hedron p. 106.

18 Paul p. 222.

19 Ibid.

20 *Fort Hartsuff 1874-1881*.

Other References

I am especially indebted to Mr. Roye Lindsay, Superintendent, Fort Hartsuff State Historical Park, and his staff for their kind assistance. Mr. Lindsay is the state's acknowledged expert on the battle and was very gracious in sharing his information.

Chapter Ten

The Battle of Warbonnet Creek

I n the mid-1870s warfare on the Plains entered its climactic phase
with the final great uprising of 1876. Clashes at Powder River
and Rosebud Creek were followed by the Little Bighorn and later,
in Nebraska, at Warbonnet Creek. Coming as it did after months of
disaster, the cavalry's victory at Warbonnet Creek began the turn-
around in the government's fortunes.

As masterfully described by Charles Robinson, the two sides
approached this defining moment in decidedly different ways.

"Covering this vast and difficult country, infantrymen
generally marched with about fifty pounds of equipment on
their backs. Cavalrymen packed their gear on mounts, but in
addition to personal equipment, each cavalryman had to carry
ten to fifteen pounds of grain for his horse. Unlike Indian
ponies, government horses could not live off the land, and
required supplemental feeding. On long marches, when the
supply of forage was exhausted, horses began to wear out, and
many cavalrymen ended up on foot. Extra food, forage, and
ammunition were carried in wagons where the terrain allowed,
and packed on mules when it did not. Often the mule train fell
behind the marching column, a problem that hindered military
operations throughout the war.

"In 1873, the army standardized weapons so that soldiers
in the Great Sioux War were generally issued two basic arms:
the .45 caliber Colt Single Action Army revolver; and the
Model 1873 Springfield rifle, in caliber .45-70 long rifle for
infantry, and .45-55 light carbine for cavalry. The Springfield
was a single-shot, breech loading weapon that fired a metallic

cartridge. It could be loaded and fired much more rapidly than its predecessors, and had twice the range of repeating rifles such as the Winchester, Henry, or Spencer.

"The improvement in firearms forced a dramatic revision of cavalry tactics. The revision, adopted in 1874, recognized that in the face of these weapons, the classic, sabre-wielding cavalry charge was suicidal. Under the new tactics, the mounted charge was used only for initial shock, the weight and speed of the horses creating confusion among the enemy, and giving the cavalryman an advantage in choosing his ground to fight. Once engaged, however, the cavalry unit dismounted and formed a skirmish line using squads of four men each. Three men with carbines placed themselves on the line, while the fourth remained on his horse behind the line, holding the horses for the others. When several companies were engaged, as was the case in most instances during the Great Sioux War, one company was held in reserve about 150 yards behind the line.

"Indian weaponry was a collection of whatever could be collected by barter, capture, theft, or various other means. Studies of cartridge cases recovered in archeological investigations of the Little Bighorn show the Indians carried at least forty-one different kinds of firearms in that fight, and it is estimated that at least twenty-five to thirty percent were armed with modern, sixteen-shot Winchester and Henry repeating rifles. After the fight, they armed themselves with captured Springfield carbines. Aside from firearms, the Indians carried traditional weapons, such as bows and arrows, hatchets, tomahawks and war clubs.

"The average Indian fought almost entirely as an individual, not as part of a larger organization. Strategy, communications, even numbers of people in a particular location—essential to any white history—were seldom noted because they did not affect most Indians as individuals."[1]

* * *

For the United States military forces sent to quell the massive uprising that had exploded across the northern plains, the first half of 1876 was an unmitigated disaster. Culminating with the catastrophe at the Little Bighorn, Indians inflicted repeated setbacks on U.S. forces led by some of the military's most famous commanders.

The fighting had begun late in the preceding year when, outraged by the intrusions of gold seekers and settlers into the Black Hills, hundreds of Sioux and Cheyennes left their reservations. When ordered to return, they refused to do so. Gathering mostly in eastern Montana and led by legendary war chiefs, they were emboldened by victories won during the spring and early summer.

Seeking to strike while the hostiles were in stationary camps and their pony herds weakened by winter weather, General Philip H. Sheridan, ordered General George Crook to proceed north from Fort Fetterman, Wyoming Territory, and attack hostile Sioux known to be wintering in the vicinity of Powder River. On March 17, 400 of Crook's soldiers under the direct command of Colonel Joseph J. Reynolds were defeated along the Powder River in the southeast corner of Montana.

Compounding that setback, Reynolds destroyed the contents of the village, burning provisions that Crook had intended to use to supply his troops for a more extended campaign. Lacking supplies, Crook's soldiers returned to their base. Significantly, the encampment struck by Reynolds that day was not a Sioux village: it was inhabited by Northern Cheyennes. The effect of the assault was to further cement an alliance between Sioux and Cheyenne.[2]

After Crook reprovisioned at Fort Fetterman, his forces put in motion a grand strategy intended to crush the major Indian threat once and for all. As conceived by Sheridan, three large columns moving from different directions would converge on the Yellowstone-Powder River area where large numbers of "non-treaty Sioux" along with other bands that had left reservations were believed to be gathering. Sheridan's plan sent Crook north from Fort Fetterman. Meanwhile, Colonel John Gibbon would move east down the Yellowstone River from Fort Shaw, Montana, and Brigadier General Alfred Terry would drive west from Fort Abraham Lincoln in Dakota Territory. Caught inside the closing pincers, the hostiles would either be destroyed or hammered into submission and forced onto reservations.

Crook's force made first contact, a brief skirmish along the Tongue River on June 9. On June 17, a much larger and more consequential engagement occurred near the headwaters of Rosebud Creek in southeastern Montana, between the Powder River and the Little Bighorn. At Rosebud Creek, Sioux and Cheyenne launched a day-long attack—unusual in Indian wars—on Crook's encampment. Casualties were high on both sides.[3] While Crook still possessed the ground at the end of the day, his losses and the need to resupply caused him to abandon his offensive.

Following the battle, Crook turned his force south to Goose Creek, Wyoming, where he waited for provisions and, with more than a thousand men already under his command,[4] asked for reinforcements. His request for additional troops would play a part in the drama that was to unfold on Warbonnet Creek the following month.

More importantly, by moving south, Crook took his army away from the vicinity of the Little Bighorn, thus foreclosing the possibility of lending assistance during the titanic combat that occurred there only eight days later, on July 25, 1876.

Believing that Crook was still moving towards him, General Terry sent Lieutenant Colonel George Armstrong Custer and the Seventh Cavalry up the Rosebud Creek to locate and pursue Indians known to be concentrating in the valley of the Little Bighorn. Custer found a huge trail and followed it west. Unwilling to wait until the rest of Terry's army closed up with him, or until Gibbon's force arrived from the west, Custer made a series of unusual—and ultimately, disastrous—moves. With troops and mounts already exhausted by forced marches, and facing one of the largest encampments of hostiles ever assembled on the North American continent, he divided his force of approximately 600 into three parts and attacked at midday instead of waiting until dawn which was standard army practice. The enormous coalition of natives that Custer sent the Seventh Cavalry against that day included Sitting Bull, Crazy Horse, and several other prominent chiefs. In the ensuing battle, Custer and every one of the more than 200 men under his immediate command were killed.[5]

The Little Bighorn was one of America's worst military disasters. News of the battle was at first slow percolating through a nation absorbed with Centennial celebration festivities. When it did, the public was thunder-struck. Custer, the flamboyant "boy general," already noted for his exploits during the Civil War, was one of the Army's most recognizable officers. By the standards of Plains warfare, the casualties were staggering. Amid the nation's shock and anger came calls for action.

For the small frontier army, the Little Bighorn represented the most recent, and most severe, reversal in a series of setbacks that had begun earlier that year at Powder River. The effect on individual soldiers was pronounced. In Crook's camp, "(t)he shock was so great the men and officers could hardly speak when the tale slowly circulated from lip to lip."[6] On the other side, the outcome induced hundreds of Plains Indians to leave their reservations to join the hostiles or begin making plans to do so.

Even before news of the debacles at Rosebud Creek and the Little Big Horn reached him, Sheridan moved with characteristic energy. Concerned by reports of Indians leaving the Red Cloud and Spotted Tail Agencies in northern Nebraska, he ordered the Fifth Cavalry to move to the region and cut the "feeder-trail" linking the reservations with the Powder River area where large numbers of hostiles were rapidly assembling.[7]

Initial elements of the Fifth Cavalry, sent from posts in the central plains, arrived in Wyoming in early June. Assembled first at Cheyenne and subsequently at Fort Laramie, eight full companies were soon in place.[8] On June 22, seven of the eight companies set out from Fort Laramie toward blocking positions along the Indian trail. Within three days, an advance party was in place. A series of extensive patrols over the next several days encountered only occasional small parties of hostiles. In the meantime, the final company had joined the group on the trail. The entire Fifth Cavalry—mounts provisioned with 75,000 pounds of grain[9]—was in place.

As the Fifth Cavalry maintained its vigil on the trail, changes occurred in two of its most important positions. First, William F. "Buffalo Bill" Cody was appointed chief of scouts. Much hyperbole —some of it generated by Cody himself—has been written about the career of the flamboyant showman, but there was no questioning his skills or his courage. His appointment had been requested by officers of the Fifth Cavalry and his presence was welcomed by its men. "(T)he soldiers trusted him as they trusted no other scout."[10]

Cody himself was eager to participate. At age thirty-one, he was already a near-mythical figure.[11] Some of his legendary reputation had resulted from adventures associated with his many previous scouts with the Fifth Cavalry—and he was a friend of Custer. When news of the Little Bighorn arrived, he wasted no time in heading west to rejoin the unit.

Cody did not move out with the Fifth when it left Fort Laramie on the June 22. General Sheridan was at the fort and asked Cody to accompany him on inspection trips to Fort Robinson and other Indian agencies. When those visits were completed, Cody joined the unit on its bivouac along the Indian trial.[12]

The second personnel change was the appointment, effective July 1, 1876, of a new commander, Colonel Wesley Merritt. Merritt, like Custer, was one of the "boy generals" of the Civil War. Highly regarded, he knew the territory well, having spent several previous months in the area serving as Cavalry Inspector for the Military Division of the Missouri—duties that enabled him to function as General Sheridan's personal investigator and trouble shooter. Merritt wasted no time in hurrying to assume his new command. On June 28, along with a company of troops, he left Fort Laramie to join the Fifth Cavalry. The group was personally guided by "Buffalo Bill" Cody, by this time freed from duties with General Sheridan.[13]

On July 1, Cody led Merritt and his escorts to the Fifth Cavalry's main camp northwest of the Red Cloud Agency in Nebraska. A brief lull followed, broken two days later when one of the Fifth's companies chased, unsuccessfully, a small group of Cheyennes, riding two horses to death and exhausting many others. Merritt responded to that event by moving the camp closer to the Indian trail and launching an aggressive series of scouts. The move to the new camp brought with it an added sign of peril: Merritt's soldiers found recently dug rifle pits and the bodies of two Black Hills miners killed by the Indians.[14]

Merritt kept his troops at the new campsite for the next several days while patrols scoured the area. Those activities ended on July 12, when Sheridan, apparently responding to Crook's continued pleas for reinforcements, ordered Merritt to return to Fort Laramie to refit and then to join Crook in northern Wyoming.[15]

The return to Fort Laramie was well under way and the unit was going into camp after a march of sixteen miles when Merritt received word from the commander of Camp Robinson that hundreds of Cheyennes were planning to leave the Red Cloud Agency and join the warring bands further north. Merritt reacted quickly. Advising Crook and Sheridan of his decision, over the next two days he back-tracked 51 miles to a point on the road between Fort Laramie and the Red Cloud Agency. There, he camped the night of July 14. Concluding that a further advance of his entire force toward the agency might provoke a fight before he was ready[16]—and determined to verify the accuracy of the information he had received[17]—Merritt sent a cavalry company to investigate the situation at the agency.

By midday on July 15 he had received word that "800 Cheyennes and a lot of Sioux"[18] were planning to leave the agency that day or soon after.[19]

Library of Congress
Colonel Wesley Merritt

After the fact information would indicate that the number was smaller, about 200 Cheyennes,[20] but Merritt had no way of knowing that, and regardless of the numbers he realized that it was crucial to shut off the flow of additional warriors to the hostiles who had already fought the cavalry to a standstill.

Within an hour of receiving the news, Merritt personally led seven cavalry companies deep into northwestern Nebraska. Merritt's goal was to get ahead of the Cheyennes and position himself across their line of march. If he could beat the Cheyennes to the trail, he intended to meet them head on and force them back to the agency.[21]

Time was of the essence. Even if they left on Sunday July 16, the Indians would need only a twenty-eight-mile ride to reach the junction in the trail.[22] Merritt would have to travel three times that distance. To do it, he needed to retrace his path to the north and turn east across the Indians' most likely route. Leaving a small detachment to guard much of his wagon train—whose commander was told to follow and catch up when the cavalry halted or went into camp—by ten o'clock

127

Photo by Nita Phillips
The Fifth Cavalary swept around the conical hill in the background on the last major cavalry charge in U.S. history. The stone monument in the foreground marks the spot where Buffalo Bill Cody fought Yellow Hair.

that night, Merritt had taken his men thirty-five miles. After a brief stop to rest and feed the horses, by five in the morning they were on the march again.

At midday they reached a palisaded camp along Sage Creek guarded by a company of infantry. There, they rested for an hour, ate a quick lunch, and further lightened their loads. Merritt's cavalrymen broke open ammunition boxes and stuffed their pockets and belts with cartridges.[23] Merritt's cavalry, as did most soldiers on the plains at that time, carried Springfield carbines, a single-shot weapon that fired a .50-caliber projectile. After 1873, many carbines were rechambered to make them compatible with a new .45-caliber round, propelled by 70 grains of powder.[24]

At Sage Creek, Merritt decided to leave his heavy supply wagons and take only light company wagons with three days rations.[25] The infantry company was loaded into the bigger wagons, and added to the contingent already assigned to guard the train. Directed to follow the cavalry, their approach toward Warbonnet Creek the next morning would influence events in the battle that followed.

That night—July 16—at 8 p.m., Merritt's cavalry reached Warbonnet Creek. They had marched eighty-five miles in thirty-one hours. . .and they had beaten the Indians to the vital crossing.[26]

Cody and his men, well out on the eastward flank as Merritt drove his force toward the junction, returned from a scout that night, assuring Merritt that the Indians were still positioned southeast—between Merritt's troops and the reservation. Large numbers of hostiles were moving towards them, however, and would probably reach the crossing early the next day.[27] As it turned out, Little Wolf's Cheyennes, having heard of the battle with Custer, were indeed on the move, hurrying to add their numbers to the hundreds already on the warpath in Wyoming and Montana. That night they were camped about seven miles southeast of Merritt's men on Warbonnet Creek.[28]

Merritt's men bivouacked in light timber on a small plateau near a line of bluffs. Shielded behind the western slope of the ridges, Merritt's encampment could not be seen by hostiles moving up the trail from the east and southeast. Only a few fires were allowed, and those were dug deep into holes so the flames could not be seen. One entire company was placed on guard duty, positioned in hollows and ravines where they could see objects silhouetted against the sky.[29]

Still in the pre-dawn hours, details in the landscape began to emerge as the blackness receded. To the west, the lightening sky revealed the rolling hills of the higher ground crossed by the regiment the night before. Immediately to the east, Warbonnet Creek extended across the Fifth Cavalry's front in a series of loops and curls that began in the southeast and traversed north before twisting back toward the left edge of Merritt's camp. A portion of the creek to the north was rimmed by a thin, snake-like tree line as the stream bent back and twisted its way to the South Fork of the Cheyenne River. Beyond the creek was a relatively flat area that extended three to four hundred yards before meeting a series of low ridges that pointed in the direction of the creek. The ridges varied slightly in height and the space between them was flat. In some places, the field of vision from these low spots and from the smaller ridges was obscured by the slightly higher ground on either side.

As the sky brightened further, almost directly to his front, looking east across the creek, the officer in charge of the sentinels, Lieutenant Charles King, was able to make out two small, sharply pointed hills that formed distinct spikes in the skyline. The southern-most one was about ninety feet high and 400 yards away. In places, this hillock and its companion blocked his view of the ground beyond. King quickly moved his outpost to it and posted a lookout on the second hill, located about 100 yards closer to camp, as well.[30]

His view now unobstructed, with two other men[31] King peered over the top of the hill, focusing mainly to the southeast, the direction from which the Indians would most likely come. The trail the Indians would use passed only a short distance to the right of the knoll where King waited. There, it crossed a shallow ravine. As the ravine and the trail wound their ways separately north, the ground between them rose sharply, concealing one from the other.

Merritt had been up since 3:30 a.m., joined within an hour by the entire Fifth Cavalry. In the pre-dawn quiet, the troopers huddled around shielded fires boiling coffee and frying salt pork. Soon, the "Dandy Fifth" was ready to mount up: 330 enlisted men, sixteen officers, a doctor, and five scouts including, and led by Bill Cody[32].

At about 4:15, as King and his men watched from the top of the small, spiked hill, several Cheyenne warriors in groups of two or three appeared at the head of a ravine about two miles to the southeast.[33] Merritt was instantly notified and came to the knoll with three of his staff, quickly followed by two scouts and about a half dozen cavalrymen.[34] They were soon joined by Cody, returning from an early morning scout during which he had located the Cheyennes' main camp.[35] The entire group had dismounted behind the hill and crawled to a vantage point at the top, peeking over at the spectacle unfolding before them. At the first sighting of Indians, Merritt ordered the Fifth to saddle up and mount, the order passed quietly from trooper to trooper. Six companies then moved forward, angling south, hidden by the sheltering bluffs as they waited in line only 200 yards from the trail and the ravine crossing.[36]

The Indians, sent by Little Wolf to scout ahead, rode slowly in the direction of King's outpost on the hillock and the Fifth Cavalry's encampment, but quite obviously saw neither. Moving in a pattern momentarily inexplicable, a number of warriors suddenly darted halfway up the wall of the ravine and began looking intently to the west.[37] The initial band moving up the draw was soon joined by additional hostiles. By 5 a.m. dozens of Indians were visible, lining the hillsides in and out of view a mile and a half away, all fixated by some occurrence out on the western horizon.[38]

Photos by Nita Phillips

Mounment atop the conical hill at Warbonnet Creek.

The explanation soon became clear. Merritt's supply train—the heavy wagons he had left at Sage Creek—were coming into view as tiny dots far out on the western rim, their presence made visible by the higher ground in that direction. In a superb logistical feat, after tending his mules and piling infantrymen on top of his supplies, Lieutenant William P. Hall had brought his train ahead on an all-night march.[39] From a distance, with the infantry in the wagons concealed beneath wagon tarps, the Indians likely believed it to be a civilian train bound for the Black Hills, and ripe for picking.

Moments after daybreak, additional excitement occurred. As Merritt and the small group with him watched, several warriors broke away from the main body on a facing ridge. Charging headlong down the slope, the party raced directly towards them at full speed. Again, the observers on the hill were left with no immediate explanation. Again, when it came, the answer lay to the west. Behind them, popping up suddenly over a high point on the prairie, no more than a mile to the southwest, two couriers carrying dispatches to Merritt galloped into view, visible not only to the cavalrymen on the hillock but also to the Cheyennes who were moving swiftly to intercept them. The Indians were not seen by the couriers who, believing Merritt's camp was near, had hurried ahead of the protection of the oncoming supply train.[40] To those on the knoll, it was apparent that the point of intercept would be near the junction where the trail and the ravine met.

Contemporary accounts credit Cody with proposing that he, along with two scouts and six troopers, cut the Indians off before they could surprise the couriers.[41] Seeing the same opportunity, Merritt immediately ordered Lieutenant King to maintain his post and signal when the time was right for Cody and his party to burst from cover and confront the fast-approaching Indians.[42]

Staying out of sight, Cody and his men scrambled down the backside of the hill, mounted their horses and, still concealed, rode to a spot near the head of the ravine. There, they waited for the signal from King. As the Indians raced headlong down the draw, the lieutenant raised his hand, delaying until the moment was right to achieve maximum surprise. When the Cheyennes were about ninety yards away, he brought his hand down, yelling for Cody to attack. Cody's party sprang from their hiding place, tore headlong around the shoulder of the bluff and, firing as they rode, charged straight towards the onrushing warriors.[43]

Startled, the Cheyennes momentarily halted and began answering the attack, firing volleys toward Cody and at the hillside outpost. Their leader, Yellow Hair, bent low over his pony's neck, fired a round that narrowly missed Merritt as he ran to join Lieutenant King at the top of the knoll.[44]

Cody's charge carried his squad straight into the advancing Cheyennes. In the melee that followed, Cody and Yellow Hair engaged one on one, although the accounts vary as to the nature and duration of their individual combat. The most intense versions describe a duel that began with rifles, transitioned to tomahawks or knives and ended with Cody scalping Yellow Hair.

The story most often credited is different, though "no less valiant."[45] In this account, as the cavalrymen charged with Cody in the lead, Yellow Hair shot and missed, but the round startled Cody's horse which reared and threw him. Cody quickly regained his feet and fired at Yellow Hair who was draped along his pony's neck and firing from underneath it. Cody's shot hit Yellow Hair's left leg, tore through it, struck the horse in the heart and killed it. Pony and rider then tumbled to the ground in a confused heap. Yellow Hair, perhaps after being knocked down again after Cody's horse stumbled over the fallen pony, jumped to his feet and was preparing to fire again when a second shot from Cody struck him in the brain and killed him.[46]

Amid the chaos, several Cheyennes tried to retrieve the chief's body but were driven off by cavalrymen. Cody took Yellow Hair's scalp, proclaiming it—according to legend and in his autobiography —to be the "first scalp for Custer."[47]

The developing clash between Cody's small force and Yellow Hair's Cheyennes caused action to erupt both west and east from the scene of their encounter. Out on the prairie to the west, at the sound of the final volley and with Indians now visible to them, Lieutenant Hall broke out his infantry from under the wagon tarps and deployed them in skirmish position to protect the supply train. To the east, the mass of Indians on the ridge opposite Warbonnet Creek began a dash to the scene of the fight.

The Cheyennes' bid to rescue their colleagues had carried them about half way across the open ground toward the creek, when Merritt ordered the Fifth's Company K to move against them. "K" was Lieutenant King's company; when it passed close to his outpost as it moved to the attack, King raced down the knoll to join it. When the company reached open ground, it spread into open order and charged. Simultaneously, sweeping both north and south around the conical hill, Company B moved to "Ks" right flank and Company I took position in line on the left. Line abreast, in a classic cavalry charge—possibly the last in American history—the three veteran companies, about 147 troopers, lit into the oncoming Indians.[48]

Stunned by the sight of the wave of blue about to slam into them, the Cheyennes turned their ponies and took flight. Merritt's cavalry chased the Indians closely for about three miles as the Cheyennes abandoned their possessions and raced in panic to the southeast toward the reservation. Sounds of the battle from Warbonnet Creek and the chase that followed carried to Little Wolf's camp seven miles away. Realizing that their path was now blocked and the goal of joining their allies was no longer attainable, they hurriedly dismantled their village and began the trek back to the Red Cloud Agency, leaving behind several lodges and hundreds of pounds of provisions.[49]

Correctly sensing that the fight had gone out of the Indians, at Merritt's direction the cavalry followed the Cheyennes in a loose pursuit over the next thirty miles,[50] intent mainly on keeping them on the move toward the agencies. Stringing out his forces over an extended front to prevent flanking attempts by groups of hostiles, Merritt's wide net rolled southeastward, folding the mass of Cheyennes within it and keeping them always pointed toward the reservations. There, without further opposition, they arrived that night and the following day.

Losses on both sides were minimal. The Fifth's only casualty occurred during the chase when a cavalryman's horse fell down an embankment, injuring the trooper.[51] Several accounts cite the Indians' only loss as Yellow Hair.[52] Others indicate that during the chase, at least six Cheyennes were killed and perhaps another five wounded.[53] In a letter to his wife written soon after the battle, Brevet Major General Eugene A. Carr, who led the Fifth Cavalry's charge that morning and participated in the pursuit that followed, indicated that three Indians were killed.[54]

The next day, July 18, Merritt telegraphed the results of the battle to Sheridan in Chicago and to Sherman and the administration in Washington. The same day, the Fifth began the trip back to Fort Laramie, arriving there on July 21. As was usual with Merritt, he did not tarry. The Fifth took on supplies and re-shod their horses on July 22. At 6 a.m. on July 23, they marched north to join Crook.[55]

* * *

Over the years, controversy has surrounded several features of the Warbonnet battle. For example, as related in Cheyenne lore, there was no individual combat between Cody and Yellow Hair and Yellow Hair was not killed by Cody. The Cheyennes' oral tradition is that Yellow Hair was struck in the midst of a heavy fire fight with several soldiers and was scalped after the firing ceased. Many days after the battle, relatives of the slain Indian went to the scene and recovered his remains. Their account, as well as several others, confirms that Yellow Hair had been scalped.[56]

Conversely, contemporary reports of cavalrymen on scene that day mostly credit Cody with killing the chief. Cody's role is attested to in several accounts written immediately following the battle, and was noted as early as the evening of July 17. The version that Cody included in his autobiography—a prolonged encounter involving knives and hand to hand combat—is almost surely overblown.

Merritt's conduct immediately following the battle deserves comment. During the Cheyennes' panic-stricken flight, it would certainly have been possible to have killed or maimed them in large numbers. Merritt chose instead to follow and push them back to their agencies. Given that Warbonnet Creek occurred less than a month after the Little Bighorn and the public's initial reaction to a more aggressive outcome would likely have been supportive, his restraint was commendable.

Merritt was initially criticized in some quarters for not immediately responding to Crook's pleas for reinforcement. Time has muted that criticism. Crook continually appealed for additional manpower although he remained static in garrison with 1,400 men[57]—already too many to chase quick moving and rapidly dissolving bands of hostiles. Merritt's victory at Warbonnet Creek prevented large numbers of Cheyennes and Sioux from combining with the hostiles that tormented Crook that summer, and provided far more effective service than joining him quickly in an already cumbersome camp.

Merritt's legacy—and that of the Fifth Cavalry—was that for more than a month they blocked the vital trail used by the Indians to reach the hostiles in Wyoming and Montana. Then, when the first major war party headed northwest, the defeat that Merritt and the Fifth Cavalry inflicted on them was decisive—both militarily and psychologically. After Warbonnet Creek, the Cheyenne and Sioux made no other significant attempts to leave their agencies and join their allies in combat.

Less than a month after achieving their greatest victory at the Little Big Horn, Warbonnet Creek was the "beginning of the beginning of the end" for the Plains Indians. Never again would they come together in such large numbers or prevail in a major battle.

For the military, and the country, Warbonnet Creek played an important role in helping restore morale and confidence. Merritt and his Fifth Cavalry outgeneraled, outrode, and outfought a dangerous foe. Their actions turned large numbers of hostiles around, prevented others from joining, and took all of them permanently out of the war. The victory at Warbonnet Creek was, in the words of one scholar, "timely, professionally executed, and desperately needed."[58]

* * *

Of all the battlefields in Nebraska, the site at Warbonnet Creek is the most hauntingly beautiful. . . and the most difficult to reach. Located about seventeen miles northwest of Harrison in the extreme northwestern corner of the state, the route to it first takes travelers to the end of paved and gravel surfaces and then over a dirt road that eventually leads to a two-rut track through a pasture. It is a marvelous vista frequented by deer and antelope in large numbers.

The battlefield remains remarkably unspoiled. The two conical hills, visible from a great distance, are instantly recognizable. The taller hill, where Lieutenant King made his observation post and around whose sides swept the Fifth Cavalry's last great charge, stands like a sentinel over the battle area. At its highest point, a monument commemorates the clash in which the hill played such a prominent role.

To the west, the bluffs where the Sioux saw the couriers and Merritt's wagon train are unchanged. To the east, past a flat area and across the dirt road, are the ridges the Indians raced down that morning, although it is likely that their original sharpness has been softened over the years by discs and plows.

Immediately east of the hill is the level, grassy area where Cody and Yellow Hair fought. A stone marker identifies the site where their combat is thought to have taken place.

As in 1876, Warbonnet Creek still meanders, looping and twisting its way south to north across the battlefield. The gullies and ravines that hid Merritt's troopers and brushed against the trail used by Yellow Hair and his warriors probably remain much the same.

The only dwelling visible on the immense horizon is the Montrose Church, across the dirt road several hundred yards to the southeast, standing stark and austere, alone on the prairie.

Endnotes

1 Charles M. Robinson III, A *Good Year to Die: The Story of the Great Sioux War*, (Norman and London: University of Oklahoma Press, 1996) p. xxviii, xxix,

2 Jerome A. Greene, *Battles and Skirmishes of the Great Sioux War, 1876-1877: The Military View*, (Norman and London: University of Oklahoma Press, 1993) p. xvi-xvii.

3 Greene p. xviii. About ten cavalrymen were killed and twenty-one wounded. Indian losses were thought to be eleven killed and five wounded.

4 Paul Hedron, *First Scalp for Custer: The Skirmish at Warbonnet Creek, Nebraska, July 17, 1876*, (Lincoln and London: University of Nebraska Press, 1980) p. 53.

5 Greene p xix.

6 Robinson, p. 222.

7 Hedron p. 34.

8 Hedron p. 33.

9 Hedron p. 47.

10 Robinson p. 229.

11 Greene p. 81.

12 Hedron p. 37,38.

13 Hedron p. 48.

14 Robinson p. 228.

15 Ibid.

16 Ibid.

17 Hedron p. 54. The information Merritt received indicated that 900 Sioux warriors were already absent from the agency.

18 Hedron p. 56.

19 Robinson p. 225.

20 Robinson p. 228.

21 Ibid.

22 Greene p. 83.

23 Robinson p. 230.

24 Michael Newton, *Armed and Dangerous: A Writer's Guide to Weapons*, (Cincinnati: Writer's Digest Books, 1990) p. 24.

25 Robinson p. 230.

26 Ibid.

27 Greene p. 84,85.

28 Hedron p. 64.

29 Robinson p. 231.

30 Hedron p. 62.

31 Greene p. 85.

32 Hedron p. 62, 63.

33 Hedron p. 63.

34 Greene p. 87.

35 Hedron p. 65.

36 Greene p. 88.

37 Hedron p. 63.

38 Hedron p. 64. Robinson (p. 230) states the greater distance.

39 Greene p. 87.

40 Greene p. 88.

41 Ibid.

42 Robinson p. 232.

43 Greene p. 89.

44 Greene p. 89, Hedron p. 67, Robinson p. 232 all contain this account.

45 Robinson p. 233.

46 Ibid.

47 Hedron p. 68.

48 Hedron p. 67.

49 Hedron p. 67,68.

50 Hedron p. 77.

51 Robinson p. 233, Hedron p. 77.

52 Hedron p. 80. Merritt's initial report to Sheridan and others on the day after the battle cited one Indian killed.

53 Robinson p. 233.

54 James T. King, *War Eagle: A Life of General Eugene A. Carr*, (Lincoln: University of Nebraska Press, 1963) p. 162.

55 Hedron p. 81.

56 Jerome A. Greene, *Lakota and Cheyenne: Indian Views of the Great Sioux War, 1876-1877*, (Norman and London: University of Oklahoma Press, 1994) p. 81-84.

57 Hedron p. 84.

58 Ibid.

Chapter Eleven

The Surrender and Death of Crazy Horse

"On all sides the Anglo Americans recognized that Crazy Horse's surrender meant that the big Indian Wars had come to an end. For history it was an epochal moment. For the people conquered it was a sad collapse of a proud way of life."[1]

Although the capture and death of Crazy Horse did not result from combat on a battlefield, the impact was so immense that any discussion of Indian warfare in Nebraska would be incomplete without it.

* * *

Crazy Horse's reputation among both whites and Indians reached its peak after the Little Bighorn. That victory and others over the years had a significant effect on many of the senior army officers sent to oppose him.

> "It suited generals to believe they were up against an Indian Napoleon and increasingly, Crazy Horse was promoted in white imagination to fit the image. As a result, he became the most important adversary. . .responsible for every army setback, and whose own defeat would mean the defeat of the Plains Indians."[2]

The Indians' concept of warfare was too individualized for all that to be true, but Crazy Horse's prestige unquestionably lent confidence and credibility to those who fought with him. For those who followed him—and as events would demonstrate, not all did—his presence and leadership were formidable assets.

Prompted by Custer's defeat, the army brought thousands of fresh troops into the Plains region. For some Indian leaders, such as Sitting

Bull, it became too much: in the face of overwhelming numbers and implacable opponents, they took their followers to Canada. Pursued from all directions, others surrendered or were defeated piecemeal during the weeks and months that followed. When Dull Knife's group was routed by Colonel Ranald Mackenzie's troopers near Barnum, Wyoming, in late 1876,[3] Crazy Horse's band was left as the only significant holdout.

Recognizing the futility of further struggle,[4] in April 1877 Crazy Horse sent word that he would bring his followers to the Red Cloud Agency, then located near Camp Robinson (the installation would be designated as a fort the following year). On May 2, a detachment from the camp met the tired, hungry Sioux about thirty miles from the agency and provided them with ten wagon loads of rations and 100 head of cattle.

On May 6, the pact was complete: Crazy Horse, with his band of 885 Oglalas and 2,000 ponies, rode in to surrender.[5] The entire group was allowed to go to the Red Cloud Agency where they were disarmed. For a time, all was quiet.

The period of calm was not to last.

Even today, many of the events that followed remain confused and controversial. Although he apparently took no action to exploit it, Crazy Horse's renown provoked the wrath of some of the other chiefs who envied the respect he was accorded by the Lakota nation and "were jealous of the psychological hold he had on the whites."[6] Important white visitors increasingly made their way to his lodge, causing resentment and prompting rumors of special favors derived from his celebrity status.[7] Other chiefs, tired of war, were fearful that he would start another round of fighting. Rumors—almost surely planted—were circulated that Crazy Horse and his followers intended to break out, perhaps while engaging on a long-promised buffalo hunt.[8]

A second fabrication was more extreme. An interpreter named Frank Grouard, who had once been held captive by the Oglalas, and disliked them intensely as a result, put forward the story that Crazy Horse intended to murder an officer at the post and take over the agency.[9]

Grouard later followed with an even more bizarre intervention. War against the Nez Perce Indians had recently broken out in Idaho. Seeking help, a senior officer at the post met with Crazy Horse and

Photo by Nita Phillips
Officers' quarters at Fort Robinson.

other agency chiefs in late August to discuss the possibility of using their services as scouts in the campaign against the Nez Perce. To the senior officer's request, Crazy Horse is thought to have replied: "We are tired of war; we came for peace, but now that the Great Father asks our help, we will go north and fight until there is not a Nez Perce left." Incredibly, Grouard translated the statement as: "We will go north and fight until not a white man is left."[10]

Another translator attempted to correct the statement, but damage had been done. Unaware that his words and intentions had been misstated, Crazy Horse continued by listing conditions for participation in the war. Meanwhile, the officer in charge grew increasingly confused and angry. Eventually, tempers flared and Crazy Horse walked out.[11] Later, he renewed his offer to help with the stipulations that he could bring his camp and engage in hunting. His conditions were not accepted and discussions ended.[12]

By this time Crazy Horse's disenchantment was growing. A promised buffalo hunt had been cancelled, adding to this disappointment. He was unused to the restrictions on hunts and the Oglalas' free-roaming lifestyle. He, and other chiefs, wanted agencies further north; some thought they had received General Crook's promise to help. When Crazy Horse surrendered, he had stated his desire for an agency east of the Bighorn Mountains or in the Powder River Country, and

141

may have been misled by other Indians into believing his group could settle where it wished.[13]

A proposed trip to Washington to discuss agency matters brought further confusion. Crazy Horse believed that a major purpose of the trip should be to confirm the site of a new agency in the north that he would choose before leaving.[14] Government representatives and most other Indian leaders viewed the situation differently and told him that first he had to go to Washington where discussions about an agency would follow.

Tribal jealousies again surfaced, further complicating the situation. Some Indian leaders felt their status threatened, fearing that if Crazy Horse made the journey he would be made chief of all the Sioux.[15] Conversely, Crazy Horse was reluctant to have certain other chiefs take part, worrying that they would agree to an unfavorable move of the agency as had happened with other delegations in the past. As the situation continued to worsen, rumors circulated that Crazy Horse would be killed or taken prisoner if he made the trip.[16]

The intrigues, rivalries, and rumors that swirled around him increasingly frustrated Crazy Horse. By some accounts, his growing discontent was obvious to friends and foes alike.[17]

The stage for what was to follow was set by the acrimonious session with the interpreter Grouard and the senior officer. The misunderstanding at the council left the army with the impression that Crazy Horse was considering a renewal of hostilities. The same day the meeting broke up, a rumor swept through the Lakotas that Crazy Horse had told an officer that he and his followers were leaving the agency.[18] For the army, the threat of 2,000 warriors[19] again loose on the plains was too much to risk.

One final fabrication destroyed any remaining hope of reconciliation. On September 3, General George Crook attempted to meet with Crazy Horse in a last attempt to settle outstanding differences. While he was on his way to the meeting, an Indian raced up to warn him of an assassination plot allegedly perpetrated by Crazy Horse. The plot story was later found to have been made up by Crazy Horse's rivals, but Crook could take no chances and his decision to withdraw sealed any hopes for a peaceful outcome.[20]

Within hours of his return to the post, General Crook ordered Crazy Horse's arrest, with the apparent intent of imprisoning him

Photos by Nita Phillips

Monument in front of restored guardhouse at Fort Robinson marks the spot where Crazy Horse was killed.

AZUSA Publishing LLC, Englewood, Cplorado
Little Big Man's role in the death of Crazy Horse, and his motives, remain uncertain.

at Fort Marion, Florida.[21] In the meantime, seeking to remove himself from the chaos, Crazy Horse had gone to the camp of Touch The Clouds, a chief friendly to him. Crazy Horse was eventually located and told that he must return to Camp Robinson. Further discussion and second thoughts followed, but by mid-morning on September 5, Crazy Horse along with some of his friends—joined along the way by several groups of warriors—were under army escort on their way to the post.

His arrival at the camp has been variously set between 3 p.m. and 7 p.m. Thomas Buecker, Curator at Fort Robinson, places it between 5 p.m. and 6 p.m.[22] Ironically, Crazy Horse and his party were met by the Post Adjutant, Second Lieutenant Frederic S. Calhoun, whose brother James was a brother-in-law of George Armstrong Custer and was killed with Custer at the Little Bighorn. Calhoun turned the party over to the officer of the day and Crazy Horse and several of his friends were taken initially to the adjutant's office and then to the guardhouse a short distance away.

The guardhouse contained two rooms: an office at one end of the building joined a barred detention area at the other. At first, Crazy Horse appeared not to understand the circumstance, then seeing the cells and prisoners in irons, he became alarmed and began to struggle. What happened next remains the subject of dispute; even those who purported to be eye-witnesses disagreed about what they saw.

One version has Crazy Horse shouting, drawing his knife, and slashing the officer of the day before dashing out the door. There, one of the soldiers instinctively lowered his bayoneted rifle to the challenge position. An Indian named Little Big Man, once an ally of Crazy Horse but recently friendlier to the other chiefs or to his own agenda, grabbed Crazy Horse and attempted to pin his arms behind him and throw him to the ground. By this account, Crazy Horse was thrown off balance, and was flung or fell against the sentry's bayonet.[23]

An Indian eyewitness, Standing Soldier, asserted that Crazy Horse was escorted to the guardhouse by an officer and four soldiers, Little Big Man and some of Crazy Horse's friends. Alarmed by what he saw inside, he drew his knife and tried to back out of the room. As he did so, Little Big Man attempted to seize his arms and was himself cut on the wrist. Despite the efforts of the soldiers, in the melee Crazy Horse managed to get outside where a guard stepped up and deliberately bayoneted him.

A second Indian eyewitness remembered the confrontation differently. The testimony of American Horse was that "in the struggle to escape from his captors Crazy Horse was held around the waist by an Indian, while Little Big Man grabbed his wrists and hands in which he held a knife. By turning his hand adroitly he gave Little Big Man a wound on his arm which caused him to release his hold, and thereupon making a violent effort to disengage himself, he surged against a bayonet in the hands of one of the guards who was standing at a guard against infantry (i.e., challenge) position and swinging his bayonet back and forth."[24]

American Horse was convinced that the soldier did not stab Crazy Horse intentionally.[25]

Thomas Buecker's research led him to believe that Crazy Horse, alarmed by the sight of the cells and the prisoners, struck wildly at his captors with his knife. Amidst the turmoil involving several people in a confined space, Little Big Man grabbed Crazy Horse's arms from behind as their struggle carried them through the door to the outside. As they grappled, Little Big Man was somehow cut on the wrist or lower arm, causing him to release his hold. Crazy Horse then broke free and in the excited crowd that had surrounded the guardhouse, he was stabbed by a guard with a bayonet.[26]

There also exists at least one account that Crazy Horse was stabbed with his own knife as he wrestled with Little Big Man.[27]

The large crowd that had assembled around the building was made up of members of the competing factions, friends and foes alike. In the chaos of that evening, violence was only narrowly averted as tempers ran high and confusion reigned.

After the stabbing occurred, the accounts become fairly consistent. The wound was in the lower right side of the back[28] below the ribs,[29] possibly piercing both kidneys.[30] Crazy Horse fell immediately to the ground, blood trickling from his mouth, writhing in pain. The assistant post surgeon, immediately on the scene, found his pulse already weak and thready. Clearly, the wound was mortal. Crazy Horse was carried next door to the post adjutant's office,[31] where the doctor administered medication for the pain.[32] At about midnight, with the doctor, Touch The Clouds, and a few other friends maintaining the vigil, Crazy Horse died.[33]

The next day Crazy Horse's father took the body to the Spotted Tail Agency[34] where it remained for a time. Later, it was carried north by his parents "where its final resting place remains a mystery."[35]

* * *

Fort Robinson has been masterfully reconstructed. The adjutant's office and the guardhouse—so significant in Crazy Horse's story—stand rebuilt and fully furnished on their original sites. A few paces in front of the guardhouse door, a stone marker identifies the spot where Crazy Horse was killed.

Endnotes

1 R. Eli Paul, editor, *The Nebraska Indian Wars Reader 1865-1877*, (Lincoln and London: University of Nebraska Press, 1998) p.175.
2 Charles M. Robinson III, *A Good Year to Die: The Story of the Great Sioux War*, (Norman and London: University of Oklahoma Press, 1996) p. 152.
3 *Famous Indian Chiefs*, *Famous Chiefs* website www.axel-jacob.de/chiefs2.html. Material extracted from website October 11, 2005.
4 Ibid. Crazy Horse is alleged to have said: "The Wai'chus (white men) outnumber the blades of grass on the prairie. It is time to take the white man's road. . . or we shall all be killed."
5 Robinson p. 332.
6 Robinson p. 337.
7 Thomas R. Buecker, *Fort Robinson and the American West 1874-1899*, (Norman: University of Oklahoma Press, 2003) p. 105.
8 Buecker p. 106.
9 Robinson p. 338.
10 Ibid.
11 Ibid.
12 Buecker p. 110.
13 Buecker p.98.
14 Buecker p. 107.
15 Ibid.
16 Buecker p. 107,108.
17 Buecker p. 108.
18 Buecker p. 111.
19 Ibid.
20 Buecker p.112.
21 Robinson p. 338.
22 Buecker p. 115.
23 Robinson p. 339.
24 Jerome A. Greene, *Lakota and Sioux: Indian Views of the Great Sioux War, 1876-1877*, (Norman and London: University of Oklahoma Press, 1994) p. 152.
25 Ibid.
26 Buecker p. 116.
27 Ibid. Mari Sandoz paints a picture of the Officer of the Day attempting to use his sword against Crazy Horse and describes multiple thrusts. Her's is the most extreme version; all other accounts report a single bayonet wound and differ only on whether or not it was intentionally inflicted.
28 Buecker p.116.
29 Greene p. 150.
30 Robinson p. 339.
31 Ibid.
32 Buecker p. 117.
33 Ibid.
34 Ibid.
35 Alan Boye, *The Complete Roadside Guide to Nebraska*, (St. Johnsbury, Vermont: Saltillo Press, 1993). p. 433.

ODYSSEY OF THE NORTHERN CHEYENNE

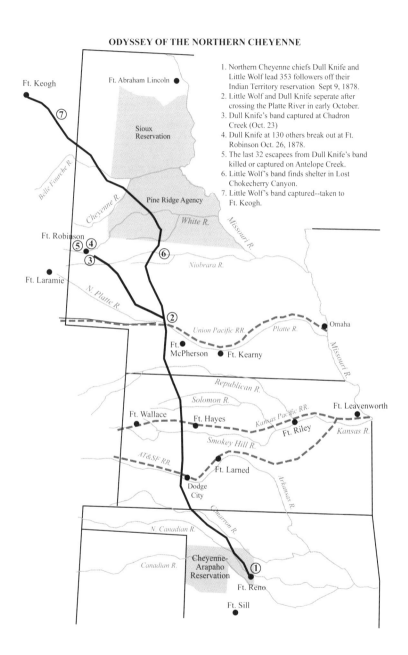

1. Northern Cheyenne chiefs Dull Knife and Little Wolf lead 353 followers off their Indian Territory reservation Sept 9, 1878.
2. Little Wolf and Dull Knife seperate after crossing the Platte River in early October.
3. Dull Knife's band captured at Chadron Creek (Oct. 23)
4. Dull Knife at 130 others break out at Ft. Robinson Oct. 26, 1878.
5. The last 32 escapees from Dull Knife's band killed or captured on Antelope Creek.
6. Little Wolf's band finds shelter in Lost Chokecherry Canyon.
7. Little Wolf's band captured--taken to Ft. Keogh.

Chapter Twelve

Dull Knife's Escape:
The Odyssey of the Northern Cheyenne

History records few sagas that surpass the epic journey of the Northern Cheyenne.

For several months through the autumn and fall of 1878 and the early, bitter days of 1879, a small group of "homesick, mistreated, half-starved Indians"[1] fought and eluded much of the mobilized strength of the army of the United States. Their desperate flight to return to their homeland is replete with examples of courage and fortitude that echo still through the corridors of time.

The final battle occurred in a legendary encounter north of Harrison in the far northwest corner of the Nebraska panhandle. It was the last major battle fought on Nebraska soil.

Although at different times several leaders played important roles, the names of two chiefs—Dull Knife and Little Wolf—are most prominently associated with the saga of the Northern Cheyenne. Dull Knife was already elderly by standards of the time, having been born in about 1810 in Montana.[2] Called "Morning Star" by the Cheyenne, the chief was venerated for his leadership and known for his peaceful intentions. For several years he had been one of the Cheyennes' four principal (or "Old Man") chiefs. These leaders represented the mystical Four Persons who dwelt at the cardinal points of the universe and were the guardians of creation.[3]

Little Wolf was famed among the Cheyenne both as a war leader and, even at age fifty-seven, for his inexhaustible ability as a long distance runner. The tribe had assigned him a special honor: he was the Bearer of the Sacred Bundle of the Northern Cheyenne, a position that carried the highest personal responsibility for the preservation of the people.[4]

149

Eventually, near Ogallala, the two chiefs parted ways. Soon after, Dull Knife and his followers were captured and imprisoned at Fort Robinson. It is their incarceration and escape that—in addition to the trek itself—form the most searing parts of the incredible story.

* * *

In the summer of 1877, Dull Knife surrendered at the Red Cloud Agency in Nebraska, believing his band had been promised food, good treatment, and an agency in the north. Sometime later, they were told that they would not be given an agency; instead, they would be moved to Indian Territory (now Oklahoma). A sizable portion of the group opposed the move. Perhaps misled,[5] or the victims of dubious translation, many believed they were later told they could return to Nebraska and to the lands they had historically roamed further north if they did not like the location in Indian Territory. Dull Knife apparently agreed to go based on that understanding—that he and his followers could return if they became dissatisfied.[6]

At Indian Territory the band shared an agency with Southern Cheyenne on land thought by some to be inadequate to sustain both groups. Although about two-thirds of the group eventually joined with their southern kin, the forced affiliation did not come without cost.[7] In Oklahoma, the Northern Cheyenne died of measles, malaria, dysentery, and starvation. Although the number is in some dispute, it is likely that fifty to sixty died the first year.[8] Whatever the number, for some —Dull Knife, Little Wolf, and others—it was too many.

The Northern Cheyenne first requested permission to leave. By one account, the agent responded by asking for a year to work on the problem. Little Wolf allegedly replied that the Cheyennes would be dead in a year.[9]

On September 9, 1878, after the Northern Cheyenne had been at the Cheyenne and Arapaho Agency in Indian Territory for more than a year, the two chiefs took their small band and slipped away. Although their camp inside a hollow was closely watched, they eluded the soldiers posted nearby. Using spies to keep tabs on army sentinels, and feigning the sights and activities of a sleeping camp, they moved quietly away from their sixty-eight lodges, hurried along by warriors sent ahead as guides. Through a final, narrow bottleneck at the head of a small valley, unseen by sentries posted on each side, the remnants of the Northern Cheyenne—ninety-two men, 120 women, sixty-nine boys and seventy-two girls[10]—moved away in the darkness. The last to leave were a small group of elite warriors—Cheyenne Dog Soldiers—a perpetual rear guard sworn never to start until the entire village was on the move. By sunrise, far from the agency, they had taken their first step on a long and improbable journey.

Moving rapidly, the Cheyennes reached horses that had been pre-positioned on the prairie. Then in patterns that would continue through their long march, they moved through gullies and kept on uneven ground or hard, dry grass to make tracking difficult.

AZUSA Publishing LLC, Englewood, Colorado

Little Wolf (left) and Dull Knife, led the Northern Cheyenne escape from Indian Territory.

They traveled often at night, laid decoy trails and further obscured their paths with horse tracks. Communicating by couriers and signal mirrors, sometimes scattered in small groups, they stayed close enough to sometimes form major camps or come together in event of danger.

Dull Knife had chosen the Cheyennes' trail, a westerly track intended to avoid settled areas. That decision was not without controversy for it was intended to avoid contact or bloodshed when possible. Some younger warriors in the party, eager to avenge the wrong-doings perpetrated on the Cheyennes, were readier than the others to attack any who might cross their path during the journey.

Provisioning 300 or more people constantly on the move required fresh mounts and livestock. Whatever Dull Knife's intentions, deaths occurred as the Cheyennes raided to acquire food and replenish their horse herds. Casualties were higher when the younger, less controllable warriors were engaged—although the numbers did not

151

approximate those shouted in the headlines of the day. On some occasions, when settlers yielded their weapons, no one was harmed.

Still, as the trek persisted beyond days and into weeks and then months, and casualties mounted on both sides, emotions and rumors increased as did exaggerated accounts of atrocities. In all, probably about 40 settlers were killed in Kansas as the Indians moved through the Sappa and Beaver valleys, the most settled regions along their trail.[11]

Pursuit from Fort Reno in Indian Territory began immediately. By the time the Cheyennes reached the vicinity of the Platte River, more than 13,000 troops, some drawn from units as far away as Utah and Florida, had been brought into the chase.

Cavalry from Fort Reno made first contact on September 13 and 14, attacking the Indians at a place called Turkey Springs. The Cheyennes made a defensive stand in a rugged area, picked off cavalry horses and lit a grass fire that spooked the army's horses and mules. Eventually, nearly surrounded, low on ammunition and almost out of water, the soldiers retreated, leaving three troopers and an Arapaho scout dead on the battlefield. Three other soldiers were wounded. It was the first in a near-miraculous series of escapes that the Cheyennes would make in the days ahead.

In a running series of clashes that lasted from September 16-22, the Cheyennes were nearly trapped several times. Once while under fire in the open, a soldier was killed and several cavalry horses were shot, causing the troopers to break off the attack. Near the Arkansas River, the soldiers again retreated after sustaining casualties. That night the Indians slipped away from their hillside positions and, using willow poles left by advance scouts to guide them, escaped across the river. A few days later, on September 27, low on ammunition, the Cheyennes were forced back into their final ring of rifle pits when troopers broke off their assault after their troop commander, Lieutenant Colonel William H. Lewis, was mortally wounded.

Early on October 3, Brevet Major General Eugene A. Carr, commander of the small garrison at Fort McPherson, received word that the Cheyennes had crossed the Kansas Pacific Railroad, about 150 miles south of Fort McPherson and the North Platte River. Carr sent warnings to the surrounding communities, telling citizens that if they kept close to the settlements and placed their horses where they would not tempt the Indians, the danger would be minimized.[12]

As the Cheyennes crossed into Nebraska, Dull Knife led them into camp at the forks of the Republican River near Benkelman.[13] Ironically, that was the same general camping area Custer had used on his expedition eleven years before. The Cheyennes' stay was a short one, but during that time they raided ranches around and south of the forks. These attacks were the last Indian raids of any substance in southwestern Nebraska.[14]

Moving north, the band crossed the Republican River near a small creek and were again caught in the open. The Dog Soldiers, with almost no ammunition, formed a rear guard screen, launching a series of spoiling attacks to shield the main party. Once again, the incredible occurred: their own horses totally "played out," the soldiers halted the attack.

Now, having crossed the Arkansas, the Smokey Hill, and the Republican Rivers, and passing over major railroad lines filled with trains shuttling back and forth in search of them, still pursued from both south and north, the Cheyennes at long last reached the Platte. On October 4, not quite a month into their journey, they crossed the river east of Ogalalla.

The Cheyennes had at this point fought four fairly substantial engagements and numerous smaller skirmishes. Only six warriors had been killed although several more had been wounded.[15]

Safely across the Platte, Dull Knife is believed to have again admonished his followers to leave the whites alone;[16] they were back in their homeland and needed to minimize the violence and the attention that it drew.

Past the river, Dull Knife and Little Wolf moved the band generally north to Whitetail Creek, sheltering finally in a secluded canyon with steep walls where they camped for a time in relative safety. There the group divided following a dispute between the chiefs.

The argument between Dull Knife and Little Wolf came as the culmination of differences between the long-time friends. Before and throughout the journey, Dull Knife generally argued for peace, steadfastly maintaining convictions he had held and advocated for more than three decades. Little Wolf was more skeptical, recalling a string of broken promises and fearing a forced return to the south. While

Dull Knife's goal was to reach the Red Cloud Agency, Little Wolf sought to continue further north and join friends and allies near the Yellowstone.

Now, as they reached a point in their journey that demanded a decision regarding where and how to proceed, their differences proved irreconcilable. Sadly, Dull Knife with 149 people—forty-six men, sixty-one women, forty-two children—131 horses and nine mules, left the next morning, heading west and north, seeking refuge in the newly established Red Cloud Agency, whose location had been moved during the Cheyennes' time in Oklahoma.

By now, some newspaper accounts were containing hints of admiration for the Cheyennes' remarkable trek, the hardships they had overcome, and—hundreds of miles into their journey—their uncanny ability to avoid capture. Tempering these accounts were articles expressing fear that the Cheyennes would join hundreds of warlike Sioux now living uneasily in agencies and renew warfare across the central and western plains. Or, more extreme, that the Cheyennes' example would inspire tribes across the continent to launch a nationwide uprising.

In actuality, Dull Knife's objective was limited: to get to the agency and shelter there until he received the agency he believed he had been promised; or, failing that, to remain with Red Cloud's people.

As Dull Knife's band traveled across the sand hills setting decoy trails and evading capture during the coldest, bitterest winter in memory, couriers were sent to Red Cloud. By Sandoz's account, the runners crept into Red Cloud's camp and reported it surrounded by troops. Still, they made contact. Red Cloud expressed his concern for them but reluctantly acknowledged that the solders' presence precluded him from doing much. He had been told that the Cheyennes would not be allowed to stay at his agency. He advised Dull Knife to surrender based on the soldiers' promises of food, shelter, and medical care.

Couriers relayed the news to Dull Knife along with reports of large numbers of troops guided by Indian scouts moving towards him. Denied sanctuary with Red Cloud, Dull Knife and his followers decided on an attempt to reach the Spotted Tail Agency further west. Cold, half-starved, with little ammunition, they continued moving in the direction of the oncoming soldiers, needing a day or so to reach terrain in which they could disappear.

They almost made it. On October 23, six weeks and several hundred miles from Indian Territory, amidst the fury of a driving blizzard, they were found by the cavalry's Indian scouts while moving in single file close to low ridges along Chadron Creek. Large numbers of soldiers soon came up—many, ironically, from the Seventh Cavalry, Custer's outfit—and were steadily reinforced over the next several hours. An extended period of bargaining then ensued, the Cheyennes insisting on their peaceful intention to move on to the Spotted Tail Agency, the soldiers refusing to allow it. Eventually, the Cheyennes agreed to move for the night to the soldiers' encampment near the creek, where they were fed. Morning brought additional parleys and reinforcements, including cannon, for the cavalry.[17]

With Dull Knife actively restraining a rebellious group of young warriors, the cavalry disarmed the Cheyennes, taking a dozen rifles and twenty sets of bows and arrows,[18] although the Indians managed to hide several weapons. The Cheyennes' horses and mules were taken away from them as well. The next morning after further talks and another near-outbreak of fighting, they were told they would receive no further food until they reached Fort Robinson. With enormous misgivings they were then loaded onto wagons and driven toward the post.

Through the bitter cold the party moved down the White Creek Valley, the wagon train lined with troopers on either side. They reached Fort Robinson late on the night of October 26, where they were searched again—an act that nearly provoked violence—before being allowed shelter. Again the Cheyennes managed to hide a few weapons, mostly under the folds of women's dresses. Heavily guarded, at long last they were taken into the warmth of a long barracks building and given coffee and food.

There, for a little while, they were mercifully dry, warm, and fed.

But only for a little while.

* * *

During the first few days the Cheyennes received medical treatment and, with the stipulation that none would leave, were given the run of the post. The women were employed on work details and were allowed to go to the river to wash clothes. Some even danced with soldiers. Although searched repeatedly, the Cheyennes managed to retain a few weapons, hidden in pieces in clothing or stashed under the floorboards of the barracks. Their period of relative serenity lasted for about two months.[19]

After a time, one of the young warriors slipped away to go after his wife who was at the Red Cloud Agency. When his absence was discovered, the Cheyennes' liberties were taken away and all of them—men, women, and children—were locked inside the single room. Although the warrior returned with his wife in a few days, the privileges were not restored and the Indians remained incarcerated around the clock under heavy guard. Eventually, some of the women were allowed to exit to perform tasks around the post. In the intense cold, despite donations from soldiers' families and pleas from officers to provide the Cheyennes with warm garments from army stores, not enough surplus items were found to clothe them all.

In December, the Cheyennes received the news they had been dreading: the decision had been made to return them to Indian Territory. Despite urging from Red Cloud and numerous officials, they steadfastly refused: "I am here on my own ground and I will never go back" Dull Knife told the post commander. Guards were increased and the Indians remained in the locked room.

On January 3, 1879, the Cheyennes were told that the time had come; they must pack up for the move south. The commander, Captain Henry W. Wessells, Jr., was ordered to move the Indians "no matter how cold the weather, but to provide everything possible for their comfort." Wessells replied to the order by saying the Indians were "resolved to die rather than to go."

In the bitter cold of the following morning, the commander came to the barracks and ordered the Cheyennes to collect themselves to begin the move. They refused.

Captain Wessells immediately cut off their food provisions and fuel to heat the barracks.

Four days later, having received no indication of submission, he offered to remove the women and children: "I shall take them out of here and they shall be fed and warmed." The Cheyennes refused.

Captain Wessells shut off their drinking water.

Now, entering their fifth day without food or heat in temperatures that would soon register twenty-eight degrees below zero, and having gone more than a day without water, it was time for the Cheyennes to act. The date was January 9, 1879, exactly four months to the day from the time the Northern Cheyenne had fled and fought their way out of Indian Territory.

Warriors had gathered together many nights to make plans. Escape would be made through sets of windows on the east side of the building.[20] The first warriors through would disable the guards, taking as many weapons as possible. Groups were assigned to move with the elderly, the women, and the children. Leaders were identified and then co-leaders as well—some of them young women—to take over as necessary. All would travel light, carrying only the barest essentials and the tribe's few remaining sacred relics. Two of the groups' best horsemen were detailed to run to a nearby ranch to attempt to capture horses. As always, Dog Soldiers would be the last to leave, fighting a rear guard action while others helped the women and children get away.

That morning, two Northern Cheyenne leaders had been manacled and taken away after again refusing to leave for the south. The Indians in the barracks became aware of the scuffle that followed and young warriors, by now influential in the Cheyennes' decision-making, had to be restrained at bayonet point from bursting out of the building. Later, iron bars and chains were placed across the doors. The Cheyennes were bolted in. Surely the time had come.

* * *

Anticipating the possibility of an escape attempt, Captain Wessells placed a cordon of overlapping sentries around the Cheyennes' enclosure.[21] That night, the officer of the day posted seven sentries around the barracks, put seven more in the barracks guardroom and more still in the main guardhouse.[22]

By 10 p.m., the moon bright on the snow cover, the Cheyennes could wait no longer. One hundred thirty Northern Cheyenne, forty-four warriors among them with five rifles, ten pistols, one only partially functional, five war clubs and assorted knives, broke for freedom. A shot from the first warrior out of the window dispatched the sentry at the corner of the building, the crack of the rifle resounding like an explosion in the cold night air. Other shooting immediately followed and two more soldiers were hit as they rushed to the scene. Two more inside the building were wounded as the Indians broke through the barrier into the guardroom to capture guns and ammunition.

One by one the Indians left the building, hurrying toward a bridge over the White River, seeking the comparative security of the bluffs beyond. Firing soon became intense as soldiers from around the post converged on the scene. Indians now began to fall as they ran through the bitter cold. When all the Cheyennes were clear of the barracks area, five Dog Soldiers formed a line behind a snow drift near the stables in a desperate attempt to hold back the troopers surging towards them. In the moonlight chaos—amidst bugles blowing, the shouts of excited men, and the noises of frightened horses; they bought precious minutes. Finally, overwhelmed by fire from every quadrant, all were slain.

By the time the Indians ran the 500-yard gauntlet of fire between the barracks and the river,[23] nine warriors were dead and many more wounded. Women and children were casualties also; bundled up, their shapes were sometimes impossible to discern as they fled in the violent disorder of the frigid night.

Many raced first towards a small bridge spanning the stream. Others, under threat from fast closing soldiers, plunged through the icy water, some stopping only for a moment to slake an almost unbearable thirst.

Here and there along their escape route, some—like three warriors near the sawmill—made brief stands. Soon, their ammunition almost exhausted, there were no more stands as the Indians, scattered now into small groups, fled first south to the river, then west toward the bluffs a half mile on the other side of the stream.[24]

The soldiers' quick pursuit made futile any attempt to get horses. The warriors sent for that purpose—those not killed or wounded— eventually abandoned the quest and sought to join the others trying to reach the line of the bluffs facing them to the west. A few hid in the tangled brush along the river. Dull Knife and a small group followed a hardened snow drift that led them away from the others and avoided the most intense pursuit.

Within the first mile, half of the warriors were down. Some of the wounded were shot of out fear that though injured or dying, they posed continuing lethal threats to the pursuers. The soldiers' concerns were not without foundation. Given the choice between death and return-

Photo by Nita Phillips

On the night of January 9, 1879, 130 Northern Cheyennes broke out of the barracks building (top left of photo). About sixty-four Cheyennes and eleven soldiers were killed during the escape attempt.

ing to Indian Territory—a fate they regarded as worse than death— they chose death, and so the night is replete with stories of wounded Indians, armed only with an empty or near-empty weapon, or a knife, or a club, attacking groups of soldiers. Some, too injured to continue, threw their weapons to others—sometimes women or children—who continued the fight.

Through the night, soldiers on foot—in places the ridge line near the post was too rugged for horses—cautiously sifted through the jagged crannies in the bluffs opposite the river and for several miles along it. Sometimes their searches discovered lone Indians or small groups who, using their empty weapons as clubs, charged at them until shot down. A few surrendered without struggle when confronted by an officer or soldier known to be friendly to them.

The numbers cited as killed or injured during that first horrific night vary according to source. Sandoz says that by morning at least thirty Cheyennes—twenty-one of them warriors—were known to be dead and the post hospital was filled with wounded Indians, often carried in by soldiers who had befriended them during their time at the fort. Two scholars place the number killed at fifty, another claims there

159

were thirty-two.[25] According to Tom Buecker, Curator, Fort Robinson Museum, at the end of the first day, the bodies of twenty-seven Cheyennes had been gathered for burial.[26]

The numbers captured on the night of January 9, also in dispute, range from thirty-five to sixty-five.[27] The commander expected more captives the next day: the deep snow, he believed, would make tracking easy and he planned to put five companies on the trail.

On the bluffs, the Cheyennes began to come together, assembled mostly by a young warrior identified by Mari Sandoz as Little Finger Nail, who traveled along the ridge, moved around and through the soldiers, and gathered the survivors. Scouts reported soldiers moving towards them from all points of the compass. They would have to move again, first across a threatening, open tableland and then, hopefully, into rugged terrain and stream beds that would provide more shelter. In a single file, about thirty-four Cheyennes[28] —all that were known to remain alive on the bluffs—began to move north.

Aided by Indian trackers, the cavalry eventually discovered their trail across the mesa. At one point on the twisted path, the Cheyennes doubled back and ambushed the pursuing troops as they moved past in single file. Believing they would capture the Indians that day, the troopers had carried no extra blankets or rations; that night under the cover of darkness and decoy fires, they returned to Fort Robinson. The Indians butchered the cavalry horses killed during the fight, roasting the meat and using the hides for warmth and as soles for their moccasins.

Along the river, soldiers continued the search, cautiously working through the jumbled timber and sorting through washouts in the embankments. Occasionally, they came across dead or wounded Cheyennes. In narrow ravines, the earlier stories repeated themselves: Dog Soldiers who would not surrender or retreat resisted to the last and were shot in vicious spasms of fire. Late in the day a cavalry troop followed a trail that led to a cave in the bluffs. Again a mini-battle erupted as five Indians refused to surrender. All but one—a young boy—were killed. Elsewhere, four women were captured as they attempted to catch up with the main party on the bluffs.

One Indian was exposed by the fire he built to warm his feet, frozen in a vain attempt to reach horses on a nearby ranch. Wounded several times, he was eventually overwhelmed after inflicting casualties on the on-rushing cavalry. Miles away, along the White River, troopers found a small girl and took her to the post. Later, two young boys were found among the buttes.

On January 11, Little Finger Nail's group was discovered again and shots were exchanged at times during a running fight; the soldiers again returning to Fort Robinson as darkness fell. The next day, two warriors were caught as they roasted meat. Firing from rifle pits, they were eventually surrounded and one, along with a cavalry trooper, was killed in the fight.

Traveling again at night, the remaining Cheyennes were pushed further west and north by the pressure of the daily pursuit. Caught again, this time between two shallow ravines, the Indians inflicted casualties before being pinned down by a steady fusillade poured into their rifle pits. After a time, the troopers pulled back a short distance and sent a courier to the post, requesting additional troops that, along with a cannon, arrived during the night.

More reinforcements came the next morning, January 13. Soon, the Cheyennes' position was surrounded and carbine and cannon fire raked the rifle pits. Only a few shots were returned during the day-long barrage, but there was no sign of surrender.

Early the following morning, the commander, Captain Wessells, moved up to the firing line to assess the situation.

The Cheyennes were gone.

They had moved the night of January 12; the troops discovered only empty rifle pits vacated before the previous day's fusillade had been unleashed upon them. By Sandoz's account, the few shots in return had been disguised by firing from under a blanket from a concealed location on a distant ridge.

Wessells waited for a resupply of rations and ammunition before resuming the pursuit. When wagons sent to replenish him overturned on the icy hillsides, he halted an additional day until a train of pack mules reached him.

The morning of January 16 dawned clear and cold. Resupplied, the soldiers in closest contact with the Cheyennes were joined by other units called to the scene. Many of them rode along the bluffs, scouring the ground, seeking the Cheyennes' trail. Now led by a Sioux and half-breed scout, both expert trackers, they eventually found it.

The Cheyennes continued to move, this time taking up positions along the rugged slope of a high bluff. There, they waited, once again in mortal danger.

When the scouts guided a cavalry unit close to the bluff the Indians fired, spooking their horses and killing a trooper. The two scouts stayed close, under cover, while the soldiers retreated a short distance down the slope. When only the two scouts remained, one of the warriors with Little Finger Nail stepped into the open and attempted to parley with them. According to Sandoz, the half-breed scout shot him and then both scouts raced down the hillside. Later, when the attack was not resumed, the body of the fallen warrior was retrieved and the cavalryman killed earlier in the fight was stripped of coat, rifle, revolver, and ammunition belt.

That night, the Cheyennes slipped away towards the bottom of the bluffs, preparing for a run across the open prairie, seeking Red Cloud, or Little Wolf, or any place that held the hope of warmth, food, and safety. As the sun rose, a Cheyenne sentry with a mirror reported columns of soldiers with a long wagon train coming from the west and more troops on the way from Fort Robinson to the southeast.

The cavalry's half-breed scout found the Cheyennes again on January 20. Scattered shooting occurred, but the rugged terrain prevented the troopers from closing in. The Cheyennes camped as darkness set in. Seeking a vantage point that might enable them to make their way through the ring of troops that was now clasped around them, the Indians climbed higher and appeared to settle for the night.

Lighting decoy fires that burned low and slow, they feigned a sleeping encampment. In the darkness, Little Finger Nail's group moved again, easing past the sentries. Trying carefully to step only on solid grass, their attempt to disguise the route was complicated by a warm night that made the ground mushy and by the presence of youngsters in the party. Their new hiding place, selected before they left the bluffs, was a washout above a dry creek bed along Antelope Creek, a tiny tributary of Warbonnet Creek. They reached it before dawn.

At that place, about thirty feet up from the bottom of the dry stream, they used knives to cut into the embankment and expand the washout. Small breastworks were built at the entrance, and then all was camouflaged with sod and brush. Having eluded the army for thirteen days and for many weeks before that, here, if necessary, was where they would make their final stand. There were thirty-two of them now—eighteen men and boys and fourteen women and children. In a hole about ten feet wide, twenty feet long, and, at the rim of the breastworks between five and six feet high, they waited, armed with newly made bows and war clubs, and a few rifles and revolvers for which they had very little ammunition.

At first light, confused that yet again the Cheyennes had slipped away, troopers rode in all directions desperately searching for a trail. Then, apparently along the soft ground of a prairie dog town, scouts picked up traces of Cheyenne children and the crutch marks of a wounded Indian. Soon, large numbers of troops began riding toward the washout.

As scouts and cavalry probed the creek bed, the Cheyennes' hiding place was detected. Troopers formed for an advance, but the Cheyennes preempted it by firing down from their lodgment, knocking down a scout and a cavalryman. More troops were drawn to the fighting; eventually, four full companies converged there under the command of Captain Wessells.

Wessells' first attempt was to dislodge the Indians by heavy fire from the relatively open front and along both sides of the washout. When this had little apparent effect, he designated a unit to pin the Indians down with covering fire and moved forces from three sides towards the embankment. Sheltered by continuous fire, a half ring of soldiers advanced, moving from each side of the washout and directly in front of it.

As the few initial return shots from the Cheyennes slackened off completely, Captain Wessells ordered a ceasefire and asked the Indians to surrender. When there was no response, he resumed the attack, again receiving only an isolated shot or two in return. Minutes later, he stopped the firing for a second time and demanded that the Indians yield. This time the Cheyennes replied with a few shots and Wessells directed the attack to continue.

As the struggle persisted, many of the soldiers crept so close to the hole—Lieutenant George F. Chase took his company within five yards of the washout face[29]—that the Indians had to peer over the top of the breastworks to see them. Exposed to fire as they attempted to aim, the Cheyennes began taking casualties. As each fell, others grabbed the guns while further inside the washout the women struggled to reload the weapons.

When an hour or more passed with only one or two shots from the Indians, Wessells and Chase led a charge to the breastworks. Repeated volleys were fired into the hideout, the shooting so heavy that smoke eventually obscured the opening. Doubting that anyone could remain alive, Wessells jumped to the rim of the fortification, again demanding the Indians' surrender. From out of the smoke came a single shot that grazed Wessells along the side of his head.

After Wessells was helped to safety, the troopers prepared for another attack that would again strike from three sides. From inside the washout, the soldiers now heard sounds of the Cheyennes' death songs. According to Sandoz, the first was sung by a single warrior—interrupted by the cry of a small girl as a woman stabbed her and then took her own life—who was then joined by all who remained alive.

When their preparations were complete, Lieutenant Chase led the soldiers as they moved off together in an all out charge to the breastworks. Firing as they moved, they ran to the embankment and then scrambled up its face. As they reached the washout, they poured repeated volleys into the cavity, jumping back only long enough to reload before firing again. Finally, the acrid powder choking and blinding them, they fell back, staring at the entrance until the smoke cleared and their vision was no longer obstructed.

Suddenly, the seemingly impossible happened: three "almost naked, dirt-streaked bloody Cheyenne" vaulted from behind the breastworks. Led by Little Finger Nail with a pistol and a knife, they charged straight at the mass of soldiers. Shooting immediately exploded from the groups of cavalrymen near the washout. Most accounts say Little Finger Nail was quickly killed by carbine fire as was a second Indian who leaped over him when he fell. The third Cheyenne managed to get deep into the midst of the surrounding soldiers before being cut down.

When the smoke from the final spasm drifted away, soldiers cautiously went to the lip of the mangled breastworks and peered into the carnage below. They found shattered bodies piled like driftwood across the floor, the blood permanently congealed, held at the surface by the frozen earth.

Seventeen dead warriors and an eighteenth mortally wounded were discovered inside and down the embankment where Little Finger Nail and his two companions were slain. Four women and two small children were also dead. Underneath the pile of bodies in the washout, seven women—one later died—and children were found wounded but alive. Moments later, soldiers carried out a six-year old girl who had been placed in a pocket dug inside the back wall of the breastworks. Wounded also, she let herself be taken to the care of Captain Wessells who she recognized from the days at the barracks.

* * *

Of the 130 or so Northern Cheyennes who broke out of the barracks on the night of January 9, 1879, the number cited for the total known killed is usually put at around sixty-four. The fate of an additional eight to ten has never been determined.[30] Many of the survivors were wounded. Eleven cavalrymen died and ten were wounded during the series of breakout encounters.[31]

* * *

The final pursuit and series of clashes were waged on difficult terrain under circumstances made more daunting by the breath-choking cold of temperatures that sometimes reached thirty degrees below zero. Amid the horrific conditions were daily examples of courage and bravery on both sides.

Company B, Third Cavalry had been sent from Fort Laramie along with another company to form part of a blocking force intended to pin down and surround Little Finger Nail's band. At dawn on January 21, Sergeant William B. Lewis and two other troopers volunteered for a dangerous reconnaissance of a position the Cheyennes had been known to occupy on the night of January 20. The Cheyennes' position, secluded high in the rocks, provided ample possibility for ambush. As Sergeant Lewis and his colleagues approached, they were taken under fire from a sheltered rifle pit by a wounded Cheyenne who had been left behind as others slipped away. In the ensuing fire fight, Lewis killed the Indian and completed his reconnaissance.

For his "conspicuous bravery and personal gallantry" that day and during another desperate encounter during the breakout, Sergeant Lewis was awarded the Medal of Honor.[32] His was the last Medal of Honor awarded for actions on Nebraska soil.

* * *

For more than two weeks after the breakout, small streams of haggard survivors struggled back to the fort. Among the first was a woman shepherding two small children. Seeing the children among the dead Cheyenne on the night of the breakout, she had hidden with them first in some brush by the river and later in a hole she had found up on the bluffs. She had carried with her a little tallow and, sheltered by the hole, used it to build small fires at night.

A starving young boy, entrusted with carrying a sacred shield on the night of the escape, made his way to the house of a settler he knew. Wounded in the leg, he still carried the relic strapped to his back.

* * *

As the captured Indians awaited their fate, a few were manacled and sent under guard through Omaha to Kansas where they were to be tried for the murders of settlers killed during the flight from Indian Territory. Eventually, in the autumn, they were released for lack of evidence and allowed to return and reunite with kinsmen.

By now, though still meshed amid occasional rumors of rampaging Indians, newspaper coverage sometimes included stories of outrage at the treatment of the Cheyennes. There was still no word of either Dull Knife or Little Wolf. Some conjectured that Dull Knife had been killed during the breakout.

He had, in fact, escaped.

With a party believed to originally number about a dozen, Dull Knife, his remaining family, and three young warriors made it past the river. Two of Dull Knife's daughters and one of the warriors were lost to gunfire before they found a frozen drift that betrayed no tracks. At that point they turned away, still moving toward the bluffs but separately from the other clusters of fleeing Cheyennes. Moving up a small ravine, they were almost discovered before a Cheyenne warrior, acting as a one man rear guard, distracted the pursuers and, before being killed, held them off long enough for the others to vanish.

Led by Dull Knife to a place remembered from his youth, they disappeared into a large chasm hidden in the rocks. There, nearly starved, subsisting on a diet of roots, moccasin leather, and sinew, they waited for ten days. Then, traveling at night and hiding in small crevasses and ravines, they moved across the panhandle of Nebraska. By Sandoz's version, they came to the house of a friend—a white man who had married a Sioux woman. The settler and his wife fed and cared for them. Soon after, Sandoz says, they slipped in with Red Cloud's Sioux and Dull Knife was taken to an isolated lodge in the vicinity of Wounded Knee. After a few days, he moved in the direction of Spotted Tail, where that chief arranged for a lodge to be prepared for him. Encouraged by some to resume the journey to the north, Dull Knife declined out of obligation to his own people, now in and around Fort Robinson, and because he had promised Red Cloud he would return. Eventually, about three weeks after the breakout, Dull Knife surrendered at the Red Cloud Agency.[33]

* * *

In the days that followed, the near-miraculous happened; aided by the direct request of General Nelson Miles, Dull Knife and his band were allowed to go north, to the country for which they had shed so much blood and struggled to reach with unmatched courage. Eventually, they received their own agency. There, a few years later, in the Rosebud Valley on what would become the Northern Cheyennes' Tongue River Reservation, Dull Knife died.

* * *

After Dull Knife and Little Wolf argued at Whitetail Creek and their bands had separated, Little Wolf took his group further north. Having by now brought "sick, half-starved, half-afoot people, old, young, men, women, and children, through 600 miles of open country, cut by three railroads, cross-hatched by telegraph—through settlers, cowmen, scouts, and the United States Army, all in less than a month," he first sought a place that offered better prospects for safety.

Pursued by as many as twenty-four companies of infantry and hard-riding cavalry—more would be sent following the breakout at Fort Robinson to foreclose the possibility of the groups' reuniting or joining Red Cloud—Little Wolf led his people deeper into the Sand Hills. Scattering his group into small clusters and setting false trails, Little Wolf brought them to a place Sandoz names as Lost Choke-cherry Canyon, a small, secluded valley with timber, grass, and a lake, located in Sheridan County near the head of the Snake River Valley, a tributary of the Niobrara River in northwestern Nebraska.[34] Surrounded by walls that offered shelter against the wind and protection against intruders, 126 people—forty men, forty-seven women, and thirty-nine children—took refuge and rested. For three months they remained there, although cavalry patrols, oxen trains, and other travelers to the Black Hills sometimes came very near.

When the Indians settled into the Lost Chokecherry Canyon area near the Dismal River, they used the region as a base for periodic raids on nearby ranches. At Fort McPherson, with most of his troops away from the fort on other duties, General Carr could at first spare but a small detail to conduct a quick scout of the area beginning on November 23. The scouts returned reporting that horses had been stolen from local ranchers.[35] Later reinforced by the return of his garrison force, General Carr conducted a ten-day, 250-mile scout beginning on December 7. The troops made no contact but caused the Indians to begin shifting to the north to avoid the cavalry.[36]

On December 20, a Cheyenne raiding party made up of about sixteen warriors stole nine horses from a Lincoln County ranch. A small combined force of cavalry, local militia, and citizens under the direction of the sheriff pursued and caught the raiders at Birdwell Creek. The Indians quickly dispersed, leaving behind a substantial portion of their supplies and seven of the horses they had stolen. The December 20 episode was the final raid in the vicinity of Fort McPherson.[37]

In January, when news reached them of Dull Knife's breakout and the last stand at the washout, it was time to leave the area. Their travels and the relative serenity they had enjoyed in the past few weeks were marred by a renegade member of the clan, perhaps demented by the journey and by the loss of family members as far back as Indian Territory. In Sandoz's account, thirsting for revenge, he and two others had on one occasion left Lost Chokecherry Canyon on a horse-stealing expedition and killed two cowboys along the Niobrara. Later, in a move that was likely to draw attention and provoke retribution, they had stolen horses marked with a "US" brand. Confronted by other Indians after his return, the renegade killed the camp's "policeman" and wounded another venerated member of the group. Banished from the band with about six others, he and another of the exiles were later captured and hanged by the cavalry after killing one trooper and wounding another as the soldiers repaired a telegraph line.

From the region of Lost Chokecherry Canyon, Little Wolf's group traveled north and west, skirting the badlands. With game increasingly scarce, his people hungry, and the soldiers' presence all around, they finally reached the vicinity of the Yellowstone, their destination since the beginning of their trek six months before. Several miles up the river, Little Wolf stopped, hoping to make contact with an officer, Lieutenant W. P. Clark, known to be friendly toward the Cheyennes. When Little Wolf's men captured two of Clark's scouts, Little Wolf set them free with directions to return to Clark and reveal the Cheyennes' location to him.

Little Wolf then moved his group—there were 114 of them left, now; thirty-three warriors among them—a short distance away to a rugged hillside where, if necessary, they could hold out for a considerable time. Additional scouts sent from Clark—Cheyennes, some of whom had relatives with Little Wolf's band—soon came to the hilltop. After a parley, the scouts returned to Clark, who immediately set out with a large contingent of troops.

Clark and Little Wolf met on a knoll a short distance from Little Wolf's stronghold. Little Wolf refused his friend's request to turn over the group's horses and guns, but after taking counsel with his people —and after a second visit from Clark, who came unarmed to the Cheyennes' camp—he agreed that his band would accompany the soldiers. In return, Clark promised them food and blankets—promises immediately fulfilled—and assured them that he would do everything possible to let them stay in the north country. That promise too was kept; Little Wolf's band was allowed to remain in the Fort Keogh area. It was a good location for them, part of their history, although reservation life was difficult for many of the wide-ranging Cheyenne who had come so far and endured so much. Twenty-five years later, after additional personal travails, Little Wolf died there in 1904.

* * *

Among the many ironies that abound in the saga of the Northern Cheyenne is that after months of bloodshed on both sides and an enormous expenditure of resources—at one point a considerable portion of the United States Army, brought from the four corners of the continent, was engaged in the pursuit—eventually the remnants of Dull Knife's and Little Wolf's contingents were allowed to remain in the north. That had been their only request when they fled Indian Territory.

A second irony was that it was the Seventh Cavalry—Custer's outfit—that formed much of the immediate pursuit and escorted Dull

Knife's group to Fort Robinson. They must have been well handled by their officers and NCOs, for there were no reported incidents, although some historians, citing Wounded Knee as evidence, believe that even a dozen years later emotions continued to run high.

Individual stories, many of them poignant, form the larger saga of the Northern Cheyenne. When the Indians were incarcerated at Fort Robinson, the young lieutenant George Chase spent much of his own pay buying tobacco and candy for them, dolls for the children, and beads for their moccasins. Yet, at the washout it was Lieutenant Chase's fate to be called upon to lead the final charge against the people he had befriended.

Known for his singing voice and his artistry, Little Finger Nail, killed at the washout, was one of the "best and brightest" future leaders of the Northern Cheyenne nation. A notebook containing his drawings was discovered on his body. The book, punctured by two bullet holes, resides now at the Museum of National History in New York City. The small pad, found in the remotest part of the Nebraska panhandle, serves as a reminder that so much promise was lost.

General Miles' intervention and act of benevolence on behalf of Dull Knife was not an isolated incident among senior army leaders. It is perhaps the ultimate irony that many of the generals who were called upon to fight the Cheyennes were often sympathetic to their cause.

General Crook:

"I do not wonder, and you will not either that when these Indians see their wives and children starving and their last source of supplies cut off, they go to war. And then we are sent out to kill them. It is an outrage."

(In 1879, General Crook assisted Ponca Chief Standing Bear at the federal trial in Omaha that declared Native Americans to be "persons within the meaning of the law" with the full rights of citizenship.)[38]

General Miles:

"The strong, industrious but degenerating tribe of Cheyennes proves the folly of the fruitless experiments and vacillating policy that has governed them for the past twenty years."

General Pope:

"In my twenty-five years on the plains in every outbreak the cause was bad faith by the government. In this outbreak there were no depredations until the Cheyennes were attacked."

One last irony: some scholars believe that the "hou" (as spelled by Mari Sandoz) phrase of the Sioux and Cheyenne—an expression that signifies acceptance, acknowledgment, or understanding—is the ancestor of the "hooah" term used today by elite U.S. military forces.[39] If so, it is perhaps part of a tribute to a small band whose indomitable courage in the face of impossible odds brought them to a remote corner of Nebraska, where their bravery became immortal.

* * *

As noted earlier, at Fort Robinson, the barracks where the Cheyennes were held has been rebuilt on its original site, part of a superb reconstruction that has taken place in recent years. The Cheyennes escape route is well marked. Ironically, their desperate flight south to the White River took them over ground that now contains a play ground and picnic area. To the west, a marker off U.S. Highway 20 identifies their general path as they hurried to the sheltering bluffs that lead further west and north. For the thirty-two who remained at the end, the bluffs traced their journey to the final struggle at the washout.

To the Indians, the battle at the washout quickly became known as the Last Hole. Located on private property seventeen miles north of Harrison, the site has become a sacred place to the Northern Cheyenne.

On the plains of Oklahoma, Kansas, and Nebraska, the Indians' resourcefulness at what would now be called "escape and evasion" even today seems remarkable in the telling. So extraordinary was the valor that the little known clashes of the Northern Cheyenne share kinship with other battles fought in heroic desperation—Massada, Thermopylae, the Alamo—whose names burn through the pages of history.

Endnotes

1 Mari Sandoz's *Cheyenne Autumn*, (New York: McGraw-Hill, 1953) forms the basis for this chapter. Material extracted from other sources is separately identified.

2 *Native American Leaders*, The National Archives Learning Curve website www.spartacus. schoolnet.co.uk/WWdullknife.htm. Material extracted from website July 12, 2005.

3 *Dull Knife Biography*, Profile of Dull Knife Biographies website www.bookrags.com/biogra-phy-dull-knife Material extracted from website July 12, 2005. By most accounts, "Dull Knife" is the closest translation of his Sioux name. One alternate version is that "Dull Knife" was a Cheyenne nickname given by a teasing relative. A second explanation is that it came after the warrior broke his knife on an opponent's buffalo hide shield -- the knife would not pierce the shield – during a fight to the death.

4 *Dull Knife (Morning Star)*, Famous Indian Chiefs website www.axel-jacobs.de/chiefs2.html. Material extracted from website July 12, 2005.

5 Thomas R. Buecker, *Fort Robinson and the American West 1874-1899*, (Norman: University of Oklahoma Press, 1999) p. 126.

6 B.W. Allred, *Great Western Indian Fights*, (Lincoln: University of Nebraska Press, 1960) p. 298

7 Buecker p. 126.

8 According to Mari Sandoz, 70 died within the first two months. Research by another scholar, Charles Robinson, led him to conclude that 41 died during the winter months. Thomas R. Buecher states that nearly 60 died the first year.

9 *Famous Indian Chiefs* website.

10 Buecker p. 127,128. Sandoz puts the number at 87 men, 197 women and children.

11 Buecker p. 129.

12 James T. King, *War Eagle: A Life of General Eugene A. Carr*, (Lincoln: University of Nebraska Press, 1963) p. 187.

13 Alan Boye, *The Complete Roadside Guide to Nebraska*, (St. Johnsbury, Vermont: Saltillo Press, 1993) p. 187.

14 Ibid.

15 Allred p. 298.

16 Ibid.

17 By a slightly different account, the two sides first camped separately after a peaceable meeting. The next day, October 24, the Indians followed the cavalry and camped near the army's bivouac. Then, before feeding the Indians, the soldiers' rounded up the Cheyennes' horses. That night additional troops arrived, bringing artillery with them. After breakfast the following morning, officers directed the Indians to surrender their guns and ammunition. After extended parleys and the near outbreak of fighting, the arrival of additional troops caused the Cheyenne to acquiesce to the army's demands that the Indians accompany them to Fort Robinson. This version is in Allred, p. 298, 299.

18 Buecker p. 134.

19 Allred p. 299.

20 Buecker p. 141.

21 Allred p. 301.

22 Buecker p. 140.

23 Correspondence (September 12, 2005) with Thomas R. Buecker, Curator, Fort Robinson Museum.

24 Buecker correspondence September 12, 2005.

25 Sandoz, relying more on Indian accounts, sets the number at thirty killed. Two other scholars, Robinson (p. 341) and Allred (p. 301) put the number at fifty. John D. McDermott, *A Guide to the Indian Wars of the West*, (Lincoln and London: University of Nebraska Press, 1998) p. 164, places the figure at thirty-two. McDermott believes the dead included "(t)wenty-two men, eight women, and two children. . ."

26 Buecker p. 142.

27 Sandoz and Buecker (p. 142) use the lower figure. Robinson states that "(s)ixty-five were rounded up and brought back in the morning ..." (p.341). Allred agrees with that number and notes that many were wounded. (p.301)

28 Buecker believes the initial group may have numbered about 50. (p. 142).

29 Buecker p. 146.

30 Allred p. 302.

31 Buecker p. 148.

32 R. Eli Paul, *The Nebraska Indian Wars Reader 1865-1877*, (Lincoln and London: The University of Nebraska Press, 1998) p. 222, 223.

33 Buecker p. 147.

34 For many years, there was a great deal of uncertainty among scholars regarding the location of Lost Chokecherry Canyon. On February 13, 2006, Sarah Polak, Director, Mari Sandoz High Plains Heritage Center, in Chadron, Nebraska, discovered a letter written by Mari Sandoz in 1953 that identifies the site precisely. The geographic coordinates are latitude 42.5347155, longitude 102.0718447, which places it in Sheridan County, "near the head of the Snake River valley, a tributary to the Niobrara. . ."

35 King p. 188.

36 Ibid.

37 Ibid.

38 Nebraska State Historical Society. See http://net.unl.edu/swi/guide/stbear.html. Material extracted July 23, 2007.

39 My thanks to Dr. Alexander M. Vielakowski, Department of Military History, Army Command and General Staff College, Fort Leavenworth, Kansas, for his remarks regarding this possibility during our September 26, 2005 conversation.

PART II

SIGNIFICANT ENCOUNTERS

SIGNIFICANT ENCOUNTERS

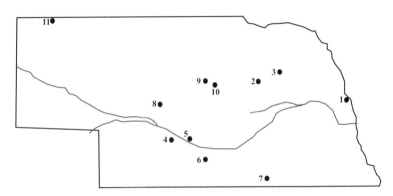

1. First military expedition in Nebraska	June 18, through summer 1823	Fort Atkinson
2. Battle of Beaver Creek	June 15 or July 17, 1855	Beaver Creek near Petersburg
3. The "Pawnee War" of 1859	July 1 - 13, 1859	Battle Creek
4. Private Lohnes' Medal of Honor	May 12, 1865	Near Gothenburg
5. Train attack at Plum Creek	July or August, 1865	Near Lexington
6. Spring Creek (Phelps County)	May 16, 1869	Central Phelps County
7. Spring Creek (Nuckolls County)	May 17, 1870	West of Ruskin
8. Buffalo Bill's Medal of Honor	April 26, 1872	Near Stapleton
9. Battle of Sioux Creek	March 1873	Ten miles west of Burwell
10. Battle of Pebble Creek	January 19, 1874	Near Burwell
11. Mackenzie's Raid	October 23, 1876	Chadron Creek, 30 miles N.of Fort Robinson

Chapter Thirteen

The First Military Expedition: Fort Atkinson

". . .(W)hen the American Revolution was a mere 36 years behind us, when not a single settler had crossed the Mississippi into Iowa, and when not a single mile of railroad existed in the entire nation, a single patch of ground a few miles north of Omaha, now surrounded by cornfields, pastures, and small town homes, was the site of the largest military post in America."[1]

* * *

Established in 1819, Fort Atkinson was built on a site identified by Lewis and Clark during their 1804 expedition. The location of the fort – on high ground on a steep bluff above the Missouri River – was influenced by Clark's favorable recommendation. Fort Atkinson became the home of the famous Sixth Infantry and an elite rifle regiment.

In 1822, a visitor, Prince Paul, Duke of Wuerttemberg, recorded the following description:

> "The fort itself was a square structure. Its sides were each 200 American yards long. There were eight log houses, two on each side. There were three gates leading into this fort. Each house consisted of ten rooms, and was 25 feet wide and 250 feet long. The roof of the houses sloped toward the interior court. The doors and windows opened upon this court. On the outside, each room has an embrasure or loophole."[2]

In 1823, the fort was both the starting and ending point for the first military expedition on Nebraska soil. On June 18, a keelboat, the *Yellow Stone*, arrived from up river carrying wounded and terrified refugees from an Indian raid on a distant trading post. More than a dozen traders[3]—by another source "about 20"[4]—had been killed by Arikara Indians in a surprise attack on William Ashley's Fur Trading Company located on the Missouri River in present-day north central South Dakota. Ashley and the remaining traders were said to be "holed up on the river and in need of aid."[5]

The cause of the raid is not certain. One version has it that an Arikara had stolen horses from the trader. The culprit was caught and the beating or horsewhipping the traders administered to him prompted the Arikara to retaliate.[6]

Within four days of the *Yellow Stone's* arrival, Fort Atkinson's commander, Colonel Henry Leavenworth, assembled and provisioned an expedition and headed upriver. Colonel Leavenworth left the fort with 220 soldiers of the Sixth Infantry and thirty members of Ashley's party who had arrived on the keelboat.[7] Along the way, Leavenworth was joined by eighty additional troopers and several hundred[8] Sioux warriors, the traditional enemies of the Arikara.

On August 9, Leavenworth's force arrived at the Arikara village which was surrounded by dirt walls bolstered with timbers dug into the ground. Leavenworth wasted no time, placing cannon on a hillside and bombarding the village while the Sioux skirmished with Arikara warriors outside the walls. The "short, sharp fight. . .ended with the Indians abandoning their village and escaping."[9] About forty Arikara were killed.[10] Seven troopers were killed during the campaign; the first casualties from a unit posted in Nebraska and in the words of one scholar "the first casualties of the Indian wars of the west. . ."[11] The "Arikara War of 1823" was the first "war" on the Nebraska frontier.[12]

* * *

Located off U.S. Highway 75 near Fort Calhoun between Blair and Omaha, Fort Atkinson is another of Nebraska's superbly restored forts. Long, fully reconstructed single story barracks—two on each side—form three sides of the large compound. The loopholes that provided firing positions for the soldiers in each room are cut into the massive timbers exactly as described in the account written in 1822. The perimeters of the fort are clearly marked. Reconstruction continues. The Missouri River has since wandered away from the bluff on which the fort stands, but the vista remains extraordinary.

Once the largest military fort in the U.S., Fort Atkinson has been superbly restored. Each of the eight main buildings was 250 feet long. The stone structure in the middle of the parade field housed the powder magazine.

Photos by Nita Phillips

Endnotes

1 Fort Atkinson, Nebraska, *The History of Fort Atkinson* website www-dial.jpl.nasa.gov/~steven/ casde/Atkinson/fort.html. The website narrative is a reprint of an article with the same name that originally appeared in *NEBRASKALAND* magazine in 1987. Material was extracted from the website November 15, 2005.

2 Fort Atkinson, Nebraska, *The History of Fort Atkinson* website .

3 Fort Atkinson, Nebraska, *The History of Fort Atkinson* website.

4 Old Fort Atkinson Nebraska by Addison Erwin Sheldon, *Legends of America* website www. legendsofamerica.com/NB-FortAtkinson.html. Material extracted from website November 15, 2005.

5 Fort Atkinson, Nebraska website.

6 Old Fort Atkinson Nebraska by Addison Erwin Sheldon website.

7 Fort Atkinson, Nebraska website.

8 Sheldon's account in Old Fort Atkinson Nebraska by Addison Erwin Sheldon cites 400 Sioux warriors.

9 Fort Atkinson, Nebraska website.

10 The figure of 40 Arikara killed is contained in Sheldon's account in Old Fort Atkinson Nebraska by Addison Erwin Sheldon website.

11 Fort Atkinson, Nebraska website. Sheldon believes there were no soldiers killed (Old Fort Atkinson Nebraska by Addison Erwin Sheldon website).

12 Old Fort Atkinson Nebraska by Addison Erwin Sheldon website.

Chapter Fourteen

The Battle of Beaver Creek:
The Death of Logan Fontenelle

D
ebate remains over the date of the battle of Beaver Creek and the struggle that resulted in the death of Omaha chief Logan Fontenelle, but there is little controversy about Fontenelle himself: he was universally regarded as an exemplary leader and a distinguished representative of his people.

Born in 1825, probably at Fort Atkinson[1] or Bellevue,[2] to a French fur trader and the daughter of an Omaha chief, Fontenelle was educated at a private school in St. Louis and spoke English and French in addition to the Omaha language.[3] At about age fifteen[4] he began serving as an interpreter for the government. Still a young man in 1853, he was elected principal chief of the Omahas.[5] The following year he accompanied other chiefs to Washington D.C. to negotiate a treaty that gave the Omaha a reservation in northeastern Nebraska in return for ceding Omaha land to the United States, thus opening Nebraska Territory to settlement.[6]

Fontenelle promoted education and agriculture, believing that survival for the Omaha tribe depended on accommodating the presence of the white man.[7] The tribe maintained excellent relations with white settlers and Fontenelle was highly respected by them. From the outset there was peace and cooperation between the tribe and the increasing numbers of emigrants flowing into Nebraska Territory. In contrast, there was war – perpetually – between the Omaha and the Sioux: "It had been for years the custom of the Sioux to come and fight (the Omahas) every summer."[8] One encounter in that endless conflict, at a date given variously as June 15[9] or July 17, 1855,[10] snuffed out the promising lie of Logan Fontenelle.

* * *

Sources generally agree on the site of the battle in which Fontenelle was slain; the clash took place along Beaver Creek near present-day Petersburg.[11] However, the details of the battle and Fontenelle's death – which have come to us through patchy writings, oral traditions of both tribes, and recollections of participants long after the event— vary considerably.

One account, though sketchy on specifics, says the battle was precipitated by the Sioux stealing some of the Omahas' horses. When Omaha warriors left camp to track the stolen animals, the Sioux, hidden in nearby hills, doubled back and attacked the camp inflicting heavy casualties that included numerous women and children. When the raid was over, the Omaha followed the Sioux for some distance until they were certain they had disappeared from the valley. Instead, the Sioux circled back again and attacked the Omahas on Beaver Creek where Fontenelle was killed.[12]

Omaha lore provides a somewhat different version: in the Omaha tradition, the hunting party saw a larger body of Sioux and retreated for two or three days[13] until they believed themselves to be out of danger. Crossing later to the south side of the Elkhorn, they found and followed buffalo tracks. The following morning, Fontenelle and two others went ahead of the main body of Omahas. As they were chasing elk, Fontenelle became separated from the other two hunters. In the meantime, the Sioux, never having ceased their pursuit, began attacking Omahas wherever they found them. Sioux history says they sighted and chased Fontenelle, thought they had lost him, and then discovered him again as he tried to free his much valued horse from the mire of a creek bed. Surrounded and surprised, he probably killed at least one (another source says three)[14] Sioux before he was "killed by about seven arrows piercing him in the breast, and by having the back part of his head broken in with a tomahawk."[15]

Fontenelle's actions are described differently in another variation. By this account, as Omaha women and children fled back to camp and Sioux suddenly appeared, Fontenelle and other Omaha warriors went out to fight the attackers. As the Sioux charged; Fontenelle did not retreat but kept on firing until he was shot and scalped.[16]

Mari Sandoz's account contains threads that are touched upon in other versions. In her description, the Sioux doubled back after seeing the Omaha scouts return to their camp. As the entire Omaha hunting party moved down Beaver Creek, the Sioux maneuvered to get ahead of them. As they did so, they found two men out hunting for elk. One ran away immediately, but the other—Fontenelle—"dropped into the high grass and fired upon the charging Lakotas," hitting one before being slain.[17]

Wikipedia
Logan Fontenelle

There are multiple references, in Sandoz and other sources, that comment on the weapon Fontenelle carried. Apparently he was armed "with a double barreled gun, one barrel rifle, the other shot gun."[18] The Sioux had not previously seen "a twice shooting gun,"[19] as Sandoz described it, and that, as well as Fontenelle's marksmanship, accounted for their casualties as they attempted to ride him down.

One other aspect of the battle deserves mention. The fight was the first for a young Sioux warrior whose name at the time was Curly. Later, his Lakota father would give him a different name: Crazy Horse. Probably thirteen years old at the time, the boy rode with Brule Sioux relatives during early and mid-summer 1855[20] and participated in the battle that Sandoz also places in July.

According to Sioux tradition, when the Sioux made their initial surprise attack on the Omaha camp, three Omahas were killed. One was slain by Crazy Horse who, when he went to scalp his victim, discovered that he had killed a woman. Although this was considered a major feat in the culture of the plains Indians—a tribe that would not protect its women and children was regarded as weak: their death or capture placed shame on the losing side—another warrior took her scalp when Crazy Horse could not bring himself to do so.[21]

* * *

The differing accounts of Fontenelle's battle make it difficult to identify its exact location. Almost all sources agree that it was along Beaver Creek, an area that now contains mostly meadows and cropland. A marker along Highway 14 in the Petersburg City Park describes the battle and is the closest memorial to the site.

Endnotes

1 *Logan Fontenelle (1825-1855)* website www.nde.state.ne.us/SS/notables/fontenelle.html. Material extracted from website October 27, 2005.

2 *Logan Fontenelle*, Nebraska State Historical Society Official Government Website Website www.nebraskahistory.org/publish/markers/texts/logan_fontenelle.htm. Material extracted From website October 27, 2005.

3 Addison Erwin Sheldon, *Sheldon's History and Stories of Nebraska –Logan Fontenelle* , Olden Times Website www.olden-times.com/OldtimeNebraska/n-csynder/nbstory/story23.html. Material extracted from website December 31, 2005. Information contained in the website is from Addison Erwin Sheldon's book, *History and Stories of Nebraska*, (Chicago and Lincoln: The University Publishing Company, 1914).

4. *Logan Fontenelle (1825-1855)* website.

5 Ibid.

6 Ibid.

7 A.T. Andreas, *Andreas's History of the State of Nebraska – Military History*, The Kansas Collection Website www.kancoll.org/books/andreas_ne/military/military-p1.html#doflf. Material extracted from Website December 31, 2005. Information contained in the website is from A.T.Andreas' book, *History of the State of Nebraska*, (Chicago: The Western Historical Company, 1882) .

8 A. T. Andreas, *Andreas's History of the State of Nebraska – Military History* website.

9 Ibid.

10 *Logan Fontenelle* website.

11 Ibid.

12 Alan Boye, *The Complete Roadside Guide to Nebraska*, (St. Johnsbury, Vermont: Saltillo Press, 1993) p. 117.

13 In the broadest and bloodiest account of the incident, the retreat was instead a three day running battle that resulted in horrific losses. In this telling, the first major skirmish occurred near Norfolk followed later by a significant encounter south of Shelton. After separate attacks on the Omahas' divided camps, one of which was on the "north side of the Elkhorn near where the Elkhorn is now crossed by a bridge at Stanton," the other south of the Elkhorn where the Omahas were "scattered out as much as five miles along the Butterfly and some out along Indian Creek." The Omahas initially struggled to make a stand "on the south side of the Elkhorn, near where Indian Creek runs into the Elkhorn." When no attack came, at midnight the now consolidated camps were "put on the move, stopping momentarily near Wisner." Over the next two days, with the Sioux ahead and behind the main column, the Omahas attempted to fight their way through. Eventually, survivors made it back to their traditional grounds along the Missouri. This account, prepared by a pioneer historian who talked several years later with Indian participants, places the number of Sioux attackers at 4,000, opposed by 1,500 Omaha and 500 Ponca fighting men in a hunting party that, counting women, children, and the aged, numbered 6,000. The historian's sources assert that over the three days, the Omaha and Ponca lost 3,000 men, women, and children (500 warriors having been slain in the first fight along the Elkhorn). This story has Fontenelle being killed just before the Omahas' final break-out to the east. The numbers and the facts are uncertain. The historian places the date as 1848 and the location near Stanton, both of which are surely incorrect. The participants were interviewed many years after the event; it is conceivable that episodes from more than one battle were intermingled in their recollections.

14 Sheldon, *Sheldon's History and Stories of the State of Nebraska – Logan Fontenelle* website.

15 *Andreas's History of the State of Nebraska – Military History* website.

16 Sheldon, *Sheldon's History and Stories of the State of Nebraska – Logan Fontenelle* website.

17 Mari Sandoz, *Crazy Horse: The Strange Man of the Oglalas*, (New York: A.A. Knopf, 1942) p. 71.

18 *Andreas' History of the State of Nebraska – Military History* website.

19 Sandoz p. 71.

20 Sandoz p. 69.

21 Sandoz p. 70.

Chapter Fifteen

The "Pawnee War" of 1859

lthough the largest and bloodiest of the Indian uprisings did not occur until the mid-1860s, misunderstandings and occasional violence took place throughout the westward migration as two very different cultures came increasingly in contact.

The causes of many of the clashes are obscure and often disagreed upon by participants. Even though most of these early encounters resulted in little or no bloodshed, their increasing frequency was evidence of the rising tensions.

* * *

On July 1, 1859, word reached authorities in Omaha, the capital of Nebraska Territory, that Pawnees in a reported strength of 700 to 800 warriors were pillaging settlements along the Elkhorn River. The Indians were said to be "driving off stock, burning fences and houses, and threatening the lives of inhabitants."[1]

The attacks, which began on June 21 when Pawnees stole several dozen cattle near the village of Fontanelle[2] (spelled from the earliest days with an 'a' instead of an 'e'), soon became bolder and more damaging. Violence later erupted when locals managed to surround several Pawnees in a house near West Point. The Indians refused to surrender and opened fire, wounding a local citizen; the settlers then responded with a heavy attack that killed four of the raiders.[3]

As was often the case, the specific incident that triggered the initial violence is uncertain. Settlers believed that a Pawnee had robbed a white man; the Pawnees said that a white man had raped an Indian woman. The most detailed settler account alleges that a settler named Uriah Thomas, who lived about twelve miles from Fontanelle, was robbed by Pawnee raiders who took "his pocket book containing $136, a package of valuable papers, including land warrants, drank up all his whiskey, and drove off a fine yoke of oxen, leaving him locked up in his cabin." According to this version, after a short time, Thomas managed to free himself and spread the alarm.

By one writer's account, ten Pawnees were killed in the various skirmishes that occurred throughout the uprising, the main encounter being a clash with settlers near Crowell in Cuming County.[4]

The courier carrying news of the escalating bloodshed arrived in Omaha only to discover that the Governor, Samuel Black, was out of the city, a full day's journey away. Only the governor was empowered to call out the militia, but Territorial Secretary J. Sterling Morton, serving as acting chief executive, assumed the responsibility. Heeding the settlers' pleas, Morton activated the militia[5] and requested help from Fort Kearny.

The fort's commandant quickly recalled Company K, Second U.S. Dragoons from wagon train escort duty and sent them speeding towards Omaha, where they arrived on July 5.[6] The Light Artillery Company from Omaha was also assembled and led by expedition commander, Major General John M. Thayer, left immediately for the Elkhorn region. Companies of militia called to duty from Fremont, Fontanelle and Columbus joined Thayer's force as it moved up the river.[7]

Arriving in the area the following day, Thayer verified that "settlements for fifty miles had been broken up." Depredations were continuing; post offices and other government properties had also been destroyed.[8]

A call for volunteers by the governor was supported by Omaha merchants who supplied horses, forage, and equipment.[9] Eventually, the combined forces—Company K, Second Dragoons; the Light Artillery Company; militia and volunteers—numbering 200 to 300 men with a six-pounder cannon,[10] came together south of the Elkhorn on the morning of July 8.[11] Governor Black, accompanying the Second Dragoons, joined the campaign there and served as commander-in-chief.[12]

The Indians were known to have camped near Fontanelle at the time of the first attacks[13] in late June and early July. The Pawnees had now moved west toward their summer hunting grounds. Thayer's force pushed forward quickly, moving up the Elkhorn in fast pursuit, each day narrowing the distance between his party and the Pawnees. By the evening of July 12, as the trail tracked west of Norfolk and into the valley of the Elkhorn,[14] the gap separating the forces was nearly closed.

Photos by Nita Phillips

As many as 2,000 Pawnees camped along the banks of this small stream about 10 miles from the forks of the Elkhorn. Near the stream, on the outskirts of the town of Battle Creek, is a historical marker describing the engagement.

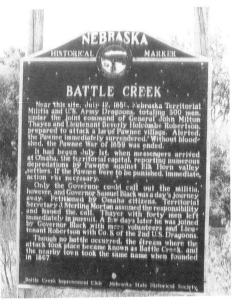

NEBRASKA

HISTORICAL MARKER

BATTLE CREEK

Near this site, July 12, 1859, Nebraska Territorial Militia and U.S. Army Dragoons, totaling 300 men, under the joint command of General John Milton Thayer and Lieutenant Beverly Holcombe Robertson, prepared to attack a large Pawnee village. Alerted, the Pawnee immediately surrendered. Without bloodshed, the Pawnee War of 1859 was ended.

It had begun July 1st, when messengers arrived at Omaha, the territorial capital, reporting numerous depredations by Pawnee against Elk Horn valley settlers. If the Pawnee were to be punished, immediate action was necessary.

Only the Governor could call out the militia, however, and Governor Samuel Black was a day's journey away. Petitioned by Omaha citizens, Territorial Secretary J. Sterling Morton assumed the responsibility and issued the call. Thayer with forty men left immediately in pursuit. A few days later he was joined by Governor Black with more volunteers and Lieutenant Robertson with Co. K of the 2nd U.S. Dragoons.

Though no battle occurred, the stream where the attack took place became known as Battle Creek, and the nearby town took the same name when founded in 1867.

Battle Creek Improvement Club   Nebraska State Historical Society

That night Thayer and his men made a forced march that brought them at daylight up against the Pawnee camp that "stretched along the bank of a small stream about ten miles above the forks of the Elkhorn."[15]

Thayer positioned his cannon and formed his men in line,[16] preparing to attack. By one account, the order to charge had been given when a Pawnee chief rushed from the camp toward Thayer, making it clear that he wished to surrender. The attack was halted.[17]

The entire Pawnee contingent, perhaps surprised by the speed and size of the government's response, surrendered immediately.

General Thayer stated that

> "(t)he troops came upon the Indians and the Indians surrendered. The line was formed, the cannon was planted and the chiefs of all the different bands came forward, throwing down their arms and raising white flags. The interpreter was directed to communicate with them, and they asked to have a council. They acknowledged that their young men had committed these depredations, and offered to give them up and did bring forward six, who were delivered up. Two of them were shot as they were trying to escape the next day. The guard so informed me. I did not see it."[18]

In addition to turning over six of the warriors as the guilty men, the Pawnee signed an agreement indicating that the property they had destroyed would be paid for by deductions from their government annuities.[19] A slightly different version says that the chief who first came forward to surrender then talked the rest of the Battle Creek encampment—whose numbers were placed at 3,000 Pawnees, Omahas, and Poncas—"into a non-violent settlement."[20]

The terms of surrender, probably laid down by Governor Black, were regarded by participants as being "just to (the Pawnees), but efficient for the protection of the settlers."[21] Other than the gunfire during the escape attempt, no other shots were fired in anger during the final confrontation.

The "Pawnee War" was over.

* * *

The small stream along whose banks the Pawnees were camped was named "Battle Creek." Eight years later, the town of Battle Creek was founded[22] a few hundred yards east of where the Pawnees had made their camp.[23]

The appearance of the creek is not much changed from 1859: it runs deeper than many of the streams that trace the Nebraska prairie and in places its sides are steeply cut. The banks are wooded on both sides. The place where the Pawnees made their camp that "stretched along the banks of a small stream" is now mostly pasture land. Fenced, grass cropped short by grazing, it lies at the edge of the town. A state historical marker on Highway 121 north of the city marks the location of the nearby encounter.

Endnotes

1 A. T. Andreas, *History of the State of Nebraska – Military History,* The Kansas Collection website Websitewww.kancoll.org/books/andreas_ne/military-p1.html#doflf. Material extracted from website October 27, 2005. Information contained in the website is from A.T. Andreas' book *History of the State of Nebraska,* (Chicago: The Western Historical Society, 1882).

2 *Semi-Centennial History of Nebraska – 1904,* NEGenWeb Project website Website www. roots-web.com/~neresour/OLLibrary/SCHofNE/pages/schn0088.htm. Material extracted from website October 31, 2005.

3 Ibid.

4 Alan Boye, *The Complete Roadside Guide to Nebraska,* (St. Johnsbury, Vermont: Saltillo Press, 1993) p. 399.

5 *Battle Creek,* Nebraska State Historical Society Official Nebraska Government Website www. nebraskahistory.org/publish/texts/battle_creek.htm. Material extracted from website October 31, 2005.

6 *Andreas' History of the State of Nebraska – Military History* website.

7 *Semi-Centennial History of Nebraska – 1904* website.

8 *Andreas's History of the State of Nebraska – Military History* website.

9 Ibid.

10 The *Semi-Centennial History of Nebraska – 1904* website states that Thayer's force consisted of 200 men. The Nebraska State Historical Society website places the number at 300.

11 *Andreas' History of the State of Nebraska – Military History* website.

12 Ibid.

13 Ibid.

14 *Semi-Centennial History of Nebraska – 1904* website.

15 Ibid. The Nebraska State Historical society dates the "Pawnee War" encounter as July 12, 1859. A second credible source places Thayer's night march on the 12th and the near-attack and surrender on the morning of the 13th.

16 *Andreas' History of the State of Nebraska* website.

17 *Semi-Centennial History of Nebraska – 1904* website.

18 *Andreas' History of Nebraska – Military History* website.

19 *Semi-Centennial History of Nebraska – 1904* website.

20 Boye p. 402.

21 *Andreas' History of the State of Nebraska – Military History* website.

22 *Battle Creek,* Nebraska State Historical Society website.

23 *Semi-Centennial History of Nebraska – 1904* website.

Chapter Sixteen

Private Lohne's Medal of Honor

"The Congressional Medal of Honor, created by Congress in 1862, has been presented many times to soldiers with Nebraska connections. In a group by themselves are fifteen men who earned the nation's highest award for gallantry while performing military service within Nebraska's borders. Those Medals of Honor, awarded between 1865 and 1879, resulted from the U.S. Army's efforts to subdue the embattled Sioux and Cheyenne during the Indians wars on the plains."

* * *

The first Medal of Honor given for service in Nebraska was earned on May 12, 1865, for actions during what would now be called a "fire fight." Private Francis W. Lohnes, a veteran of the Civil War battles at Fort Donelson and Shiloh, was assigned to Company H, First Nebraska Veteran Volunteer Cavalry when, in August 1864, the unit was sent to guard stage stations and road ranches against massive Sioux and Cheyenne raids then threatening the Platte valley. Early 1865 found the company in the vicinity of Gothenburg, where in February of that year they built a military camp at Midway Station, a key site on the stage route. Operating from that location, Company H moved up and down the valley, patrolling, skirmishing, and providing a security screen for settlers in the area and travelers moving along the trail.

On the morning of May 12, Lohnes, in charge of a small wood-gathering detail, took his men from the Midway Station camp and moved toward stands of timber that lay at some distance to the west. After about ten miles, their path took them close to Dan Smith's ranch, where their seemingly routine duty brought them into the midst of a battle.

As Lohnes and his men came upon the scene, an outnumbered contingent from Company A of the First Battalion of Nebraska Cavalry was engaged in a violent struggle with a large band of Indians raiding through the area. Lohnes led his men straight into the fight and was wounded during the ensuing melee. As the troopers struggled to break free, Lohnes, surrounded at one point by as many as ten Indians, fought off the attackers and enabled his troopers and the cavalrymen from Company A to successfully retreat to Dan Smith's Ranche.

Lohnes recovered from his wound and during a ceremony at Fort Kearny on August 15, was presented with the Medal of Honor. His was "the only Medal of Honor awarded to a member of a military unit bearing Nebraska's name."

* * *

Today, the place where Lohnes fought his battle and won the Medal of Honor is indistinguishable from the surrounding landscape. Like much of the ground in that vicinity, it is mostly level. Only a few rolling hills of low elevation shape the valley and occasionally break the horizon. The tall grain elevators that reflect the area's rich agricultural base are the features most visible from a distance.

Material in this section is drawn primarily from James E. Potter's marvelous chapter, *The Pageant Revisited: Indian Wars Medals of Honor in Nebraska, 1865-1879*. Mr. Potter's work is contained in *The Indian Wars Reader 1867-1877*, R. Eli Paul, editor, (Lincoln and London: The University of Nebraska Press, 1998). See pages 217 – 227. The introductory quote is on page 217. Potter's chapter contains a wealth of information on the circumstances surrounding each medal and on the soldiers who received them.

See Appendix E for a location map and other details on Medals of Honor earned in Nebraska.

Chapter Seventeen

Attack on a Train at Plum Creek

T he 1864 "Plum Creek Massacre" was not the only notori-
ous incident associated with the stream of that name. Three
years later, not far from Lexington, another event equally as
horrific took place near it.

* * *

On a date given as July[1] or August[2] 1867, a large band of Cheyennes ripped up a section of railroad track near present-day Lexington. The damage to the tracks derailed an on-coming train which the
Cheyennes then ambushed, plundered, and burned. Several members
of the train crew were killed.

The careful trap was laid by Cheyennes led by a chief named
Turkey Leg. The place chosen for the ambush was about four miles
west of Plum Creek Station where the tracks traced a gentle curve and
passed over a small bridge or culvert spanning a shallow gully. At
the small trestle the Indians removed the rails and tilted them so that
one end of each protruded two to three feet above the track bed. Ties
were piled against the rails for support and the entire structure was
lashed together by wire cut from the telegraph line that paralleled the
tracks.[3] The Indians apparently hoped that the barricade arrangement
would rip out the underside of the train carriage as it passed over, or at
the minimum, rupture the cylinders on each side of the locomotive.[4]
When the barricade was in place, the Indians hid in nearby tall grass
and ravines and waited for traffic along the track.

The first activity came after midnight in the form of a hand-car sent
ahead of the train. Accounts vary as to the number of men on the car
and their immediate fate. One source says there was a six-man repair
crew on the vehicle. Distracted by the sight of Indians, they did not

see the barricade. The hand-car slammed into the barrier and all six men were thrown from it. The Indians swarmed over them and by this account five of the six were killed almost instantly. The sixth was hurled some distance from the car and tried to hide in the prairie grass. Caught by one of the Cheyennes, he was knocked unconscious and scalped. Something then caught the attention of the Indians, perhaps the approach of the train, and the warrior dropped the scalp and rode off elsewhere. The railman, whose name was William Thompson, awoke, found his own scalp, and after passing out again eventually revived in the cool night air. Finding a place to hide, he watched a disaster unfold as the Indians destroyed the train and slaughtered its crew. Later, with the Indians drunk from liquor pilfered from the freight cars, he made his way to Plum Creek Station where his wounds were treated.[5]

A slightly different version has three workers in the hand-car. When the car hit the blockade, it slammed to a stop at the bottom of the gully. All three railmen were stunned and bruised, but as the Indians raced towards them, two managed to escape in the darkness. Frightened and hiding in close proximity to the Indians, they could not warn the approaching train. The third member of the hand-car, Thompson, was scalped by the Cheyennes. By this version, in his fear and delirium he waved his arms wildly, grabbed his scalp back from the warrior, and somehow managed to scramble away in the blackness.[6] Both accounts have him eventually resuming his career with the railroad.

Meanwhile, unaware of the peril that awaited it a short distance down the tracks, the train was fast approaching. As the train sped towards the blockade, the crew eventually saw the barrier and the dislodged rails in the engine's headlights. The engineer tried to reverse the locomotive, but the train was moving too fast to stop. A series of catastrophic events soon took place, each adding to the horror that preceded it.

As the train, brakes screeching, slammed into the barricade, the fireman was flung against or into the locomotive's open firebox and was "literally roasted alive."[7] In the chaos of the derailment, the engineer was hurled through the locomotive's window and was nearly disemboweled as he struck a metal object in the cab. His charred body was later found surrounded by burning cars and cargo. It is uncertain whether he died as a result of his injuries or if he was killed by the Cheyenne attackers who quickly swarmed over the wreckage.

Within moments, the area around the ravine was transformed into a nightmarish scene. Shattered cars and freight were strewn over the landscape. Fires quickly began, started partly by the flames ejected from the locomotive's mangled firebox. Two flat cars fully loaded with bricks were catapulted over the engine and landed several feet beyond it while the remainder of the train telescoped against the engine and ground itself apart. The conductor, riding at the back of the train, jumped free. The crewman hurried toward the locomotive, saw what had happened to the engineer and fireman, and ran into the night to escape capture and warn a second train known to be following along the track only a short distance behind.

The conductor managed to escape marauding Cheyenne and flag down the second train, which he rode back to Plum Creek, arriving there at about two in the morning. Attempts to form an immediate rescue party were not successful, and it was mid-morning before a force from the local area made its way to the ambush site.

They found total devastation. Scattered amidst the burned out hulks of train cars were pillaged boxes of merchandise and opened bolts of cloth spooled out along the ground. There is a description of Cheyenne warriors taking bolts of loosened material "and with one end tied to their ponies' tails or the horn of their saddles (riding) at full gallop up and down the prairie just to see the bright colors streaming in the wind behind them."[8]

Plains warfare often consisted of a vicious cycle of attacks and counter-attacks. In the case of the train incident at Plum Creek, retribution was soon forthcoming—and it came from a most interesting source.

Major Frank North, commanding a company of the famed Pawnee Scouts and a few soldiers, brought his contingent to the scene of the attack. He followed the attackers' trail long enough to confirm they were Cheyennes. North chose not to pursue them, believing that if they were not followed, the Cheyennes would return to raid again in the same area. Accordingly, he went into camp at Plum Creek and waited for them to reappear.

They did so, about ten days later. Warned by one of his detached scouts that the Cheyennes were moving towards Plum Creek from the south, Major North moved his force to the Plum Creek overland stage station. There, he intended to rest his men and horses overnight.

The Pawnee Scouts, however, wanted to identify the approaching party before darkness set in. North consented and allowed forty-eight scouts led by two young cavalry officers and accompanied by two sergeants to move out and locate the incoming raiders. Leaving quickly, the company rode almost directly south, crossed the Platte and followed the river bank in an easterly direction until they were within about a mile and a half of Plum Creek.

There, they collided with the Cheyennes.

For generations, the Cheyenne along with their traditional allies, the Sioux, had been the bitter enemies of the Pawnee. It was a struggle fought with little quarter given: both sides found inventive and horrific ways to torture prisoners, raid, and terrorize their opponents. Now, at the sight of their mortal enemies, both parties eagerly readied for a clash.

The Cheyennes—about 150 in all, by most estimates—quickly mounted and the mayhem occurred as opposing sides met on the banks of Plum Creek. Though the Scouts numbered only fifty-two total (counting the two cavalry officers and two NCOs), they charged at full fury. The speed of their attack and the cohesion of the smaller group carried them into and through the Cheyennes who broke, overwhelmed by the ferocity of the assault, and fled in panic and confusion. The Pawnees' wrath was not soon abated and they raced after the Cheyennes, pursuing them for miles as they rushed toward the Republican Valley. The killing and scalping ceased only when nightfall put an end to the chase.

When the blood lust was over, fifteen Cheyenne warriors had been killed and scalped. The Pawnee also returned with thirty-five horses and mules. Two captives—one, a sixteen-year old nephew of Turkey Leg— were also taken and later exchanged for six settler hostages held by the Cheyenne.[9]

The encounter had an important consequence; the victory of Major North's Pawnee Scouts put an end to Cheyenne attacks on the railroad.[10]

* * *

The present day train tracks run close to the original road bed that was the scene of the slaughter in 1867, although the actual site of the attack is not marked. The surrounding landscape, mostly virgin prairie at the time pockmarked only by a few widely scattered settler cabins, is today farmland lush with corn and grain.

Not many miles from the scene, the Johnson Reservoir and Tri County Supply Canal alter the general appearance of the region as it existed when the fight occurred. The Platte River itself is considerably changed. Where early accounts speak of a broad, though shallow stream coursing across wide swathes of the prairie, today irrigation and other diversions siphon off its flow, often reducing it to tiny rivulets and small channels.

Endnotes

1 Richard Crabb, *Empire on the Platte*, (Cleveland and New York: The World Publishing Company, 1967) p. 27.

2 Harrison Johnson, *Johnson's History of Nebraska*, (H. Gibson, Herald Publishing House, 1880) p. 324.

3 Johnson p. 325.

4 Johnson p.324.

5 Crabb p. 27.

6 Ibid.

7 Johnson p. 325.

8 Johnson p. 325-326.

9 Johnson p. 326-327.

10 Johnson p. 327-328.

Chapter Eighteen

Spring Creek (Phelps County) May 16, 1869

T here is irony, sometimes, in the way history unfolds.
Almost every other waterway in the state is better known
than the two small streams, one in southeast and the other in
south central Nebraska, that share the same name. Other regions west
and north are more renowned for their battle sites. Yet, the nation's
highest honor for valor was awarded—multiple times—for actions
along both streams. Near one of the tiny creeks, more Medals of Honor
were won than at any other place in Nebraska. Indeed, per square
mile, at few places in the world have as many Medals of Honor been
earned than along the banks of Spring Creek.

* * *

Spring of 1869 found the Fifth U.S. Cavalry in the process of
transferring from Fort Lyon, Colorado, to Fort McPherson,[1] near
North Platte from where they would take part in the Republican River
Expedition. On May 14, soon after the unit had crossed into Nebraska,
scouts came across an Indian trail of considerable size near Medicine
Creek. Still some distance south of the fort, Brevet Major General
Eugene A. Carr, the Fifth Cavalry Commander, sent his pack train on
to Fort McPherson[2] and detailed seven companies of cavalry to follow
the trail.

The troopers, led by their most famous scout, William F. Cody,
pursued the difficult trail for two days, tracking the Indians many
miles to the east into what is now Phelps County. While the rest of the
command watered its horses at a ford along Spring Creek, Carr sent a
small group that included Cody on an advance scout to check on five
Indians who had been seen in the far distance.[3] A short time later, Carr,
anticipating trouble, sent a full cavalry company under the command

of an experienced Civil War veteran, Lieutenant John Breckenridge Babcock, to support the reconnaissance.

Two miles from Spring Creek, as Babcock's troopers made contact with the scout party, both groups were ambushed by an estimated 200 Indians who poured into the cavalrymen from concealment in nearby gullies and ravines. Within minutes, the soldiers were surrounded and under heavy attack. In the face of the furious assault, Babcock had his troopers dismount and make a stand on high ground.[4] The inexperienced troopers, initially shaken by the swiftness and ferocity of the onslaught, were rallied by Babcock who "encouraged and steadied his men," setting a conspicuous example of coolness and courage under fire by calmly riding up and down the lines. Under Babcock's astute leadership, the isolated troopers held the Indians at bay for a half hour until reinforcements sent by General Carr arrived on scene. Seeing substantial numbers of troops streaming towards them, the Indians broke off the attack and withdrew.

One scholar described the encounter as "unremarkable": three troopers were wounded in the skirmish[5] and after it was over, the Fifth Cavalry resumed an uneventful journey to Fort McPherson. Two events, however, lent a special quality to the engagement. The first was the presence of Buffalo Bill Cody, who was grazed by a bullet during the fighting. (When General Carr reached the battlefield, Cody was wrapped in a bloody bandage covering a scalp wound.[6]) The second was that Lieutenant Babcock received the Medal of Honor for his extraordinary leadership during the fight. It was the first Medal of Honor awarded for action along a stream named Spring Creek.

A year and a day later, further to the east at a different creek bearing the same name, many more would follow.

* * *

The tiny creek that flows through Phelps County probably hasn't changed much over the years. Amid the surrounding farmland, gullies and ravines still cut the area close to the stream. The battle site is not marked.

Endnotes

1 Unless otherwise identified, material in this segment is drawn from R. Eli Paul, editor, *The Nebraska Indian Wars Reader 1865-1877*, (Lincoln and London: University of Nebraska Press, 1998) p. 218-219.

2 James T. King, *War Eagle: A Life of General Eugene A. Carr*, (Lincoln: University of Nebraska Press, 1963) p. 97.

3 King p. 98.

4 Ibid.

5 King's research led him to conclude that one trooper was killed in the action. King p. 98.

6 Ibid.

Chapter Nineteen
Spring Creek (Ruskin, Nuckolls County) May 17, 1870

To protect the growing number of settlements in southern Nebraska along Spring Creek and the Little Blue and Republican Rivers, in 1870 a temporary cavalry post called Camp Bingham was established on the Little Blue River west of present-day Hebron. Company C, Second U.S. Cavalry, was sent from its permanent base in Omaha to garrison the small post.[1]

In mid-May, about a month after the camp was activated, several horses wandered away from the bivouac, and five cavalrymen—Sergeant Patrick Leonard and Privates Heath Canfield, Michael Himmelsbach, Thomas Hubbard, and George Thompson[2]—were sent to look for them. Two days later, on the morning of May 17, while searching for the horses along Spring Creek west of present-day Ruskin,[3] about seven miles southwest of his camp,[4] the five men were suddenly attacked by a band of fifty Indians, who rushed at them from concealment in ravines along the creek.[5] The cavalrymen's horses were shot from under them, killed by the first burst of heavy fire from the Indians. The troopers quickly made makeshift breastworks from the carcasses.[6] Firing from behind the tenuous shelter, the five soldiers fought for their lives.

For the next two hours, pinned against brush and shrubs near the creek, the cavalrymen beat back a series of attacks that wounded Private Hubbard and threatened many times to overrun their position.

Finally, repeatedly repulsed by the steady fire from the five soldiers, the Indians withdrew when they mistook a party of surveyors for a military force sent in relief. When the Indians departed, the soldiers made it back to Camp Bingham on foot, carrying the wounded soldier with them.[7] The number of Indian losses is not known.

While the savage struggle was going on at Spring Creek, other Indians took horses and killed a settler along the Little Blue. The rest of Company C pursued the raiders who escaped south, across the Republican River. Although the skirmishes were seemingly not of major consequence, the long term effect was substantial. "Despite the turmoil the raid created among the settlements in the region, it was

Photos by Nita Phillips

On May 17, 1870 this rugged landscape along Spring Creek was the scene of a fierce encounter between five troopers searching for lost horses, and about fifty Indians. All five soldiers were awarded Congressional Medals of Honor.

the last Indian foray into southern Nebraska."[8] Camp Bingham was abandoned a few months later.[9]

Though the encounter was small, history associates an extraordinary event with the bitter fight at Spring Creek. When a description of the encounter reached the Secretary of War, William W. Belknap, he ordered that all five cavalrymen involved in the battle be awarded Medals of Honor.[10]

Thus, in the fire and tumult of two desperate hours along a small creek near Ruskin in Nuckolls County, "more Medals of Honor were won than at any other incident in Nebraska's military history."[11]

* * *

All too often the specific locations of early battles along the frontier are not known and their sites are not identified. Fortunately, neither circumstance applies regarding the Spring Creek fight near Ruskin. The location is precisely known and the place is well marked.

Today the ground where so much violence occurred is separated to the north by a cornfield and to the south, closest to the stream, by pasture. As it was in 1870, the land nearest the stream is cut by sharp ravines, probably not much different from the time the Indians poured from them to attack the five troopers on that May morning. Spring Creek, where the soldiers were pinned against the shrubs and bushes that lined it, has in many places rather rugged, steep sides, surprising for a stream whose small channel trickles along at the bottom of its sharp banks.

A marker on Highway 136 west of Ruskin identifies the scene.

Endnotes

1 R. Eli Paul, *The Nebraska Indian Wars Reader 1865-1877,* (Lincoln and London: The University of Nebraska Press, 1998) p. 218.

2 *Skirmish at Spring Creek,* Nebraska State Historical Society website. Website www.nebraskahistrory.org/publish/markers/texts/skirmish_at_spring_creek.htm. Material extracted from website April 9, 2005.

3 *Skirmish at Spring Creek* website.

4 Paul p. 219.

5 Paul p. 217.

6 Ibid.

7 Paul p. 219.

8 Paul p.220.

9 *Skirmish at Spring Creek* website.

10 Paul p. 220.

11 *Skirmish at Spring Creek* website.

Chapter Twenty

Buffalo Bill's Medal of Honor

In chapters written about Nebraska's early history, a surprising number of pages contain references to William F. Cody. Well remembered for his world-renowned Wild West show, "Buffalo Bill"—aided by massive and effective self-promotion—was an internationally known entertainer. But Cody was far more than a showman; at a relatively early age his marksmanship, scouting, and fighting skills made him a legend along the frontier. The record is clear that on numerous military expeditions, particularly those involving the U.S. Fifth Cavalry, Cody was much sought after as a scout and advisor.

* * *

By 1869, William F. Cody's name was already tied to Nebraska through his actions at Spring Creek, where he was wounded and Lieutenant John Babcock won the Medal of Honor. Later that year Cody scouted for Brevet Major General Eugene A. Carr and the U.S. Fifth Cavalry, "the Dandy Fifth," on the Republican River Expedition. The future would place him with General Wesley Merritt and the Fifth Cavalry at Warbonnet Creek where he would, by many accounts, slay the Indian warrior Yellow Hair in individual combat and claim "the first scalp for Custer."

The spring of 1872 found Cody scouting near present-day Stapleton with a contingent of the Third Cavalry. Based at Fort McPherson, on April 26 they were engaged in their second day of tracking a band of Minneconjou Sioux that had stolen horses from a nearby Union Pacific Station. The trail eventually brought the force—Company B of the Third Cavalry, led by Captain Charles Meinhold, to the banks of the South Loup River.

AZUSA Publishing LLC, Englewood Colorado
William F. "Buffalo Bill" Cody

As the troops approached the stream, Meinhold divided his command, detaching Cody, Sergeant John H. Foley, and ten other enlisted soldiers to scout along the south side of the river. Meinhold, with the remainder of the main force, crossed the stream and moved along the north bank.

Cody's reconnaissance soon discovered Indians camped near the stream. There, "under Cody's skillful guidance, Foley's party managed to approach within fifty yards of the Indian camp before it was discovered."

Firing began when the Minneconjou finally caught sight of the approaching troopers. In the brisk clash that followed, Cody killed one Indian and two others were shot down as they fled the campsite into the path of the Meinhold's main force coming from the north. Six other Indians, who happened to be away from the camp hunting when the attack occurred, made a safe escape.

The conspicuous actions of several members of the party during the sharp encounter induced Captain Meinhold to recommend four of the attackers for award of the Medal of Honor. One of the group, First Sergeant Leroy Volkes, was with Meinhold and the main body of troops that converged on the Indians from the north. The remaining three were with the smaller contingent that found and assaulted the Indian camp.

- Sergeant John H. Foley: "charged into the Indian camp without knowing how many enemies he might encounter";
- Private William H. Strayer: "bravely closed in on an Indian while he was fired at several times, and wounded him";
- The final recommendation was for William F. Cody: "Mr. Cody's reputation for bravery and skill as a guide is so well established

that I need not say anything else but that he acted in his usual manner."

Colonel Joseph J. Reynolds, Commander of the Third Cavalry, approved Captain Meinhold's recommendations and the medals were issued on May 22, 1869.

* * *

For a short distance a mile or two north of Stapleton, the South Loup flows almost straight east. The scene of Cody's encounter was likely along that stretch of river, before the stream bends briefly north and then falls away to the south and east. The river's course has remained essentially the same over the years, as in all likelihood has its appearance. Like most such streams on the Nebraska prairie, timber and brush line the banks. The trees are heavy in places but sometimes thin out leaving gaps in the timber. It was probably at one of those places, or a short distance from the river where the brush gives way to open prairie, that Cody came upon the Indian camp. The site is on private property.

Endnotes

1   Material for this section is primarily drawn from James E. Potter's remarkable chapter *The Pageant Revisited: Indian Wars Medals of Honor in Nebraska 1865-1879*. Mr. Potter's work forms the epilogue to *The Indian Wars Reader 1865-1877*, edited by R. Eli Paul (University of Nebraska Press, 1998).

Chapter Twenty-one

Battle of Sioux Creek

T he exact date has been lost, but in late March, 1873, the first serious trouble in the North Loup Valley erupted between marauding Sioux and settlers in the region. For a number of years groups of Sioux had periodically stolen away from their agency along the South Dakota border. Once outside the reservation, they hunted, raided Pawnee settlements further south, and made off with settlers' livestock.

* * *

The theft of a mare and colt from a settlement near Turkey Creek precipitated what came to be known as the Battle of Sioux Creek.[1] The unique encounter was fought a bit more than 10 miles west of Burwell,[2] a short distance southeast of present-day Taylor.[3] It was an unusual fight: there were no casualties and the settlers' lack of military competence and poor preparations were apparent to all. Nonetheless, the skirmish was to have important consequences for the region.

Spoiling for a fight and frustrated by continued thefts of valuable livestock of which the loss of the mare and colt was only the most recent example, a group of eleven settlers quickly formed after the Turkey Creek incident was reported. Led by Jack "Happy Jack" Swearenger, a trapper and reputed Indian fighter and scout,[4] the group picked up the trail at the Turkey Creek farmstead where the tracks of the stolen animals, along with those of about a dozen Sioux ponies, were clearly discernible.

Nine of the eleven members of the settler party were mounted. The other two rode in a spring wagon that carried camping equipment and other provisions. The group carried a variety of weapons that, as would soon be shown, were generally inadequate to the task. Most had only muzzle-loading guns, old fashioned muskets, or shotguns loaded with buckshot. One carried a loaded musket but had no extra ammunition. Another with a Spencer needle gun started the expedition with twenty-seven rounds of ammunition but lost twenty of them during the excitement of the running battle that eventually followed. Two of the group had Spencer carbines. The Sioux were better equipped: apparently all of them carried Winchester repeating rifles.[5]

After posting a guard at the Turkey Creek farm to protect the women and preclude the theft of the homestead's remaining horses, Swearenger's party set out trailing the raiders north along the creek. After a few miles the Indians split up, their tracks making it clear that the largest group had crossed the stream and moved south, while two or three warriors escorting the stolen horses continued to trek generally north, following the creek.[6]

Focused on retrieving the stolen animals, the settlers decided to pursue the latter group.[7] The surrounding landscape was rugged, deeply cut by gullies and sharp ravines, but Swearenger's men disregarded the possibility of ambush and pushed forward after the fleeing Indians. The trail continued past the head of Turkey Creek, traced mostly west and north to Sioux Creek, and then followed that stream towards the valley of the North Loup. The settlers tracked the Sioux until dusk and then made camp along the creek in a grove of cottonwoods.[8]

The chase resumed before sunrise and had progressed for several miles when a commotion broke out towards the rear of the column. There, about 400-500 yards away and coming fast were eight to twelve Sioux warriors, apparently the group that had split away during the early part of the pursuit. The Indians maneuvered between the main body of settlers and their supply wagon, momentarily cutting it off from the rest of the party. Swearenger dismounted, placed his horse between himself and the Indians and then stood behind it. Declining an opportunity to open fire, he perhaps thought he could parley or that the absence of shooting from the settlers might dissuade the Sioux from attacking.[9]

It did not. One of the warriors jumped from his horse and, using the animal's back as a firing platform, began shooting at the settler party. Within moments, his opening shots were followed by volleys from the rest of the Sioux.[10]

A running fight soon developed, induced partly by the settlers' horses—some shied from the noise and bolted away—and by the settlers themselves as they sought more defensible ground.[11]

As the fight continued over areas of open ground, clusters of settlers sometimes halted momentarily and fired at the onrushing Indians. The attempts to break up the pursuit had only brief effect, however. The Indians would initially stop, dismount and return aimed fire, and then remount, circle, and resume the attack. Meanwhile, the supply wagon surged through the melee, its two occupants keeping up a constant fire from the back of their vehicle, even though the stock of one of their rifles had caught in a wagon wheel and broken.[12]

Finally, about eight miles from where they had camped the night before, the settlers reached a steep bank bordering the stream.[13] There, they came together and made a stand. As one of the group held the horses, the others fired at long range from their elevated vantage point. The Sioux eventually broke off the attack and moved off in the direction of their three companions with the stolen colt and mare.

Other than a mule that died west of present-day Burwell on the settlers' way home—it is uncertain whether it had been wounded in the battle—there were no casualties on either side.[14] There was, however, one additional surprise awaiting Swearenger's group back at Turkey Creek: the larger group of Indians that had split off from the initial party had hidden out, waited for their pursuers to pass by and then returned to the farmstead to steal the remaining horses.[15]

The consensus among the settlers was that the Sioux could have inflicted more serious damage on them had they chosen to do so. Apparently, however, the raiders were content to steal livestock and, having succeeded in doing that, departed without taking lives as well.

The loss of livestock to Indian raids like the one at Turkey Creek posed a considerable financial burden on the settlers. For a time, immigration into the North Loup Valley slowed as a result of the attacks. In the days after the Sioux Creek encounter, settlers petitioned the government to send a military expedition through the valley. The army responded almost immediately and in April a cavalry company from Fort Omaha scouted the North and Middle Loup regions. As they reached Loup City on their return, they were caught in a horrific blizzard. All sixty cavalrymen took shelter in a tiny store building (one of two houses in Loup City at the time) through the massive storm that began on April 13 and lasted in full, unabated fury until April 16. After it was over, the troopers found that twenty-five horses and four pack mules had been suffocated by the snow.[16]

A second expedition followed the next month and when it too returned to Fort Omaha, some settler families banded together to construct their own fortifications. Eventually, after continued raids and Indian "scares" and the small but furious battle at Pebble Creek, the government agreed to the settlers' request for a permanent military presence in the region.

* * *

Today, the battle site stretches over private ranch land in a sandhills landscape that provides some of the state's most attractive scenery. The area's rolling hills, water, and plentiful grass make it superb cattle country. Other than for occasional fence lines and country lanes leading to scattered ranches, the ground over which the running battle was fought is little changed. Not far north of the battleground the Calamus Reservoir now provides water and recreation to the region that Lakota and settlers once contested so bitterly.

Endnotes

1 H.M. Foght, *The Trail of the Loup*, (Ord, Nebraska, 1906) p. 111.
2 Anna M. Cameron, *Garfield County Who's Who in Nebraska 1940*, NEGenWeb Project website. _Website www.rootsweb.com~negarfie/whowhoge.htm. Material extracted from website November 12, 2005.
3 Thurman A. Smith, *Who's Who in Nebraska 1940 – Loup County*, NEGenWeb Project – Loup County website. Website www.rootsweb.com/~neresour/OLLibrary/who1940/co/loup.htm Material extracted from website April 9, 2005.
4 Ibid.
5 Foght p. 111.
6 Foght p. 113.
7 Ibid.
8 Ibid.
9 Ibid.
10 Foght, p. 114.
11 Ibid.
12 Ibid.
13 *Who's Who in Nebraska 1940 – Loup County* website.
14 Foght p. 114.
15 Foght p. 115.
16 *Dead Horse Creek*, Sherman County Historical Society, Nebraska State Historical Society website. Website www.nebraskahistory.org/publish/markers/texts/dead_horse_creek.htm. Material extracted from website April 9, 2005

Chapter Twenty-two
Battle of Pebble Creek

Near Burwell on a January morning so cold that shells sometimes stuck in rifle barrels, a small but lethal encounter was fought where Pebble Creek flows into the North Loup River. There in 1874, Lakota Sioux waged a pitched battle with trappers and settlers from nearly ranches and homesteads. The battle resulted in the construction of Fort Hartsuff to provide protection to settlements in the valley of the North Loup.[1]

* * *

During the two years preceding the Pebble Creek fight, the frontier shifted, visibly and quickly, west across the plains. Settlers moved into the North Loup Valley in substantial numbers during that time, but major trouble had been avoided even though parties of Sioux periodically moved through the area to hunt or raid the Pawnees at their reservation near Genoa.[2]

The onset of winter brought increased contact. "(H)unters and trappers began to encounter small parties in the hills east of the (North Loup) river. Soon bands returning from unsuccessful raids upon the Pawnees, driven by hunger, openly entered the settlements, begging and stealing."[3]

During the afternoon of January 18, settlers on a hunting expedition near Willow Springs observed from a distance a large party of Indians surrounding a settler's residence. The Indians were seen to dismount and enter the home. Once inside, they ransacked the house. After devouring everything edible, they moved back outside and began scouring the farm, eventually killing the chickens, a valuable commodity on the frontier. The four members of the settler family, named McClimans, were left shaken but unharmed.

The Indians left the looted ranch at about three in the afternoon. Moving north, within a half mile they came across a cedar cabin, home to a group of trappers. The Sioux found the place unoccupied: all but one of the residents was away hunting and trapping; the other was cutting wood up a canyon a quarter of a mile from the house.

The Indians broke into the cabin, and as at the McClimans Ranch, looted it, leaving with pelts, clothing, blankets, and food. As the last Indian came out of the shanty with his arms full of plunder, he was fired upon by one of the trailing party of settlers who had first seen the Sioux at the McClimans place. The warrior dropped the loot, jumped on his horse and raced away to join the rest of his party. The interior of the cabin was left in a shambles, stripped of the trappers' accumulated hides and possessions.[4]

The Indians, thought to be about forty in number, continued in a northerly direction up the valley, finally stopping along Pebble Creek about three miles away. There, they erected an enormous tepee and made camp after butchering a cow taken from a nearby farm.

Meanwhile, the remaining cluster of trappers had returned home, having noticed the Indian encampment at Pebble Creek. Their cabin that night was the site for a meeting attended by nearby trappers, ranchers, and settlers. A runner was sent by the assembly to notify other settlers. Eventually, sixteen men were gathered and placed under the command of Charles "Buckskin Charley" White. The plan was to make contact with the Indians the following morning, demand the return of the stolen goods and, to the extent possible, seek restitution for items damaged or destroyed.[5]

The morning of January 19 dawned clear and bitterly cold. By sunrise, White had led his group to within 300 yards of the huge tepee. After posting his men, White walked into the camp to parley. He found the Indians at breakfast and in a belligerent mood. White attempted to talk with the leader of the warriors, but the situation became immediately threatening.[6]

After a short time, with tempers ready to erupt, White hurried back to his men and ordered them to take cover. As they were positioning themselves along the bank of the North Loup River, the Indians opened fire. White's group quickly responded and shooting erupted between the settlers scattered along the riverbank and the Sioux advancing toward them from the encampment. The intense cold added to the

Photo by Nita Phillips

Sioux attacked settlers in a defensive position at this junction of Pebble Creek and the North Loup River.

misery of the scene; until rifles warmed up, shells sometimes stuck inside them[7] and had to be dislodged with pocket knives.[8]

The settlers' vantage point along the river bank was well chosen; White's party had an excellent view of the ground leading from the campsite and the ledge shielded them from the Indians' fire. Several minutes into the fight, recognizing the settlers' strong position, the Indians split their attacking force. Half remained north and west of White's group in the direction of the camp and sought to keep the settlers pinned down. The remainder, under cover of a low ridge that cut through the area parallel to the river, crawled around to the rear of White's group and brought the settlers under fire from the southeast as well.[9]

Heavy firing continued for about a half hour.[10] Before the shooting ended, one of the settlers, Marion Littlefield, was killed instantly, shot in the head as he raised up to fire. Soon afterward, the Indians broke off the attack,[11] perhaps content that vengeance had been extracted or concerned about their own mounting losses, thought by the settlers to be three killed and others wounded.[12]

The settlers waited for a time on the battlefield, warming their weapons, anticipating additional attacks that never came. A pre-arranged supply wagon reached them later that morning and was used to transport Littlefield's body to the nearest settlement. Soon after, a reconnaissance confirmed that the Sioux had departed the area having left behind two wounded ponies.

The Battle of Pebble Creek resulted in the construction of a military post—Fort Hartsuff—in the valley of the North Loup. After the fight, residents in the region, worried about continued attacks, petitioned federal authorities to build a fort.[13] Congress quickly passed the enabling legislation and construction began in the fall.[14] By December, the first of Fort Hartsuff's major buildings was complete and the post was operational.[15]

* * *

Pebble Creek is a small rivulet almost obscured in places by the lush vegetation, brush, and trees that line its banks and extend over its tiny channel. A marker off Highway 91 sets in a flat, open area where the Sioux made their camp and erected the enormous tepee that was mentioned in accounts of the battle. During most of the year, the heavy foliage along Pebble Creek and the surrounding crop land obscure the battle site (now on private property) at the point where the stream flows into the North Loup. However, the view from the Highway 91 bridge on the west outskirts of Burwell looking further west up the river provides not only a scenic vista but also a view of the area where the streams come together and the fight occurred.

Endnotes

1 H. W. Foght, *The Trail of the Loup*, (Ord, Nebraska, 1906) p. 124, 125.
2 *The Pebble Creek Fight*, Nebraska State Historical Society website. Website www.nebraska-history.org/publish/markers/texts/pebble_creek_fight.htm. Material extracted from website April 9, 2005.
3 Foght p. 124.
4 Ibid.
5 Foght p. 125.
6 Ibid.
7 Ibid.
8 Foght p. 126.
9 Ibid.
10 *The Pebble Creek Fight* website.
11 Foght p. 127.
12 *The Pebble Creek Fight* website.
13 Anna M. Cameron, *Garfield County Who's Who in Nebraska 1940*, NEGenWeb Project website. Website www.rootsweb.com~negarfie/whowhogc.htm. Material extracted from website November 12, 2005.
14. *The Pebble Creek Fight* website.
15. Foght p. 130-135.

Chapter Twenty-three

Mackenzie's Raid

Fort Robinson played a significant role in the annals of the American West. While the surrender and death of Crazy Horse and the Cheyenne Outbreak are the events most often associated with its history, in reality the fort was the focus of activities that although less well known and often more mundane, were essential to the opening and safeguarding of America's new frontier.

Beginning with its establishment in 1874, "Fort Rob's" soldiers patrolled trails, guarded mail routes, shielded wagon trains, secured the nearby Red Cloud and Spotted Tail agencies, and served in the numerous campaigns that eventually brought peace to the plains. Many of these duties, while but little remembered, involved sizable numbers of troops and had important consequences, sometimes tipping the balance between war and peace.

One such instance occurred during the fall of 1876.

* * *

After a failed attempt the previous year, in 1876 government commissioners met with Indian representatives for a second time at the Red Cloud Agency to negotiate the treaty that would relinquish Sioux claims to the Black Hills.[1] In late September, after several days of confusion and bitter disputes, commissioners secured sufficient signatures from the reluctant and sometimes bewildered chiefs to claim dubious title to the Black Hills region.

The negotiation process was hostile from the start; after one particularly angry session, an embittered Sioux chief walked out, taking his followers with him. More importantly, after the treaty was signed, two influential Indian leaders, Red Cloud and Red Leaf, infuriated by the results, took their followers away from the Red Cloud Agency.

Thirty miles from the post, at Chadron Creek, they established new camps and demanded that government rations be delivered to them at those locations rather than at the agency.

General George Crook arrived at Camp Robinson in mid-October. Perhaps fearing the precedent and a potential breakdown in the government's reservation system if the situation was left unaddressed, Crook concluded that the Indians must return to the agency, even if force was required to make them do so. Concerned also that the bands might break away to join still-hostile groups further north, Crook decided that immediate action was necessary.

On October 22, a sizable force under the command of Colonel Ranald Mackenzie left the post on a rapid, night march that took them to the Chadron Creek area. There, close against the potentially hostile camps, eight companies from the Fourth and Fifth United States Cavalry accompanied by forty Pawnee Scouts waited for daybreak. At sunrise, in a daring and well-conceived strike, the Scouts captured the pony herds while four companies of cavalry surrounded each camp.

Both camps surrendered immediately. The firearms of 150 warriors were confiscated along with more than 700 horses. That same day, the Indians were taken back to the agency. Women and children and the aged and infirm were permitted to ride. Warriors, who in other circumstances comprised "the best light cavalry in the world," were required to walk the entire thirty miles.

As best as can be determined, not a shot was fired; but, for the Indians the defeat was crushing, total, as surely as if bodies had been left strewn on the battlefield.

The effects were felt almost immediately.

Red Cloud from this point resumed his role as an advocate for cooperation, and the door was slammed on the much-feared possibility that the bands would unite with Crazy Horse or other groups still at war.

Mackenzie's actions that morning epitomized the highest in military professionalism. "Supreme excellence," Sun Tzu said thirty-five centuries before in *The Art of War,* "consists in breaking the enemy's resistance without fighting[2].

In the early dawn hours of October 23, 1876, Mackenzie and his men attained Sun Tzu's high standard.

Endnotes

1 Material for this section is drawn primarily from Thomas R. Buecker, *Fort Robinson and the American West 1874-1899*, (Norman: University of Oklahoma Press, 1999) p. 88.

2 James A. Clavell, editor, *The Art of War: Sun Tzu* (New York: Dell Publishing, 1983) p. 2

Part III

Skirmishes, Incidents
and the
Shadows of History

SKIRMISHES, INCIDENTS, AND THE SHADOWS OF HISTORY

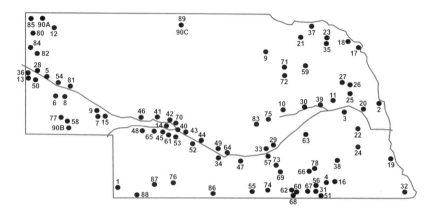

1. Sioux vs. Arapahos - date unknown, near Haigler.
2. Treaty Expedition - 1825, Fort Atkinson.
3. Sioux vs Pawnees - circa 1830s, Skull Creek, Butler County.
4. Sioux vs Pawnees - 1832, junction of Big Sandy, Little Blue.
5. Fur Trapper Battle - 1833, near Scottsbluff.
6. Sioux vs Pawnees - pre –1835, near Courthouse Rock.
7. Sioux vs Pawnees - 1835, Ash Hollow.
8. Sioux vs Pawnees - 1835, Courthouse Rock.
9. Wagon train attack - 1837, near Ash Hollow.
10. Sioux vs Pawnees - pre –1846, Loup River, near mouth of Cedar Creek.
11. Wagon train attack - 1849, Twenty miles west of Fremont.
12. Sioux vs Crows - 1849, Crow Butte (near Crawford).
13. Peace Council - September 1851, mouth of Horse Creek, near Scottsbluff.
14. Brady's Island - 1853, near North Platte.
15. Mail Station attack - 1854, Ash Hollow.
16. Jefferson County strife - 1854 and after, Jefferson County.
17. Dakota County incidents - September 1855, Dakota County.
18. Poncas vs. Omahas - circa 1856, Near Ponca, Dixon County.
19. The Whitmore Scare - April 1856, Weeping Water, Cass County.
20. Threatened Attack on Fremont - October 1856, Fremont.
21. Tensions in Knox County - 1856 – 1859, Knox County.
22. Mrs. Warbritton's vengeance - 1857, Saunders County.
23. Incident at Cedar Creek - 1858, Cedar Creek.
24. Pawnees vs Settlers, Lancaster County - 1858-1859, Lancaster County.
25. Raids along Elkhorn River - June 21 – early July 1859, Fontanelle, other sites along river.
26. Pawnee uprising - June 29-July 4, 1859, West Point, Cuming County.
27. Pawnee raid - June or July 1859, Near Crowell, Cuming County.
28. Attack on Pony Express rider - 1860, near Mitchell Pass.
29. Sioux vs Pawnees - September 1860, Grand Island.
30. Sioux vs Pawnees - 1860-1863, near Genoa, Nance County.
31. Early Incidents in Thayer County - circa 1860-1861, Thayer County.

32. Precautions in Richardson County - 1861-1865, Richardson County.
33. Smith Family massacre - February 5, 1862, Wood River, 12 miles from Grand Island.
34. Heywood Ranch attack - circa 1862, 22 miles west of Ft. Kearny.
35. Slaying of the Wiseman Family -1863, Cedar County.
36. War Council - Fall 1863, Horse Creek Valley, near Scottsbluff.
37. Bentz Hill Massacre - 1864, three miles northwest of St. Helena.
38. Depredations at Patton Farm - early 1864, Northern Saline County.
39. Sneak attack at Looking Glass Creek - early 1864, Platte County.
40. Stage Coach attack - May 23, 1864, near Fort McPherson.
41. Attacks near Fort McPherson September 1864 Lincoln County
42. Attack on soldier detail - September 8, 1864, near Fort McPherson
43. Stage coach attack - November 1864, between Fort Kearny and Fort McPherson
44. Indian scares, Dawson County - 1864-1867, Dawson County.
45. Attack on O'Fallon's Bluff station - January 7, 1865, two miles south, four west of Sutherland.
46. Widespread attacks on stations - January, 1865, Fort McPherson west along trail.
47. Attack on stage coach - May 1865, east of Fort Kearny.
48. Attack on Alkali Springs Station - October 28, 1865, ten miles east of Ogallala.
49. Attack on Elm Creek Station - 1865, 22 miles west of Ft. Kearny.
50. Battle of Horse Creek - 1865, seven miles southeast of Henry.
51. Raids in Thayer County - 1865-1866, Thayer County.
52. Attack on Miller's Ranche - 1866, 60 miles west of Fort Kearny.
53. Attack on Midway Station - 1866, 75 miles west of Ft. Kearny.
54. Attack on wagon train - 1866, near Scottsbluff.
55. Clashes in Republican River Valley - 1866-1871, Franklin County.
56. War returns to Thayer County - Summer 1867, Thayer County, multiple locations
57. Attacks at Campbell Farm - July 24, 1867, west of Doniphan.
58. Violence in Cheyenne County - 1867, Cheyenne County.
59. Depredations in Madison County - 1867-1869, Shell Creek, Madison County.
60. Haynie Fight - 1868, eastern Nuckolls County.
61. Hinman Farm and other attacks - 1868, Lincoln County.
62. Otoes vs Sioux/Cheyennes - 1868, Liberty Creek, Nuckolls County.
63. Pawnees/Omahas/Poncas/Otoes vs. Sioux - 1868, York County.
64. Tobin Indian Raid - August 29, 1868, one and a half miles west of Overton.
65. Attacks in Lincoln County - 1869, Lincoln County.
66. Shawnee raid, Fillmore County - 1869, Fillmore County.
67. Military activities near Hebron - 1869-1870, Hebron area.
68. Thain attack - May 7, 1870, eastern Nuckolls County.
69. Attack on settlers - summer 1870, Near Kiowa Ranch, Adams County.
70. Buffalo Bill's pursuit - September 1870, near Fort McPherson.
71. Settler incident - 1870, Antelope County.
72. Raid near Cedar Creek - November 1870, Antelope County.
73. Wagon Train attack - Fall 1870, near Spring Ranch, Adams County.
74. Fortifications in Webster County - 1870-1871, Guide Rock, Red Cloud, Elm Creek.
75. Military presence, North Loup - Summer 1871, Howard County.
76. Temporary post at Red Willow - early 1872, mouth of Red Willow Creek.
77. Attack in Cheyenne County - Summer 1872, Pumpkin Seed Creek.
78. Exeter Indian scare - Fall 1873, Fillmore County.
79. Incidents of a different nature - Fall 1874, Holt County.
80. Attack on Mail Wagon - May 16, 1876, 10 miles west of Fort Robinson.
81. Freight Wagon Ambush - May 27, 1876, near Bridgeport.
82. Wagon Train attacks (2) - 1876 south of Fort Robinson.

83. Sherman County Scare - Summer 1876, Sherman County.
84. Tensions in Sioux County - Summer 1876, Sioux County.
85. Black Elk wagon train attack - July 1876, along Warbonnet Creek.
86. Cheyenne Scare, Furnas County - Fall 1878, Beaver City area.
87. Death in Hitchcock County Fall 1878 Hitchcock County
88. Raids in Southwestern Nebraska - October 1878, Benkelman area.
89. Fort Niobrara - April 22, 1880, one and a half miles east of Valentine.

Ghost Dance Scare
90A. Conical Hill Fortification - Fall 1890, near Montrose.
90B. Fort Sidney staging area - October – December 1890, Sidney.
90C. Fort Niobrara - Fall 1890, east of Valentine.

* * *

SIOUX VS. ARAPAHOS: NEAR HAIGLER

The date is uncertain, as is the outcome, but about one and a half miles west of Haigler was the site of a battle between the Sioux and the Arapaho. Losses were apparently significant. A mass burial ground located a few hundred yards west of the battleground likely contains casualties from that battle.[1]

"TREATY EXPEDITION" FROM FORT ATKINSON: 1825

In 1825, 500 men under the command of Colonel Henry Leavenworth moved up the Missouri from Fort Atkinson with the aim of negotiating treaties with tribes along the upper reaches of the river. Aided by the impressive show of force, the expedition was an exceptional success: "(t)reaties were concluded with the Ponca, Arikara, Mandan, Minataree, Oto, Missouri, Pawnee, Omaha, and several clans of the Sioux."[2]

SIOUX VS. PAWNEES: SKULL CREEK, BUTLER COUNTY, CIRCA 1830S

The Pawnees had apparently lived for generations on Skull Creek near present-day Linwood—this was probably the village seen by Villasur's Expedition in 1720—as well as around Bellwood and Savannah. According to stories told to the first settlers, the Skull Creek area was the location of frequent bloody clashes between the Pawnees and Sioux. The Sioux were said to often raid the Pawnee villages, demolishing their dwellings and "leaving squaws and papooses strewn around the village, mangled and dead." These forays occurred at the time of the Sioux ascendancy and, by one account, were vengeance raids in retribution for the terror inflicted upon the Sioux when the Pawnees were more powerful.[3]

Sioux vs. Pawnees: junction Big Sandy and Little Blue, 1832

Numerous pioneer diaries mention the lush hunting grounds of the Republican River and Little Blue valleys. These areas were the disputed domains of several tribes who fought "many and fierce" conflicts over access to the grass and the region's plentiful herds of buffalo and deer.

An early Jefferson County history describes an enormous struggle between the Sioux and the Pawnee, thought to have been fought near the junction of the Big Sandy and the Little Blue rivers. While there is no way to corroborate the date or the very large numbers of participants mentioned in the report, the account provides a vivid description of the scale and ferocity of major battles between the tribes.

"In 1832 one of the most desperate battles ever waged on the American continent between savage tribes was fought in Jefferson County. . .within the borders of contested hunting grounds. Sixteen thousand Indian warriors, it is said, were arrayed in deadly combat for three days. . . .The Pawnees and their allies were arrayed against their deadly foes, the Sioux and their confederate tribes, and as both leading tribes were noted for their prowess and desperation in battle, the fearful conflict can be better imagined than described. After a desperate struggle the Sioux were compelled to withdraw from the battlefield, but not until 3,000 of their braves had fallen in the fatal, fruitless struggle for mastery over the disputed territory. But the Pawnees paid dearly for their victory, 2,000 of the warriors in their confederation having fallen before the arrow and tomahawk of the desperate Sioux. But the infuriated Pawnees sought revenge by burning 700 prisoners at the stake during the engagement."[4]

Fur trapper battle near Scottsbluff: 1833

Courthouse Rock appears in several stories associated with the region. Long before wagon trains rolled along the Platte and used the place as a reference point, "the Court House" surfaced in the traditions of local tribes and in the tales of early mountain men.

One of the later that survived decades of telling concerns a trapper, possibly named Gonneville, who was killed by an Indian or died during the course of a battle near the confluence of two streams west of the rock. The event has been variously dated as 1830 or 1833 with the latter the more likely. The majority of the tribes were not overly hostile at the time, so it is possible that the death occurred not in a battle but as a result of a quarrel between two individuals. Regardless, it was evidence yet again that at any stage, life on the frontier was seldom benign.[5]

As traders and trappers moved into the area, some intermarried with local Indian tribes. Coalitions arose and quarrels sometimes developed between opposing combinations. "A few traders and trappers (lost) their lives, but the total loss of property at Indian hands was quite small through the period of the 1800-1840s."[6]

* * *

Courthouse Rock is about six miles south of present day Bridgeport off State Route 88. Along with Chimney Rock, twelve miles farther west, it became an important landmark for early travelers. A feature of the Oregon National Historic Trail, it is now part of the National Trails System as designated by the National Park Service.

Sioux vs. Pawnees near Courthouse Rock: Pre-1835

A pioneer historian credits an early, but undated, battle between the Sioux and the Pawnee fought not far from Courthouse Rock "at a point nearly opposite the opening in the hills now known as Round House or Riddington Gap." The battle, thought to have occurred before 1835, was reputed to have been a fierce one from which the Pawnee emerged victorious.[7]

Sioux vs. Pawnees. Ash Hollow: 1835

At Ash Hollow during the winter of 1835, the Sioux and Pawnee waged a day-long battle. The Pawnee's devastating losses—by one account, the Pawnee were thought to have suffered sixty killed in the fight—caused the tribe to move south, out of the region.[8]

Sioux vs. Pawnees. Courthouse Rock: 1835

In Pawnee lore, a story exists that relates to the historic struggles between that tribe and its bitter enemy, the Sioux. The date would likely have been around the year 1835 and the setting for the episode may have been the time immediately following the Sioux's major defeat of the Pawnee at Ash Hollow. It is a tale that reads remarkably like the saga told of Crow warriors at Crow Butte a few years later.

Steve Mulligan Photography
Courthouse Rock, about six miles from Bridgeport, appears in several stories associated with the area.

{See Bordeaux and the Sioux vs the Crow, Crow Butte: 1849} Both are stories of heroism and both involve unique geographic features in the same region of the Nebraska panhandle.

In the Pawnee account, a band of Pawnee is fleeing the Sioux, probably after the debacle at Ash Hollow. To shield the larger party from the on-rushing Sioux, the Pawnee form a small rear guard led by a young chief. The skirmishers engage the pursuers and keep them away from the main party, but the size and ferocity of the Sioux attack eventually drive the retreating Pawnee to Courthouse Rock where, in desperation, they climb to the top to save themselves. The Sioux surround the rock, camping at its base with the intention of starving out the Pawnee or destroying them as they come down.

According to Pawnee lore, the young leader of the rear guard finds a narrow, secluded crevasse that extended from the top of the monolith down the inside of the rock face. Stringing together a series of lariats to make a "rope" long enough to reach the base of the bluff, the chief explores the chasm. At the bottom, he discovers a small slit large enough to crawl though. The niche opens to the outside. The Sioux have left it unguarded.

In the blackness of the second night, one by one the Pawnee shinny down the "rope," squeeze through the small opening at the bottom, and slip away in the darkness.[9]

SIOUX ATTACK ON WHITMAN WAGON TRAIN, ASH HOLLOW: 1837

In 1837, near Ash Hollow, a large party of Sioux attacked members of the Whitman Expedition on their journey to Oregon. The party's scout, William Gray, asserted that large numbers were killed and wounded.[10]

SIOUX VS. PAWNEES, CEDAR CREEK: PRE-1846

" . . .The emigrants followed (a trail) southwestward along the Loup past the mouth of Cedar Creek, where the pre-1846 Pawnee town was destroyed by the Sioux."[11]

ATTACK ON WAGON TRAIN NEAR FREMONT: 1849

There is testimony from one source that in the valley of the Platte along the banks of Shell Creek, twenty to twenty-five miles west of Fremont, a wagon train of '49ers was attacked by Indians. No further details of the resulting fight are given.[12]

BORDEAUX AND SIOUX VS. CROWS, CROW BUTTE: 1849

Triggered sometimes by unusual events, historic enmities between many of the tribes of the Great Plains often erupted into violence. In 1849, a band of Crow Indians, said to have been led by a warrior named White Bear, raided a trading post established by a Frenchman named James Bordeaux about twenty-five miles east of present-day Crawford. The raid was successful and the Crows were believed to have made off with forty-seven horses and thirty-five mules. Bordeaux quickly assembled a nearby band of Brule Sioux warriors and went after the Crow raiders.

Some miles north of the trading post along the banks of the White River, Bordeaux and the Sioux ran down the Crows. A major fight ensued, won generally by the Sioux. Some of the Crows escaped entirely; others fled south. Eventually, the Sioux backed the remaining Crows up against the north face of Crow Butte, located east and a bit south of Crawford.

As the story goes, the Crows abandoned their horses and climbed the bluff along a narrow path that led to the top. The Sioux responded by camping along the base of the butte, waiting for the Crows to run out of water. For three days and nights the Sioux watched the Crows' night fires, listened to them sing, and sometimes saw them dancing on top of the butte.

On the fourth day, on a secluded part of the butte, a Sioux scout found a "rope," a line made of rawhide, hair, and horse livery. The Crows, the majority of them, had used it to slip unnoticed down the precipice. At the base of the cliff near the descending line, the Sioux found the body of a Crow warrior, the apparent victim of a long fall down the near-vertical wall.

Nita Phillips photo

Scene of a legendary battle between the Crow and the Sioux.

To cover the escape, some Crow warriors had remained at the top of the butte to light the nighttime fires and distract the Sioux. They were almost assuredly killed.[13]

* * *

A state historical marker located four miles east of Crawford on U.S. Highway 20 describes the Crow Butte encounter and other notable features of the surrounding area.

PEACE COUNCIL: SEPTEMBER 1851

In 1851, the largest Indian Peace Council ever held on the Plains took place a few miles from Scottsbluff. In September of that year, between 8,000 and 12,000 Sioux, Cheyennes, Arapahos, Crows, and members of other tribes met near the mouth of Horse Creek. Five years earlier, in 1846, the United States government had placed Thomas Fitzpatrick, an able old mountainman in charge of the Upper Platte and Arkansas Agency. Fitzpatrick was extremely effective, and until his death in 1854, there was comparatively little trouble with the Indians.

It was Fitzpatrick, along with Father DeSmet, Jim Bridger, Robert Campbell, D. D. Mitchell and a few others, who arranged the Peace Council gathering. After first assembling at Fort Laramie, the entire group moved en masse to camping grounds near Horse Creek. "Due

231

to the presence of DeSmet and Fitzpatrick (the two most trusted white men on the Great Plains) the Treaty Council went smoothly and the Indians promised peace and free passage of emigrants through their lands in return for annual allowances."[14]

DEATH AT BRADY'S ISLAND: 1853

Although tales of strife in Lincoln County (sites of North Platte, Fort McPherson, and important venues along the Overland Trail) are generally associated with the uprisings that occurred a decade or more later, one of the first recorded Indian attacks in the county took place as early as 1853. In 1852, a pioneer named Brady built a house of cedar logs on the south side of the Platte River at a place that came to be known as Brady's Island. Brady was believed to have been killed by Indians about a year later. [15]

ATTACK ON ASH HOLLOW MAIL STATION: 1854

In 1854, a U.S. mail station situated in the vicinity of Ash Hollow was attacked and destroyed by a Sioux war party.[16] There were thought to be fatalities among the station employees.

STRIFE IN JEFFERSON COUNTY: 1854 AND AFTER

One of the first histories written after Jefferson County was officially organized listed it as one of the counties in Nebraska Territory that had suffered most from Indian raids during the early settlement period. As with its companion counties along the Kansas border, Jefferson was situated near the Republican River Valley, "the best hunting ground" for the Plains Indians.

The native tribes did not cede the valued region without contest. For a period of time in 1854 all of the very early settlements were abandoned because of pressure and deprivations from persistent raids. Emotions were typically high and ran so close to the surface that in one instance a squabble over a cow led to the death of a settler and an Indian.

Strife continued for more than a decade. Indeed, as it did elsewhere along the border, the Civil War brought an increased number of attacks as the warring tribes sought to take advantage of the government's difficulties in the east and the reduced numbers of troops in the Plains region that sometimes resulted from it. As an early history notes, the

Civil War brought a period of general lawlessness to the area, attributable to white renegades as well as native raiders.[17]

DAKOTA COUNTY INCIDENTS: 1855

During the summer of 1855 in the northern part of Dakota County, three Ponca Indians entered and ransacked the cabin of a settler named Adam Benner, while Benner was away. His wife, very ill and bedridden, was at the cabin as was the Benners' infant child. The Indians threw the bed on the floor and demolished the family's possessions in the house. Mrs. Benner died a short time later. "General Harney was at the time (nearby) at Fort Randall. The three Indians were delivered up to him by their tribe, and were tried, condemned and executed for their crime."

"In September 1855, 21 Sioux warriors came upon (a small) company of settlers at the mouth of Clark Creek, stole all their provisions, and also their boat, thus cutting off communication with the Iowa side of the river, their source of supplies." Three or four days later, a party of Poncas' came upon the scene and attempted to steal clothing. The settlers fired several shots and drove the raiders away. Later, a member of the company came from the Iowa side of the river with food and provisions.[18]

OMAHAS VS. PONCAS: NEAR PONCA, DIXON COUNTY CIRCA 1856

"Previous to the advent of white settlers in 1856, Dixon County was the abode of several tribes of Indians, chief among which were the Dakotas (Sioux), Omahas, and Poncas. The Poncas were the most numerous of the these three tribes. Their principal village was near the present location of Ponca. . .The principal village of the Omahas was near the "lone tree," a few miles above the mouth of Dailey Creek. These Indian tribes had frequent battles with each other, sometimes resulting in great slaughter. In one of these savage conflicts between the Omahas and the Poncas, which occurred about a mile north of Ponca, near the Missouri, the Omahas, who were on a raid, were ambushed and defeated with great slaughter, almost everyone on the raiding party being slain."[19]

THE WHITMORE SCARE: APRIL 1856

In the spring of 1856, the Whitmore family, early settlers who lived near the Salt Basin in the vicinity of present-day Lincoln, were driven from their home by Indians (likely Pawnees). The family fled towards the Missouri River, raising the alarm along the way. Reports (false) of alleged atrocities were quickly forthcoming, apparently embellished as the news spread from settlement to settlement.

Eventually, 500 men from Omaha, Nebraska City, and all parts of Cass County assembled at Weeping Water. General Thayer sent a six-pounder cannon from Omaha to Plattsmouth on a boat called the *St. Mary's*. Thayer arrived in person soon after and took command of the force from Douglas County. Scouts were soon organized, some venturing as far as the Salt Basin. On the night of April 16, a scouting party took an Indian prisoner, who escaped the following morning.

Further reconnaissance revealed that the Pawnees were not on the war path, although a small band had robbed and killed a white man. On April 17, the forces that had assembled at Weeping Water disbanded and returned to their homes.[20]

THREATENED ATTACK ON FREMONT: OCTOBER 1856

The new settlement of Fremont was situated three miles north of a major Indian village, home to about 1,500 Pawnees. In October 1856, alarmed by the continued number of white settlers moving into the Fremont area, Pawnee chiefs advised the settlers that "unless they abandoned their evil intention of founding a city, they would be annihilated. . . ." The Pawnees gave settlement leaders three days to decide. A council was quickly held and a settler was sent to Omaha (the territorial capital) to request help. The governor provided a box of muskets, ammunition and a squad of eight soldiers. Eventually enough armed men were collected from around the county and the nearby settlements to form a company of about twenty-five troops. Those soldiers, "by marching and counter-marching, by bonfires and torchlight processions and by the burning of haystacks, produced the impression upon the Pawnees that it was a vast army, and had the effect of over-awing them. So that at the end of three days they sent a flag of truce and a messenger saying that the chiefs had reconsidered the matter and concluded to let them go unmolested for the present."[21]

TENSIONS IN KNOX COUNTY: 1856-1859

"I will not be responsible for injury done to white men or their property on this side of Aoway Creek.

(Signed) Michel Sayre, Chief Poncas"

When the Omaha tribe moved from the "Niobrara Country" in the mid-1850s, the land they vacated was opened for settlement. Arguments over disputed claims quickly developed between newly arriving settlers and the Ponca tribe who "began strenuously to urge their claims" on the region.

The Poncas' opposition to white settlement continued for many years, but despite the ominous tone of the Ponca chief's note, "strangely and happily" no bloodshed took place. In May 1858, the Poncas were moved by treaty to the north side of the Niobrara River, but their close proximity to white settlements continued to prompt frequent "scares."

One such incident, apparently typical of many others, occurred in the fall of 1859. As on other occasions, settlers "collected at (a hotel in the county) to sleep and put out guards."[22]

MRS. WARBRITTON'S REVENGE: SAUNDERS COUNTY 1857

Even the most threatening circumstances can sometimes provide surprising and humorous outcomes. The following account comes from an early history of Saunders County.

"The marauding. . .Pawnees were a constant source of annoyance (to the settlers), and their homes and families were subject to any of the red men's desperate needs. . . .On one occasion, Mrs. Reubin Warbritton, provoked beyond endurance by the thefts and insolence of a Pawnee brave, seized a good goad (i.e., a sharp-pointed stick used for driving oxen) and thrashed him into obedience, to the pleasure and delight of his companions. The lady at once became a heroine in their eyes and was considered by them as a 'much brave squaw'."[23]

INCIDENT AT CEDAR CREEK: 1858

In 1858, in northeastern Nebraska, five oxen belonging to settler families were stolen by a party of Ponca Indians. Word quickly spread through Cedar County and forty-nine settlers assembled to track the raiders. Within a day or two they came upon the Ponca band—about thirty in number—camped on the opposite bank of Cedar Creek drying the flesh of the oxen, all five of which had been killed. The settlers were prevented by the creek from making a quick attack and the Poncas, surprised and outnumbered, fled leaving behind only one woman with a small child. The settlers took the woman and infant to the local Agency and reported the theft. The Ponca chief whipped the woman, whose life was saved by the intervention of the agent. The chiefs then sent several warriors to bring in the raiders and compensated the settlers for the loss of the oxen. The episode was somewhat untypical; though sometimes strained, the relationship between the settlers and the Poncas was generally positive.[24]

PAWNEES VS. SETTLERS, LANCASTER COUNTY: 1858-1859

At a date unspecified but probably around 1858, a settler named Davis, newly arrived at the small Olathe settlement in Lancaster County, killed one of the two Pawnees who had burst into his cabin. The Indians were outraged and their threats of retribution forced several early settlers "to retreat to the Missouri River."

For a time in 1858 while treaty negotiations were ongoing, most of the Pawnee tribe camped near the Great Salt Basin. Their presence there brought them close to the cabin of Captain Joseph M. Donavan and his family. Frictions were frequent and "the utmost vigilance (was) required on the part of the family to keep peace and protect themselves." Though no shooting occurred, the Pawnees' intrusions eventually became so frequent that Captain Donavan moved east in the county to Stevens Creek. The family remained there until 1861, when they returned to the Yankee Hill area near the present State Regional Center.

Not all episodes in Lancaster County ended as peacefully as the Donavan's. Two violent incidents took place in 1859. The first, early in the year, happened at the Olathe settlement. Settlers there were periodically harassed by marauding Pawnees, and on one occasion a steer was stolen from the herd of a pioneer named Jeremiah B. Garrett. Livestock was a precious commodity—the gold of the frontier—and cattle theft, regardless of who perpetrated it, was considered a capital offense. Garrett immediately organized a party of settlers who found the Indians about three miles away skinning the stolen steer. In the clash that followed, Garrett was struck by an arrow and at least one Indian was killed and another wounded. The Indians were said to have left the area "leaving their dead on the field."

Not long after, a band of about fifteen Pawnees robbed and ransacked an empty cabin shared by two settlers. A group of neighbors soon met at the cabin of a settler named Sophir, located on Salt Creek east of the present-day Regional Center, and made plans to confront the raiders who were known to be camped near the present site of the State Penitentiary. The following morning when the Indians returned to the cabin area, one of the settlers, Joel Mason, met them in a parley, requesting that the stolen goods be returned. Mason's attempt was met with derision, and the Pawnees jabbed the threatened settler with their rifles. As Mason was forced close to the cabin door, he gave a pre-arranged signal to the other settlers who were hidden inside. The rest of the group burst out of the door, firing as they charged toward the Indians. Their attack startled the Pawnees, three of whom were killed and five wounded before the rest could race away. "The suddenness of the attack so surprised the Indians that they did not succeed in inflicting even a wound in return for their loss."

After the encounter at Sophir's cabin, no further bloodshed was reported in Lancaster County.[25]

Raid along the Elkhorn River: 1859

On June 21, 1859, several hundred Pawnee raiders began pillaging settlements near Fontanelle, West Point, and other locations along the Elkhorn River. The escalating violence precipitated the "Pawnee War" of 1859, described more fully in the "Pawnee War of 1859" section of the preceding chapter.

Pawnee Uprising: June 29-July 4, 1859

During the summer of 1859, the Pawnees aggressively raided through the Elkhorn Valley, plundering and stealing on a scale that culminated in "The Pawnee War of 1859." The area around West Point in Cuming County was the scene of widespread deprivations.

While events in Cuming County were related to the actions that precipitated the Pawnee War, and certainly contributed to the climate of fear and foreboding that afflicted the settlers in the region, militarily they were separate from the excursion led by General Thayer that eventually ended the "war."

In late June, Pawnee Indians, numbering perhaps a thousand total, moved north through the Elkhorn Valley. Ostensibly on a hunting expedition, "they seemed to be in a half starved condition and in order to satiate their hunger commenced systematic warfare upon the settlers' pigs, poultry, and stock . . . ."

237

"After having committed numerous deprivations further down the valley," the Pawnees arrived in the vicinity of West Point on June 29, where they killed a tethered heifer belonging to a local citizen. That same night, a company of volunteers from the surrounding area reached the settlement. Riders were sent to warn farmers and ranchers of the threat. Through the night and into the following day, many settlers brought their families to West Point.

Indian sightings and scares continued through the day, but eventually the Pawnees noted the size of the settler force assembling in the community and moved further north up the river. A company of thirty armed settlers followed them, staying on the east side of the Elkhorn, attempting to shield settlers in the vicinity of the small settlement at DeWitt.

Shortly after arriving at DeWitt, the company was approached by eleven Pawnees. Under the ploy of inviting the Indians to eat with them—when they hoped to capture the Pawnees and make them prisoners for later exchange—the assembly arrived for dinner at the residence of a settler named B. B. Moore. There, some members of the militia company waited unobserved in a partitioned part of the house, while others blocked the only escape route. Firing soon broke out—it is not known who started it—as the Pawnees burst from the house and broke through the militia line meant to block their escape.

Several Pawnees were killed or wounded. One was left dead at the Moore's house. Two others, badly wounded, were also left behind. Later, Pawnees allegedly told settlers that only three of the original eleven returned to their camp and that one of them later died of his wounds. One member of the militia company was wounded.

Rumors that the Pawnees would exact vengeance for their losses immediately surfaced. Panic—"such a one as the citizens of West Point have never witnessed since"—ensued. After consultation, almost all decided to "abandon West Point and go to Fontanelle with all of their effects they could take." A few remained behind for a short while, hiding valuable articles that could not be taken along. Cattle were collected and after further tribulations and scares, were eventually driven to Fontanelle. For a time, only two settlers were left in the entire county.

On July 4, a small party of ten to fifteen settlers left Fontanelle to return to West Point and DeWitt to scout and check for damage.

Author's photo

Scottsbluff, a famous landmark on the Oregon Trail, was the scene of several enouncers between emigrants and natives--including at least one attack on a Pony Express rider.

Returning to the Moore house, the scene of the initial clash, they found a dead Indian, furniture and dishes broken, and the contents of the home strewn around the house and grounds. In the midst of their patrol, a shouted alarm—false—induced further panic. In the rush to retrieve their weapons from nearby wagons, a gun accidentally went off killing one of the company instantly. The settler party then returned to Fontanelle and events associated with the "war" moved to a climax further north and west along Battle Creek.[26]

PAWNEE RAID: 1859

In June or July, the skirmishes between Pawnees and settlers that eventually led to the "Pawnee War" of 1859, culminated in a major clash near Crowell in Cuming County. Casualties from the Crowell engagement are not known, but about ten Pawnees were believed to have been killed in the series of raids that began in June. (See "The Pawnee War of 1859" for details.)

ATTACK ON PONY EXPRESS RIDER: 1860

There is an unattested story of an attack on a Pony Express rider named Charles Cliff that dates from 1860 or 1861. The ambush is alleged to have occurred around Mitchell Pass. Although wounded, the rider is said to have escaped and made his way to the Scottsbluff Station.[27]

SIOUX VS. PAWNEES: GRAND ISLAND SEPTEMBER 1860

The Hall County area in south central Nebraska was a frequent battleground in the continuous struggle between the Sioux and the Pawnees. In September 1860 an especially large, violent battle between the tribes was found on the Grand Island in the Platte River, observed by settlers watching along the banks of the river.[28]

SIOUX VS. PAWNEES: NANCY COUNTY 1860-1863

Nance County was first settled in 1857 by a colony of about 100 Mormon families. After early hardships the settlement, close to present-day Genoa, prospered until 1860 when Pawnees arrived to take possession of the nearby reservation assigned to them by treaty. For the next three years constant strife between the Pawnees and Sioux war parties that came to raid their ancient enemy placed the Mormon colony in peril. Finally, in 1863 the settlement broke up and members dispersed to several other locations.[29]

EARLY INCIDENTS IN THAYER COUNTY: CIRCA 1860-1861

A German emigrant named Christian Luth was thought to be the first settler in Thayer County. After establishing a prosperous farm, he was killed by Indians in 1860 or 1861.

Luth's death would be one of the first of many to follow in Thayer County. During the Civil War, settlements in the county were generally made only at or near the fortified ranches. "But (many) settlers were either killed in the great raids of 1864 and 1867, or compelled through fear to seek places more secure."[30]

PRECAUTIONS IN RICHARDSON COUNTY: 1861-1865

The onset of the Civil War brought fear of Indian raids throughout the frontier settlements. In Richardson County, an early settler, Stephen Story, responded to the threat by organizing a militia company. However, no attacks are known to have taken place inside the county.[31]

SMITH FAMILY MASSACRE: NEAR GRAND ISLAND, FEBRUARY 5, 1862

The number of raids on Nebraska settlements increased as Indian leaders began to recognize the depth of the Federal government's preoccupation with the life or death struggle being waged on the Civil War battlefields in the east. On February 5, 1862, one of the first in a long series of horrific attacks took place about twelve miles from Grand Island along Wood River, on the farmstead of a settler family named Smith.

Four male members of the Smith family were killed while away from the house felling timber. The father and two of his sons were found in close proximity, having clustered together to defend themselves. The neck of the oldest son was broken and his skull crushed. The second child died soon after he was found, his throat having been slit from ear to ear. The body of the third boy was found a short distance away with a broken skull.[32]

ATTACK ON HEYWOOD RANCH: CIRCA 1862

Among the biographical sketches of early residents of Johnson and Pawnee counties there are notes concerning an early pioneer named Asa E. Heywood who, for a time, operated a ranch west of Fort Kearny "where he carried on an extensive ranch business furnishing meals and feed for stock and having stable room for 300 horses. After living there two years he was driven out by Indians who stole his property and killed some of his neighbors. He was obliged to evacuate his premises on a few moments warning. He left on the stage, traveling until he met soldiers, when he returned with them, and for two weeks assisted in burying the dead and hunting the savages."[33]

SLAYING OF WISEMAN FAMILY: CEDAR COUNTY 1863

One of the most savage episodes in Cedar County history took place in 1863, at a time when many of the men in the county—having joined Company I of the Second Nebraska Cavalry the year before—were away on army duty in Dakota Territory. A band of Yankton and Santee Sioux chose that time to attack the home of a settler named Henson Wiseman. Wiseman was one of the Cedar County men serving with the cavalry and, ironically, on the day of the attack his wife was also away from the house. Left at the home were five children. The Sioux killed them all. The oldest, a boy of seventeen, had apparently battled desperately in defense of the family. He, his thirteen-year-old brother and an eight-year-old sister were killed outright. A five-year-old boy lived three days. A girl aged fifteen—shot through the abdomen with an arrow and having had a cartridge exploded in her mouth—lived for five days after the attack.[34]

WAR COUNCIL: NEAR SCOTTSBLUFF, FALL 1863

The greatest war council in the history of the Plains Indians took place in the fall of 1863 in Horse Creek Valley, not far from present-day Scottsbluff. It is possible that the mass uprising that began the following year with the Plum Creek Massacre was discussed or planned at the council. Ironically, the meeting took place not far from where the great Peace Council had been held twelve years earlier.[35]

BENTZ HILL MASSACRE: 1864

Far to the north, below Yankton, South Dakota, about midway along the enormous bend of the Missouri that forms Nebraska's northeastern boundary, sits the present-day hamlet of St. Helena. In 1864, an event occurred near the village that carries lessons about the climate of the times and the dangers of life on Nebraska's early frontier.

A little more than three aerial miles northwest of St. Helena (four and one half miles when driven on the mostly-gravel roads), one of the early pioneers in the area, Dr. Lorenzo Bentz, was attacked and killed by Indians. Bentz's slaying was intended as a signal: a warning to potential settlers not to move into the area. Set in the context of the Great Sioux War that was about to erupt across the plains, the incident provides a stark example of how tenuous was existence along the frontier.

Since the time of the incident almost a century and a half ago, the small elevation where the slaying occurred has been known as the site of the "Bentz Hill Massacre."[36]

DEPREDATIONS AT PATTON FARM: SALINE COUNTY, EARLY 1864

Early relations between whites and Indians in Saline County were generally positive. A horrific exception occurred early in 1864 in the northern part of the county when a Sioux raiding party ravaged the house of a settler family named Patton. The male members of the family were tied up and Mrs. Patton, though several months pregnant, was repeatedly raped by members of the war party. The Sioux slaughtered the family's flock of sheep before making their escape.[37]

SNEAK ATTACK AT LOOKING GLASS CREEK: EARLY 1864

Sometime early in 1864, prior to the great uprising of the Plains Indians that was to come in August, a party of Sioux Indians killed

Wagon ruts are still visible near Mitchell Pass.

Author's photos

Chimney Rock was a landscape feature often mentioned in pioneer diaries.

243

several members of a government-contracted hay crew along Looking Glass Creek in Platte County.

A local resident named Pat Murray had received a contract to put up hay for government troops posted at the nearby Pawnee Agency. Murray, at his home near Columbus when the incident took place, hired several workers who were lodged in tents in a meadow alongside the creek. After sunset, their work done for the day, and having picketed the teams of horses and mules, most were at their tents when a dozen Sioux warriors approached the campsite. Pretending to be Pawnees, they demanded food from Mrs. Murray, who cooked for the workers.

While they were eating, one of the hay crew, a veteran of life on the Plains, recognized the Sioux dialect. The Sioux claimed to intend no harm, saying they were on their way to raid at the Pawnee reservation. Subsequently, however, they began to examine the hay crew's weapons as if out of curiosity and later untied a "fine span of mules." When members of the hay crew began to resist, one was immediately tomahawked and the owner of the mules was shot with eight arrows. Others, the exact number is not known, were also killed. Mrs. Murray was shot with five arrows as she fought with a pitchfork trying to save the crew's horses, all of which were taken by the Sioux.

A young boy on the hay crew escaped by hiding in a hay stack. The next day the boy brought help from the Pawnee agency. Mrs. Murray was found alive in the tall grass where she had crawled away to hide. She eventually recovered from her wounds. The Sioux raiders were never caught.

Although the killings occurred before the outbreak in the fall, the memory of it further heightened the sense of panic when full-scale war broke out later in the year.[38]

ILLUSTRATIVE EVENTS FROM THE GREAT SIOUX UPRISING

May 23, 1864: Stage attack near Fort McPherson {traveler's note}

"We noticed a wagon going up the river on the other side; who the people were we do not know, but the Indians made a dash upon them right opposite the Post in broad daylight, killing two men, set fire to the wagon, and ran off with the horses."[39]

September 1864: Attacks near Fort McPherson

September, 1864 was a bloody month in Lincoln County. It began when a "number of men working on W. M. Hinman's farm" were surprised and killed. Soon after, a squad of soldiers gathering plums near Fort McPherson were attacked and several "were killed and scalped." Spotted Tail was thought to have been the leader of the war party. A short distance from the fort, a stage was attacked with officers on board. One horse pulling the stage was killed, another wounded. Through the period of the uprising, "stage coaches, though generally guarded, were frequently captured and the occupants killed. Freight (wagon) trains were attacked and plundered, and unless they could escape by flight, the entire wagon party would be killed and scalped."[40]

September 8, 1864: Soldier killed Near Cottonwood Springs

". . .we got news that (Private Bluford) Starkey had been killed by Indians while in a fight with them among the cedars in Cottonwood Canyon."[41]

November 1864: Stage attack between Fort Kearny and Fort McPherson

"Lieutenant Williams and an officer named Hancock were riding west on a stage between Fort Kearny and Cottonwood Springs (Fort McPherson). It was a bright moonlight night. It was a four-horse stage. After they had got well out of Plum Creek (Lexington) coming west, and were out on the broad plains, all at once about a dozen shots came from the Indians, and they killed two horses that were in the lead, and those two horses dropped in their tracks. This was part of the Indian plan, and then they commenced shooting into the stage. Williams and Hancock with Smith & Wesson carbines, and the other two (i.e. driver and guard) with Sharps' Rifles, got down flat on the ground and kept up a fire with the Indians, who besieged them all night. The two dead horses kept the stage from being run away with, and the Indians soon killed the other two. As the Indians skirmished around, the men lay on the ground and got in between the horses, and when morning came they had fired off a greater share of their ammunition, and had succeeded in getting two or three Indians, but were themselves unharmed.

They were reinforced in the morning by a party who had been warned by someone who had heard the shooting."[42]

1864-1867: Indian scares, Dawson County

The early pioneer history of Dawson County records that for at least three years after the Plum Creek Massacre, Indian scares were frequent. When the peril seemed imminent, settlers sought refuge at the Plum Creek Station. "To them the windmill at the railroad water tank, towering as it did, high above all else, was ever a beacon of safety. At Plum Creek the citizens. . .formed a company of militia to be ready to fight the Indians . . . ."[43]

January 7, 1865: Attack on O'Fallon's Bluff Station

"The Commander at O'Fallon's Bluffs telegraphed that the Indians had run all across his post, and had halted a train and killed several persons."[44]

(O'Fallon's Bluff Station was located about two miles south and four miles west of Sutherland.)

January 1865: Widespread destruction and deaths

"All the time companies and cavalry were arriving from the East. The Indians had disappeared, having committed great depredations all along the route from within fifty miles of Denver to Cottonwood Springs (Fort McPherson). Almost every ranch had been besieged or had had a fight with the Indians. The Indians had captured a number of horses, killed a lot of people, and had disappeared, going south. And while this was (occurring) on the Platte, they had raided the Arkansas River, and had done great damage. They had burned trains, and great quantities of stores and supplies."[45]

May 1865: Attack on stage coach east of Fort Kearny

Although Indian attacks on stagecoaches have long been a staple of Western fiction, authentic instances of such attacks are rare. One of these is given by Samuel Bowles, who reports an incident that occurred east of Fort Kearny in May, 1865:

"Today's news shows that some of the Indians had broken through or run around the military lines. They had commenced by ambushing a party of some 12 to 20 soldiers, mostly converted rebels, on their way from Fort Leavenworth to Fort Kearny, but without arms. Two of these they killed outright, and most of the rest they wounded so savagely they will probably die. The next day they assaulted the incoming stage which had six to eight passengers. . .circling around and around the vehicle on well-mounted horses, and shooting their arrows fast and sharp. . .at horses and passengers. The horses were whipped up, the men on the stage had two rifles and kept them in play, and thus the Indians were held at bay until the protection of a station and a train was secured, when the attacking party, finding themselves baffled, retired. They numbered about 25 in all." [46]

October 28, 1865: Attack on Alkali Springs Station

"Alkali Stage Station was located about ten miles east of the present town of Ogallala, Nebraska. There was a post office at the Alkali as well as a telegrapher. The station was raided on October 28, 1865, the Indians destroying considerable property and killing four men. General Herman H. Heath led troops in pursuit, eventually killing twenty-nine of the raiders."[47]

1865 (date unknown): Station burned

" . . .a traveler found a station 22 miles west of Fort Kearny, six miles southeast of Elm Creek 'a smoking ruin.'"[48]

1865 (date unknown): Battle of Horse Creek

About seven miles southeast of Henry in extreme western Nebraska, in an area that has since borne the name "Horse Creek Battle Ground," soldiers from nearby Fort Mitchell were sent to intercept a party of warring Indians. In the sharp encounter that followed, casualties occurred on both sides. "A number of soldiers, including the captain" were reported killed. Soldier fatalities were buried near Fort Mitchell.[49]

1865-1866: Raids in Thayer County

The killing raids of 1864 were savage in the extreme. Heavy raids continued in Thayer County but over the next two years the level of violence slackened. "The raids of 1865 and 1866, although of considerable consequence to the settlers, were attended with but little loss of life. . .and no lives, we believe, were taken in Thayer County; but there was considerable loss of property, many of the settlers losing all their stock."

For Thayer County the period of relative peace was brief. In 1867, violent raids would again bring death and large scale destruction to the county.[50]

1866 (date unknown) Station burned

". . .a passerby observed that Miller's Ranche, 60 miles west of Fort Kearny and due south of Willow Island was 'abandoned and burned to the ground.'"[51]

1866 (date unknown): Station burned

". . .a traveler found Midway Station, 75 miles west of Fort Kearny burning from an Indian raid."[52]

1866 (date unknown): Attack on wagon train near Scottsbluff

The "Battle of Scottsbluff Mountain Pass," another story otherwise undocumented, is alleged to have taken place sometime in 1866. An "old-timer" account tells of an encounter in which a wagon train composed of emigrant and freight wagons was attacked by Indians somewhere near Mitchell Pass in proximity to the present-day national monument. Thirty-eight persons were alleged to have been killed.[53] This account, like many others, is unattested. The large number of deaths, unreported in other accounts, may cast doubt on portions of the story.

CLASHES IN REPUBLICAN RIVER VALLEY: 1866-1871

For many years, hunters and trappers had been active in the area of what is now Franklin County. Conflicts with the Indians were frequent and at different times many trappers and member of hunting parties were killed. As early as the winter of 1866-1867 "a settlement in the western part of (Franklin) county. . .had to be abandoned on account of the hostility of the Indians.

The year 1870 saw concerted attempts to settle the central and western Republican River Valley. "Prior to that time, the Republican Valley had been the very best hunting ground for the Indians, and their occupancy of it, with their hostility, had rendered settlements previous to this time impracticable."

Even after General Carr's defeat of the Sioux at Summit Springs, Indian scares sometimes surfaced. During the winter of 1870-1871, the small settlements in Franklin County applied to the state governor for arms and ammunition for defensive purposes. The governor agreed, but only if the settlers formed themselves into a militia company. When the entire county was organized, the company was enlisted in the Second Nebraska Cavalry. "The Governor issued commissions to the officers elected, and ordered that they should be armed and placed on a war footing immediately."

During the summer of 1871, a company of soldiers was stationed about two miles above the mouth of Turkey Creek to guard against Indians, but no attack occurred.[54]

War returns to Thayer County: Summer 1867

Along the frontier settlements, the new state of Nebraska (statehood was achieved March 1, 1867) was baptized in fire. During the summer of that year, another large uprising occurred that spread death and terror along the overland trail. "(Indians) again raided down on the settlements, driving off stock and carrying away scalps."

In Thayer County, deprivations were severe. The bloody season began in June with an attack on a site known as Old Hackney Ranch. There, raiders drove off seven horses and the two ranchers barely escaped with their lives riding a horse that had been left in the barn unnoticed by the raiders. After the closest of calls, they managed to reach safety at a settlement on the Big Sandy.

On the same day at the nearby Kiowa Ranch, sixteen horses were stolen in a hit and run attack. The first settler death occurred as the war party continued down the valley of the Little Blue. About a mile from present-day Hebron they came to a farm occupied by a settler named Haney. After a parley, and after pleading with the marauders not to take his horses, Haney was shot and killed. In a desperate race to safety, Haney's three daughters somehow managed to escape to a nearby settlement despite the raiders' attempt to take them prisoner.

The next day, June 10, attacks continued with a raid near Thompson's Ranch on the "eighteen-mile ridge" in Thayer County. Thompson and his family had fled the night before, but the following day another settler, Captain S. J. Alexander (later Nebraska's Secretary of State), believing the Indians had taken their plunder and left the area, came to the ranch hoping to preserve what he could on behalf of the Thompson family. Alexander loaded Thompson's remaining possessions on a wagon and set out for safety, only to discover that he was being stalked by eight raiders whose path would intersect with his at an ambush site a short distance ahead.

Momentarily secluded behind a bluff, Alexander cut the harness from his team. Climbing on the fastest horse, he set out across a four-mile stretch of open ground toward the nearest settlement. The Indians quickly captured the loose horse, but the distraction took enough time for Alexander to reach a draw that he turned into hoping to throw the pursuers off his track. The ruse temporarily delayed the Indians and as they searched for his trail, Alexander crossed over another ridge out of sight and made it to safety.

In August, at the foot of a steep hill west of the Hackney Ranch, raiders attacked members of a three- or four-person party who were taking a herd of sheep to Colorado. One person was killed and later buried at that site. The others fought a running battle over the "eighteen-mile ridge" and eventually reached safety at a settlement on the Big Sandy. The Indians slaughtered the entire herd of sheep.

Continuing down the valley, the raiders came to the farmstead of a settler called "Poland Pete" and made prisoners of two of his children, a boy of about eight and a girl fourteen. As the party with their captives moved back up the valley of the Little Blue, the boy "overcome by fatigue and fear," began crying. At a bluff on the north side of the river, in the presence of his sister, the child was shot and killed with an arrow. Some time later, the girl was among the prisoners exchanged for Indian captives at North Platte.

Not far from the hill where the boy was slain, two settlers named Bennett and Abernathy resided in times of threat in a cave on a limestone bluff. The cave contained a spring and the two men had enlarged the cavity and built a fortified addition at the front of the cave consisting of logs and branches. The Indians apparently attacked and laid siege to the cave, approaching it through trees and underbrush that ran along the base of the bluff. The attackers set fire to the logs at the front of the cave. It is uncertain if the settlers were smothered by the flames and smoke, burned alive, or killed after their ammunition ran out. The cave was later sealed when soldiers found the bodies so charred and mutilated they could not be moved elsewhere for burial.

The depredations continued as the raiders passed west through the county before killing two emigrants called "Polish Albert" and

"Polish Joe" near the Oak Creek Ranch in Nuckolls County, "taking away their teams and other effects."

Two weeks later, the war party returned, first killing a settler named "Polish Jack" in eastern Thayer County where the final deaths from the 1867 raids took place. Near the residence of a settler named William Nightengale, raiders killed a farmhand named Ignatz Tenish.[55]

ATTACKS AT CAMPBELL FARM: JULY 24, 1867

On July 24, 1867, west of Doniphan about ten miles south of Grand Island, Sioux and Cheyenne raiders attacked the home of settler Peter Campbell. "Campbell and his eldest son were away from home helping a neighbor with his harvest. The Indians. . .captured two of Campbell's nieces (another account says they were his daughters), aged seventeen and nineteen, and his twin sons, aged four. A nine-year-old daughter escaped." A credible account says Mrs. Campbell and a small boy were killed.

The captives from the Campbell farm form part of the full story of the Plum Creek saga. (See "Attack on Train at Plum Creek.")

"In mid-August of that year (1864), the Pawnee Scouts, led by Frank North, fought a Cheyenne band near Plum Creek and took a woman and a boy prisoner. The boy was a nephew of Turkey Leg, a Cheyenne Chief.

"A month later, a meeting was held in North Platte between a government peace commission and Sioux and Cheyenne leaders. Turkey Leg recognized Major Frank North, commander of the Pawnee Scouts, and offered to exchange some white prisoners for the two Indians captives. The children were exchanged unharmed in late September, 1867 at North Platte."[56]

On the same day the Campbell farm was attacked, a German emigrant named Henry Dose was killed and scalped at a nearby ranch. Dose's home was plundered and his stock taken. In the same area, Indians killed Mrs. Thurston Warner, the wife of a settler, and wounded one of her children.[57]

VIOLENCE IN CHEYENNE COUNTY: 1867

"Troubles with Indians were kept up for many years. Stock was run off from the ranches. Settlers were attacked and killed, stages and emigrant trains were attacked, and, unless the greatest caution was used, there was great danger that small and unprotected parties would be surprised by Indians. At one ranch—that of a French Canadian, known as French Louis—attacks were made and stock run off, at intervals of every few weeks, until, when nearly ruined, and about the time of the completion of the Union Pacific Railroad in 1867, he moved to Sidney. . .and started a store, selling supplies and whiskey to the men engaged in the construction of the railroad."[58]

DEPREDATIONS IN MADISON COUNTY: 1867-1869

Indian problems for the early settlements in Madison County were generally not severe. In the midst of a bitter winter in 1867, hungry Indians poisoned and ate a settler's cow, "killed and ate five dogs belonging to the settlement, and upon discovering the carcasses of seven timber wolves which had been killed by the settlers three weeks previously. . .dressed them as well as they could and devoured the flesh."

In 1869, as Sioux Indians moved through the settlements along Shell Creek, livestock were killed and the wife of a settler was wounded during an exchange of fire.[59]

HAYNIE FIGHT, NUCKOLLS COUNTY: 1868

In northern Nuckolls County, a "man by the name of Haynie was killed, and his daughter, a girl of fifteen," was captured by Indians. The Indians carried their captive across the Republican River into Kansas. That night, just below Superior, she escaped after the Indians had made camp. After moving about two miles downsteam, she waded across the river, eventually reaching safety at a settlement in Thayer County, "only a half hour before the Indians came in sight, following her trail."[60]

HINMAN FARM AND OTHER ATTACKS: 1868

The uprising that began in 1864 would not end in a substantial way until General Carr's victory at Summit Springs in July 1869. In Lincoln County, Indian attacks actually increased during 1868. "Attacks on small numbers of white men became alarmingly frequent. Several small parties were attacked, killed, and scalped." At the Hinman Farm, the site of a raid in 1864, five men were killed when the farm was attacked for a second time.

Around Plum Creek and Fort McPherson, the railroad provided favorite ambush locations for Indian attackers. In 1868, a train engineer

Harper's Weekly
Train engineer "Dutch Frank" foils Indian attack.

known as Dutch Frank became famous for foiling a potentially lethal attack. As his train was rounding a curve, Frank saw hostile Indians on each side of the road bed and a number crowded in the middle of the tracks intent on blocking the train. Deciding that stopping would mean certain death, Frank instead increased the speed of the train and plowed through the Indians on the tracks, killing several. The train and crew somehow made it unscathed through a hail of bullets fired from both sides of the train. At the next stop it was found that the front of the engine was covered with blood.[61]

OTOES VS. SIOUX/CHEYENNES: LIBERTY CREEK 1868

During 1868, near the head of Liberty Creek in Nuckolls County, "there was a battle between sixty-five Otoes. . .and forty Cheyenne-Sioux. (The fight) lasted for several hours and resulted in favor of the Otoes, who obtained six ponies and five scalps from their adversaries."[62]

INTERTRIBAL WAREFARE: YORK COUNTY 1868

In 1868, York County formed a loose focal point for a conflict that involved several tribes. In that year, the Pawnee, Omaha, Ponca, and

Otoe combined to fight their common enemy, the Sioux. The line of battle was thought to be on the south side of the West Blue, about eight miles south of the York. No settlers were known to have been injured, but the depredations caused by the raids and the movement of war parties across the region made life difficult for the residents. Settlers were unexpectedly aided by the presence of a large herd of buffalo that came into the area and provided much-needed food. Ironically, it was said to be the last year that buffalo were seen in York County.[63]

TOBIN INDIAN RAID: APRIL 29, 1868

Between 1864 and 1867, the Union Pacific Railroad was completed from east to west across Nebraska. To maintain the tracks and keep the adjacent telegraph wires repaired, section crews were stationed at intervals along the line. The crews were the subject of frequent attacks by Sioux and Cheyennes. One well-documented incident occurred in the spring of 1868, about one and a half miles east of present-day Overton.

"Mrs. Timothy Tobin and Mrs. William Costin, wives of section foremen, and their families were threatened by an Indian raiding party on April 29, 1868. Shortly afterward the warriors attacked and killed Mr. Tobin and section hands Schultz and McCarthy. A third employee named Williams, though seriously wounded, escaped to the section house. Fearing for her husband and his crew, Mrs. Costin bravely set out to warn them of the danger. A passing train picked up the survivors. . . . ."[64]

ATTACKS IN LINCOLN COUNTY: 1869

Troubles persisted in Lincoln County until eased by Carr's victory at Summit Springs in July. Although the presence of military posts in the county prevented hardships of the extent then being inflicted on areas further south, "a good many small parties. . .were killed, and stock and horses run off by the Indians, and many deprivations continued."[65]

SHAWNEE RAID, FILLMORE COUNTY: 1869

An account left by John Ziska, an earlier pioneer who lived in a dugout near the Fillmore County boundary, asserts that Shawnee Indians made a raid through the region in 1869. Reports reached settlers that the Indians had reached Hebron and were coming further down the Little Blue. "Everyone in the district. . .packed up ready to make an escape, when some of them went over to investigate. . . and found that the Indians had gone home after killing some men and stealing thirteen head of horses."[66] Accounts left by early arrivals are sketchy, and Ziska's story is difficult to corroborate.

Military activities near Hebron: 1869-1870

In June 1869, Company A, First Nebraska Cavalry, eventually numbering about sixty-five troopers, was organized in Thayer County for protection of the frontier. The company built a stockade on the bank of Spring Creek, about one mile south of present-day Hebron. The fortification "greatly aided the early settlement."

The following year a company of regulars relieved Company A. Posted near Kiowa, about twelve miles northwest of Hebron, it was five members from this unit who were awarded Medals of Honor for their activities along Spring Creek in Nuckolls County.[67]

Thain attack: May 7, 1870

A settler named Thain, living in the eastern part of the county, was the last man killed by Indians in Nuckolls County. Thain was surprised by Indian raiders, murdered, scalped, and robbed of his horses. "Thain's Branch, a tributary of the Little Blue, on which he lived, received its name in honor of him."[68]

Attacks on settlers: Adams County, Summer 1870

Despite its location along the Overland Trail, attacks on settlers in Adams County were comparatively rare. One recorded instance happened in the summer of 1870, when groups of settlers near Kiowa Ranch were attacked by marauding bands of Indians, likely Sioux and Cheyennes. Soon after the attacks began, "a company of United States regulars under Captain Spalding" arrived at the scene and drove the attackers away. One soldier was wounded during the clash.[69]

Buffalo Bill's pursuit: September 1870

Although the great uprising of the mid-1860s had ended, Indian raiders sometimes returned to the Lincoln County area on horse stealing expeditions. In September 1870, in a sizable raid on a stock ranch near Fort McPherson, attackers made off with twenty-one of the best horses, including one named "Powder Face," a favorite of Buffalo Bill Cody.

Cody guided the pursuit that quickly formed, leading sixty soldiers from Fort McPherson to a location about sixty miles southwest of the fort near Medicine Creek. There, Cody believed, the marauders would camp for the night. Cody correctly anticipated the attacker's plans. Scouting through the night, he found the raider's camp and posted soldiers around it. At sunrise the troopers attacked, surprising the Indians in "a short, sharp fight.' A number of Indians were killed at the scene and during the pursuit that followed. Cody's men recovered most of the stolen horses (but not "Powder Face") and captured several Indian ponies as well.[70]

SETTLER INCIDENT: ANTELOPE COUNTY, 1870

With a few exceptions—mostly thefts of horses, chickens, and ducks, and episodes of persistent begging—early settlers in Antelope County generally "suffered but little molestation from the Indians."

The first recorded violence took place in 1870, when a raiding party of ten Sioux appeared at the house of a settler named Louis Petras. Becoming increasingly belligerent as the day wore on, the raiders eventually fired several shots into the house and stole nine horses.[71]

RAID NEAR CEDAR CREEK: NOVEMBER 1870

By far the most serious of the early frontier incidents that occurred in Antelope County happened in November 1870 when, shortly after attack on the Petras' home, raiders struck the county for a second time. On the second occasion a large war party broke into the home of a settler named Robert Horne, who lived near the head of Cedar Creek. The attackers stole the goods they could carry with them and destroyed the rest.

Pursuit was soon organized. Fourteen settlers tracked the raiders, eventually finding and catching them a few miles south of O'Neill. In the sharp battle that followed, two Indians were killed and two or three more were wounded. Two of the settlers' horses were killed and others were injured. The settlers' response halted further raids into Antelope County.[72]

ATTACK ON WAGON TRAIN: FALL 1870

In late 1870, a small California-bound wagon party consisting of five travelers was attacked along the trail in Adams County. Four of the five members of the party were killed during the fight. The fifth

256

managed to escape, finding safety at nearby Spring Ranche. In the same general area, at a point on the trail four miles south of present-day Juniata, evidence of an earlier massacre was discovered. "There were traces of graves and remnants of articles of hardware, showing that, in all probability, parties had been murdered, and the articles they had with them, such as were considered useless to the assailants, were burned."[73]

FORTIFICATIONS IN WEBSTER COUNTY: 1870-1871

In April 1870, settlers reached the fertile Republican River Valley and selected a promising location on the north side of the river, near the mouth of Soap Creek. "The place was called Guide Rock, from a large rocky bluff on the opposite site of the river, which being so high above the surrounding landscape made a conspicuous landmark." Eventually a settlement formed, and to protect themselves the settlers built a one room, forty foot square, stockade.

In August, a second group of settlers constructed a fortification near present-day Red Cloud. The Guide Rock location became known as the lower stockade and that at Red Cloud as the upper stockade.

The following spring, a third fortification—known as the Elm Creek Stockade—was erected on the farm of a settler named M. L. Thomas.

As at most new settlements, "scares" were frequent. For settlers in Webster County, the most serious took place in 1871. "During (that) year there was still great fear of Indian attacks, and there were serious scares and frights. At one time the Indian Chief Red Cloud was said to be camped about eight miles above the Red Cloud stockade, accompanied by a band numbering all the way from many hundreds to many thousands, and all were bent on driving white people from the county. There was for a time great confusion among the settlers. The rumor, however, proved to be without foundation. The Indians rarely appeared and when they did, it was in small numbers and they were perfectly friendly."[74]

MILITARY PRESENCE, NORTH LOUP: SUMMER 1871

Settlers began arriving in number in Howard County during early 1871. The first arrivals were in frequent fear of attack by marauding Sioux. The Pawnee Reservation was on the county's eastern boundary, and the settlements were along the route of the attacks and counterattacks between the historic, bitter enemies.

In response to pleas by settlers, a unit of soldiers, Company C, Ninth Infantry, was "ordered to duty in the Loup Valley. (The) company arrived when the Loup bridge was building on May 12, 1871, and remained—and assisted with the bridge until it was completed on June 10, when they removed to the North Loup, some distance above St. Paul, and went into camp there. Here they remained for a long time, and the relationship formed between the soldiers and the settlers were of the most pleasant and friendly nature. . . ."[75]

TEMPORARY POST AT RED WILLOW: EARLY 1872

Although major problems with Native tribes in the Republican Valley had ended after Summit Springs, newly arriving settlers continued to voice concerns about the possible renewal of fighting. In response to requests from the emigrants, in 1872 the army sent two companies—one cavalry and one infantry—to "guard against any surprises by the Indians." The soldiers camped at the mouth of Red Willow Creek. "Late in the year (1872), however, finding that there was little danger from the Indians, the soldiers were ordered away."[76]

ATTACK IN CHEYENNE COUNTY: SUMMER 1872

"After the organization of the county, the Indians gave no particular trouble, except an occasional attack on herders or surveying parties unprotected by soldiers or small parties who ventured out. . . . There were many such incidents as these, where parties were killed and scalped, though there was no real Indian outbreak. . . . In the summer of 1872, Professor I. W. LaMunyon. . .had charge of a surveying party, surveying the lands along Pumpkin Seed Creek, being attended by a company of cavalry from Fort Sidney. No hostile Indians having been seen, and apprehending no danger, this company took occasion one day to ride off to Sidney, leaving the surveyors unprotected. Some time during the day, while engaged in their labors, the party was attacked by a band of Indians. A hole several feet in circumference and about two feet in depth had been dug for the purpose of storing casks of water, etc., and to this Professor LaMunyon led his men, where they took refuge, putting up their water casks and provisions about the sides for better protection. Here they endured an attack of several hours' duration. The plan of attack was that generally adopted by Indians —to put their ponies on a full run, and, riding in single file, throwing themselves on the outer side of their ponies, shooting under their necks, while describing a circle about the besieged. Though a sharp firing was kept up on both sides for several hours. . .none of the surveying party was hurt. Many of the ponies of the Indians were killed, and several Indians were slain. Finally, the soldiers appearing in sight, the Indians fled, and, though pursued, made good their escape."[77]

EXETER INDIAN SCARE: FALL 1873

In the fall of 1873, telegraphed reports reached Exeter that Indians on the war path seventy-five to one hundred miles west of the city had killed homesteaders and were headed towards the settlement. Only two able-bodied men were left in the hamlet at the time. The men took what defensive precautions they could and waited for an attack that never came.[78]

INCIDENTS OF A DIFFERENT NATURE: HOLT COUNTY, FALL 1874

In an era when descriptions of encounters between Natives and settlers so often ended in bloodshed, two stories from Holt County provide refreshing outcomes.

In the fall of 1874, Indians visited the home of a settler, requesting flour. The settler gave him half his supply, for which the Indians offered to pay. When the settler refused the payment, the Indians returned the flour.

In the western part of the county, a band of forty Indians came to the home of John O'Connell "when there was no one at home but the women, two little girls, and a little boy. The Indians formed themselves in a circle around the house, and then in a file rode up to the door, demanding of Mrs. O'Connell something to eat. She gave them the best she had of coffee, bread, meat, etc., prudence suggesting that their demands must not be refused. After partaking of the frugal offering, they, very much to the surprise of their enforced hostess, presented her with a large quantity of buffalo meat, mounted their ponies, rode up one by one, shook hands with her, and galloped away over the plain."[79]

MAIL, WAGON TRAIN ATTACKS NEAR FORT ROBINSON: 1876

In the fall of 1875 a government commission met for the first time with various Indian representatives for the purpose of purchasing the Black Hills and prohibiting hunting in Wyoming's Big Horn country. Held near the Red Cloud Agency in northwestern Nebraska, the council was troubled from the outset by dissension between the parties and among the Indian bands. The absences of powerful chiefs —neither Crazy Horse nor Sitting Bull chose to participate—further confused the proceedings. The talks failed amidst considerable bitterness.

In the volatile situation that followed—it was evident, for example, that the government could not keep miners out of the Black Hills—the military was ordered to force the non-treaty Indians on to the agencies. To comply with that directive, the army launched a campaign that led in the following spring and summer to the engagements at Powder River, Rosebud Creek, the Little Bighorn, and, in Nebraska, Warbonnet Creek.

Even before the major engagements, however, the Indians' dissatisfaction provoked a series of smaller clashes that instilled a climate of terror across Nebraska's panhandle.

On May 16, 1876, ten miles west of Camp Robinson, a mail wagon traveling from Fort Laramie was attacked. The driver was killed, shot six times. The raiding party of four Indians was chased a considerable distance but the pursuit was unsuccessful. The killing of the mail carrier escalated the level of violence; up to that point, similar attacks had been limited to theft or the killing of horses on the wagon teams.

Ambushes of freight wagons were frequent. On May 27, a wagon train was attacked near present-day Bridgeport, ten miles north of the North Platte River Bridge. Two mules and a horse were killed. Two wagon trains carrying freight were ambushed between the Red Cloud Agency and the North Platte Bridge at about the same time. "Travelers were warned that the trail was unsafe and were encouraged to travel in large, well-armed parties." Depredations around the Red Cloud Agency occurred frequently: corrals were burned, stock run off, and supply trains were increasingly the target of attacks.

To the extent that depleted cavalry forces would allow (most had been diverted for duty with the Big Horn and Yellowstone Expeditions), roads and trails were patrolled and aggressive reconnaissance conducted throughout the area.[80]

It was a very dangerous summer.

SHERMAN COUNTY SCARE: SUMMER 1876

In 1876, the Battle of the Blowout, the Little Big Horn, Warbonnet Creek, and other encounters both near and far away brought a renewal of the Indian scares that, while never ending, had subsided somewhat following the Civil War and Carr's victory at Summit Springs. The Loup Valley was the scene of one such major "scare." Reports of massacres, though unfounded, "aroused so much terror that a large number of the inhabitants left (Sherman) county."[81]

TENSIONS IN SIOUX COUNTY: SUMMER 1876

Sioux County was a flash point for trouble in the mid-1870s. "Previous to 1876, Sioux County, as well as the northern portion of Cheyenne County north of the North Platte River, was occupied by the Ogallala and Brule Sioux as their reservation and hunting grounds, the country then abounding in game. This being about the last suitable hunting grounds in the west, the Indians were very jealous of any encroachments of white men into their territory, and it was only after the discovery of gold in the Black Hills, and then only with the greatest difficulty, and only through fear of being driven out by force that they were prevailed upon to relinquish by treaty their exclusive right to their reservation. This treaty was formed in 1876."[82]

The 1876 treaty was highly disputed by the Indians, many of whom did not agree with the provisions – particularly the ceding of the Black Hills to white settlement – or the questionable manner in which the treaty was negotiated. The bitter aftermath was one of the contributing factors to the 1876 uprising that led to the Little Big Horn and, in Nebraska, to Warbonnet Creek.

Because of the large number of Indians in Western Nebraska and the persistent tension between the groups, for much of the time Sioux County was the location of two military posts: Fort Robinson and Camp Sheridan.

BLACK ELK WAGON TRAIN ATTACK: 1876

The name of Warbonnet Creek surfaces several times in Nebraska's military history. The small stream was the location for the significant battle in July 1876, during which Wesley Merritt's cavalry defeated Indians attempting to join Crazy Horse, and Buffalo Bill Cody is believed to have scalped the Sioux warrior Yellow Hair, thus taking "the first scalp for Custer." Three years later, north of Harrison in a dugout along Antelope Creek, a small tributary of Warbonnet Creek, the last holdouts of Dull Knife's band of escaping Cheyennes were killed or captured in a death struggle with the cavalrymen who surrounded them.

A lesser known encounter occurred along the stream three months before Merritt fought the major battle nearby. The episode is significant because it was the first battle for a thirteen-year old named Black Elk. Later, his story would be made famous by John Neihardt in *Black Elk Speaks*.[83]

In May of 1876, Black Elk rode with a war party of Sioux and Cheyenne and was with them when they attacked a wagon train moving along Warbonnet Creek.

As related by Alan Boye,

"Black Elk used a "six shooter" given to him by a relative to fight his first battle. He rode bareback, hanging onto the horse's neck and leaning under the beast's head to shoot at the wagons. The wagon train had circled its wagons and placed oxen in the center for defense. The wagon train consisted of prospectors headed to Sioux lands in the Black Hills in search of gold. Black Elk's band was headed to the Rosebud to join up with Crazy Horse. They had left Red Cloud's band because they believed he had sold out to the whites by signing a treaty relinquishing the Black Hills.

"A month later Black Elk would be present to watch Crazy Horse and others wipe out Custer at the Little Big Horn. . ."[84]

CHEYENNE SCARE, FURNAS COUNTY: FALL 1878

During the "Cheyenne Autumn" odyssey, as the Northern Cheyennes were making their desperate trek from a reservation in Oklahoma to their historic grounds in northeastern Nebraska, their route took them for a time to Beaver Creek, just south of the Nebraska border in Kansas. There, several settlers were killed.

In Furnas County, scouting parties were formed to watch for approaching Cheyennes, but the first alarms were little heeded. Soon after, a report came in that 2,000 Indians (the actual number that had left the reservation in Oklahoma was about 350) were five miles from Wilsonville in the western part of the county. This time the panic was profound, and many of the settler families west of Beaver City fled the county.

At Beaver City and east through the county, preparations were made for defense. "A wagon corral was made on the public square, the horses and women were placed inside and guards stationed all around to prevent a surprise." The townspeople, joined by arriving settlers, waited for an attack.

It never came. Within twenty-four hours it was learned that "the reported 2,000 Indians were 2,000 Texas cattle driven by cowboys." The Indians were, in fact, gone from the area.[85]

DEATH IN HITCHCOCK COUNTY: FALL 1878

The approach of the Northern Cheyennes following their breakout from Indian Territory, terrorized Republican Valley settlements all along the Kansas-Nebraska border. The Cheyennes' escape route took them near Hitchcock County and caused turmoil as settlers fled or prepared themselves for defense. No one from the border settlements was known to have been harmed, although a rancher, George Rawley, was killed near Stinking Water Creek. Rawley was one of the few persons killed after the Cheyennes reached Nebraska.[86]

RAIDS IN SOUTHWESTERN NEBRASKA: OCTOBER 1878

The path taken by the Northern Cheyennes brought them across Nebraska's southwestern border and into camp at the forks of the Republican River near Benkelman. Before moving further north, they raided nearby ranches, seeking horses, cattle, and other provisions. These were the last raids in southwestern Nebraska.

The chapter "Dull Knife's Escape: The Odyssey of the Northern Cheyenne" provides a complete discussion.

FORT NIOBRARA: APRIL 22, 1880

In 1876, treaties sent the Ogallala Sioux under Chief Red Cloud and the Brule Sioux led by Chief Spotted Tail to the Pine Ridge and Rosebud Agencies, respectively. While no major flare-ups occurred, problems persisted with a frequency that frustrated and alarmed the settlers who were coming to the area in ever-increasing numbers.

One pioneer history of Brown County says "(the Sioux were) continually wandering from their reservations, robbing and killing any white men they could find. As an added safeguard it was decided to send troops to keep the Indians in bounds."

In early 1880, General George Crook dispatched soldiers to a site on the Niobrara River south of the Rosebud Agency. The new post, named Fort Niobrara, eventually became the home of three companies of the Fifth United States Cavalry and one company of the Ninth Infantry.[87]

GHOST DANCE SCARE: 1890

"Late in the 1880s. . .Indians were heartened by news of a savior, an Indian John the Baptist whose heralds came out of the wilderness and went among tribes offering a miraculous regeneration of their pride and a new and glorious independence. All they had to do was to perform a magical rite—a special Ghost Dance."[88]

The Ghost Dance was part of a mystical set of beliefs preached by a Paiute shaman named Wovoka. Wovoka, also known as Jack Wilson, prophesized that "the whole Indian race, living and dead. . .would be reunited upon a regenerated earth, to live a life. . .free from death, disease, and misery."[89] When the cosmic event occurred, the buffalo would be restored and the white man would disappear. The dance was an important part of the prophecy; the more often it was performed, the sooner the prediction would come to pass.[90] There were variations in the dance ritual. Unique to the Sioux was the belief that Ghost Shirts would protect them from soldiers' bullets.[91]

The Ghost Dance originated in Western Nevada among the Paiute tribe.[92] By the spring of 1890, it had reached the Pine Ridge Reservation in South Dakota, just across Nebraska's northern border. The dance provoked enormous concern, sometimes bordering on hysteria, from many settlers and some agents, who interpreted the dance and the promised disappearance of the white man as a violent threat to their safety.

In response to appeals for protection, during the fall and early winter the United States government moved large numbers of additional troops into the region. Because of its location on the railroad, Fort Sidney was used as a staging area. Fort Niobrara, east of Valentine, also was the scene of heightened activity. The fort was established in 1880 to guard the Rosebud Reservation just across the border in South Dakota. Now, troopers were alerted in event trouble spilled out of Pine Ridge and Wounded Knee further to the west. Throughout the panhandle, ranchers barricaded homes and banded together for protection. Atop the conical hill near Montrose, where Lieutenant King had his observation post during the Battle of Warbonnet Creek, settlers hollowed out a wide trench, preparing for an attack that never came. (A small cavity near the top of the hill remains today, a likely remnant of the settlers' fortification.)

On December 15, the famed Sioux leader Sitting Bull was killed by tribal police during an attempted arrest. Sitting Bull's death added to the already-high tensions that culminated in confusion and tragedy at Wounded Knee Creek on December 29, 1890.

Although scattered outbursts of violence such as occurred at the Chippewa Reservation at Leech Lake, Minnesota, in October 1898, took place for the next decade or so,[93] Wounded Knee was the last major encounter between soldiers and Indians in the United States. The Ghost Dance movement died out soon after.[94]

Endnotes

1 Alan Boye, *The Complete Roadside Guide to Nebraska,* (St. Johnsbury, Vermont: Saltillo Press, 1993) p. 290.

2 *Fort Atkinson, Nebraska,* The History of Fort Atkinson website. Website www-dial.jpl.nasa. gov/~steven/casde/Atkinson/fort.html Material extracted from website January 3, 2006

3 The website www.kancoll.org/books/andreas_ne links to A.T. Andreas, *Andreas' History of the State of Nebraska,* (Chicago: The Western Historical Company, 1882). Andreas's work provides a county by county portrait of Nebraska's earliest frontier counties. Andreas' references are especially valuable in describing the early days of the following counties: Adams/ Antelope/Blackbird/Boone/Buffalo/Burt/Butler/Cass/Cedar/Chase/Cheyenne/Clay/Colfax/ Cuming/Custer/Dakota/Dawson/Dixon/Dodge/Douglas/Dundy/Fillmore/Franklin/Frontier/ Furnas/Gage/Gosper/Greeley/Hall/Hamilton/Harlan/Hayes/Hitchcock/Holt/Howard/Jefferson/ Johnson/Kearney/Keith/Knox/Lancaster/Lincoln/Madison/Merrick/Nance/Nemaha/Nuckolls/ Otoe/Pawnee/Phelps/Pierce/Platte/Polk/Red Willow/Richardson/Saline/Sarpy/Saunders/ Seward/Sherman/Sioux/Stanton/Thayer/Valley/Washington/Wayne/Webster/ Wheeler/York. This footnote was extracted from Andreas' commentary regarding Butler County.

4 Andreas (History of Jefferson County)

5 Merrill J. Mattes, *The Great Platte River Road,* (Lincoln: The Nebraska State Historical Society, 1964) p. 342.

6 Donald D. Brand, *The History of Scotts Bluff Nebraska,* (Berkeley, California: U.S. Department of the Interior, National Park Service, Field Division of Education, 1934)

7 Mattes p. 374.

8 Boye (p. 359) and Mattes (p. 311), both contain references to the battle.

9 Mattes p. 374.

10 Mattes p. 285.

11 Mattes p. 132

12 Eugene F. Ware, *The Indian War of* 1864, (Lincoln: University of Nebraska Press, 1960) p. 14.

13 Boye p. 429, 430.

14 Brand, *The History of Scotts Bluff Nebraska.*

15 Andreas (History of Lincoln County).

16 Mattes p. 310.

17. Andreas (History of Jefferson County).

18 Andreas (History of Dakota County).

19 Andreas (History of Dixon County).

20. Andreas (History of Cass County).

21. Andreas (History of Dodge County).

22. Andreas (History of Knox County).

23. Andreas (History of Saunders County).

24 Andreas (History of Cedar County).

25 Andreas (History of Lancaster County).

26 Andreas (History of Cuming County).

27 Mattes p. 462.

28 Andreas (History of Hall County).

29 Andreas (History of Nance County).

30 Andreas (History of Thayer County).

31 Andreas (History of Richardson County).

32 Andreas (History of Hall County).

33 *Portraits and Biographical Sketches of Johnson and Pawnee Counties, Nebraska,* (Chicago: Chapman Brothers, 1889) p. 505.

34 Andreas (History of Cedar County).

35 Brand, *The History of Scotts Bluff, Nebraska,* "Last Stand of the Indians" chapter.

36 Boye p. 443.

37 Andreas (History of Saline County).

38 Andreas (Platte County History).

39 Ware p. 142.

40 Andreas (History of Lincoln County).
41 Ware p. 325.
42 Ware p. 269-270.
43 Andreas (History of Dawson County).
44 Ware p. 320.
45 Ware p. 323.
46 Mattes p 232, 233.
47 Ware p. 468.
48 Mattes p. 272.
49 Nebraska History & Record of Pioneer Days website, www.rootsweb.com/~neresour/OLLi-brary/Journals/HPR/Vol01/nhrv01p9.html. Material extracted from website April 7, 2007.
50 Andreas (History of Thayer County).
51 Mattes p. 273.
52 Ibid.
53 Mattes p. 462.
54 Andreas (History of Franklin County)
55. Andreas (History of Thayer County)
56. www. nebraskahistory.org/publish/markers/texts/conflict_of_1867.htm. Material extracted from website June 18, 2007.
57. Andreas (History of Hall County).
58. Andreas (History of Cheyenne County).
59. Andreas (History of Madison County).
60. Andreas (History of Nuckolls County).
61. Andreas (History of Lincoln County).
62. Andreas (History of Nuckolls County).
63. Boye p. 83. See also *Andreas' History of the State of Nebraska (History of York County)*
64. Nebraska State Historical Society website: www.nebraskahistory.org/publish/markers/texts/tobin_indian_raid.htm. Material extracted from website June 18, 2007.
65 Andreas (History of Lincoln County).
66 G.R. Keith, *Pioneer Stories of the Pioneers of Fillmore and Adjoining Counties*, (Exeter, Nebraska: Press of Fillmore County News, 1915).
67 Andreas (History of Thayer County).
68 Andreas (History of Nuckolls County).
69 Andreas (History of Adams County).
70 Andreas (History of Lincoln County).
71 Andreas (History of Antelope County).
72 Ibid.
73 Andreas (History of Adams County).
74 Andreas (History of Webster County).
75 Andreas (History of Howard County).
76 Andreas (History of Red Willow County).
77 Andreas (History of Cheyenne County).
78 G.R. Keith, *Pioneer Stories of the Pioneers of Fillmore and Adjoining Counties*.
79 Andreas (History of Holt County).
80 Thomas R. Buecker, *Fort Robinson and the American West 1874-1899*, (Norman: University of Oklahoma Press, 1999) p. 77-82.
81 Andreas (History of Sherman County).
82 Andreas (History of Sioux County).
83 John Neihardt, *Black Elk Speaks*, (Lincoln: University of Nebraska Press, 1979).
84 Boye p. 196.
85 Andreas (History of Furnas County).
86 Andreas (History of Hitchcock County).
87 Lilian L. Jones, *Days of Yore: Early History of Brown County, Nebraska*, (Ainsworth, Nebraska, 1937) p. 9.
88 Alistair Cooke, *Alistair Cooke's America*, (New York: Alfred A. Knopf, 1976) p. 240.
89 Dennis Tedlock and Barbara Tedlock, *Teachings from the American Earth: Indian Religion and Philosophy*, (New York: Liverlight, 1975) p. 75.
90 Maria Elena Garcia, *A Natural Reaction of Human Beings*, http://www.loyno.edu/history/journal/1992-3/Garcia.htm. Material extracted from website March 9, 2007.

91 Portland Independent Media Center, *Wounded Knee*, http://www.portland.indymedia.org/en/2006/11/349679.html. Material extracted from website March 9, 2007.
92 Campfires: Nevada Historical Timeline, http://www.nevada heritage.com/timeline/timelinemainpage.htm. Material extracted from website March 8, 2007.
93 John D. McDermott, *A Guide to the Indian Wars of the West*, (Lincoln and London: University of Nebraska Press, 1998) p. 168.
94 Ibid

Closing Thoughts

While spasms of violence such as Dull Knife's escape with the Northern Cheyenne sometimes erupted after the final Great Sioux War ended, these outbursts tended to be isolated in nature, not part of a general conflagration.

By the end of the decade of the 1870s, the war on the Nebraska plains was over.

Although a specific date and time cannot be attached to the moment when the pendulum swung from war to peace, for Nebraska, and for the country, the absence of war on the frontier was a watershed event.

From Nebraska's earliest existence as a territory, violence or the threat of violence had been part of the fabric of its existence. Now, that chapter had ended.

* * *

Today, the battlefields at the Blue Water and the Blowout sit in the middle of farm or ranch land; relics occasionally kicked up by a steer or turned over by a plow the only hints of the fury that once occurred there. Where Villasur fought near Columbus, a bridge spans the river and the grass moves softly in the wind likes waves on an ocean swell. The hills around Massacre Canyon keep silent vigil where the noise of battle once filled the air. Warbonnet Creek still draws us, twice fascinated, to Buffalo Bill's encounter and the last great charge of the Fifth Cavalry. Further north and west, lies the hallowed ground of the Northern Cheyenne where the final stand of a desperate few made them immortal. The two Spring Creeks, where uncommon valor was a common virtue, lie placid in Nebraska's summer and frozen over in the winter, giving no hint of the gallantry that once took place along the banks of the tiny streams. The Platte and the Loup and the Republican roll unvexed across the prairie.

The legacy of the soldiers, settlers, and Native Americans who rode through the state's history—told in stories of courage, bloodshed, terror, fortitude, and heroism—reach across the decades to surprise, instruct, or inspire the generations that have followed and those that are yet to come.

APPENDICES

Appendix A
Perspective:
Civil War and the Great Sioux Uprising

The Civil War had enormous consequences for the defense of the frontier during the Sioux uprising. The titanic struggle in the east influenced the number of soldiers available for duty and the type of soldier—volunteer or Regular Army—that could be called upon.

* * *

"(In 1861) (t)he impact of the Civil War is immediately felt in the far west by disruptions of garrisons, the defection of Southerners, and the withdrawal of regulars for front line duty. Volunteer troops take over guard formations."[1]

"The incursions of Indians, and the vast damages which they had done in Nebraska, raised such an outcry that the Government had to send Nebraska troops home for the protection of Nebraska. . ."[2]

"In this final year of the Civil War (1865), volunteer troops such as the Seventh Iowa and Eleventh Ohio cavalries, which performed so valiantly guarding the Great Platte River Road, are gradually replaced by U.S. Army Regulars, veterans of the Civil War."[3]

"On the Union side. . .Confederate prisoners were successfully recruited to fight against the Sioux and other Plains Indians. These so-called 'Galvanized Yankees' were organized into six regiments of approximately 6,000 men. . .and many remained in service in 1866."[4]

273

Appendix B
Perspective:
Stations, Ranches, Camps and Forts

"Late in the year (1858) fortified ranches, serving travelers with crude lodgings and provisions, began to spring up along the Platte, frequently in the vicinity of U.S. mail stations."[5]

"It was not until 1859, however, that civilians began to settle along the Platte in quantity, in fortified adobe or cedar-log structures. If these were initiated by overland stage or Pony Express operators, they were called stations. If they were launched privately, as hostelries or groceries and saloons, they were called ranches, in the singular sometimes spelled 'ranche'. If the army built or occupied an outpost to protect telegraph facilities (or later, Union Pacific railroad construction), it would be designated a military post."[6]

"A ranche is not a dwelling, nor a farm-house, nor a store, nor a tavern, but all of these, and more. It is connected with a large corral, and capable of standing an Indian siege. You can procure entertainment at them. . .and they keep for sale liquors, canned fruit, knives, playing-cards, saddlery and goggles. . .

"These ranches are seen at a distance of from four to six miles on these dead levels, and loom up like a Fortress Monroe or Castle St. Angelo. A stable or house with its square openings for light and air resembles, at a short distance, a brown stone fort, with embrasures. The dwelling is sometimes adobe, but more frequently. . .log. . .and a corral of pickets or adobe construction constitute the prairie castle.

"Strictly speaking, (the adobe) is not adobe. . .being simply prairie sod, cut in blocks. They are laid, grass down, in walls three feet thick, and make the coolest house in summer, and warmest in winter, known in this region. . . . It is impossible to fire it, and arrows can do no damage." {James Meline, a traveler on the trail, 1866}[7]

"Ranches provide alike for man and beast. . . . A large yard is surrounded by a stockade paling, with stabling, feed-troughs, and hayricks, with here and there loop-holes for the rifle. In places of imminent peril from Indian attacks. . .the wall of the upper stories and every angle of the house or stable has its outlets for firing upon an approaching foe. The log or adobe house is often small; but like an eastern omnibus or street car, is unlimited in accommodations for all who seek shelter." {M. Carrington, a traveler on the trail, 1866}[8]

Military installations were labeled 'camps' if their intended occupancy was to be temporary (even if for an extended duration) and 'forts' if the facilities were designated to be permanent.

Appendix C
Perspective:
Nebraska units organized during Civil War

First Battalion, Nebraska Cavalry

Organized at Omaha January to August, 1864. Attached to District of Nebraska. Operated against Indians in Nebraska and Colorado; guarded Overland Mail routes. At Fort Cottonwood, Nebraska, October and November 1864; at Gillman's Station until January, 1865; at Cottonwood Springs until February, 1865; and at Gillman's Station until July, 1865. Company B at Dakota City until July, 1865. Scout from Dakota City April 12-16, 1865. Scout to Middle Bow River April 22-27. Company C at Fort Cottonwood, Nebraska, until July, 1865. Scout from Cottonwood May 12-14, 1865. Company D at Omaha until February, 1865. Moved to Fort Kearny, Nebraska, February 25 with duty there until April; at Fort Laramie, Wyoming, until July. Consolidated with lst Nebraska Veteran Cavalry July 10, 1865.

First Regiment, Nebraska Cavalry

Organized from First Nebraska Infantry October 11, 1863. Attached to District of Southeast Missouri, Department of Missouri, to November 1864. District of Northeast Arkansas, Department of Missouri to January, 1864. District of Northeast Arkansas, Seventh Army Corps to May 1864. Third Brigade, Second Division, Seventh Army Corps, Department of Arkansas, to October, 1864. Fourth Brigade, Cavalry Division, Seventh Army Corps, to October, 1864. District of Nebraska and District of the Plains, to July, 1866. Designated First Nebraska Veteran Cavalry from July 10, 1865.

SERVICE: Duty at St. Louis, Missouri, until November 30, 1863. Moved to Batesville, Arkansas, November 30-December 25. Operations in Northeastern Arkansas January 1-30, 1864. Action at Black River January 18. Jacksonport January 19. Expedition after Freeman's forces January 23-30. Sylamore Creek January 23 (Detachment). Sylamore January 24. Scout to Pocohontas February 9-20. Morgan's Mills, Spring River, February 9. Pocohontas February 10. Expedition from Batesville after Freeman's forces February 12-20. Spring River, near Smithfield, February 13. Expedition to Wild Haws, Strawberry Creek, etc., March 10-12. Scout from Batesville to Fairview March 25-26. Spring River, near Smithville, April 13 (Detachment). Moved to Jacksonport, Arkansas, April 17-19. Attack on Jacksonport April 20. Expedition to Augusta April 22-24. Near Jacksonport April 24. Moved to Duvall's Bluff May 25-30. Veterans on furlough June 10 to August 13. Left Omaha for Fort Kearny, Nebraska, August 15, arriving there August 23. Operations against Indians in Nebraska and Colorado until July, 1866, participating in numerous affairs with hostile Indians at Plum Creek, Spring Ranch, Julesburg, Mud Springs, Elm Creek, and Smith's Ranch. Also engaged in scout and escort duty. Operations on Overland Stage route between Denver and Julesburg, Colorado, January 14-25, 1865. Operations on North Platte River, Colorado, February 2-18. Scout from Dakota City April 12-16 and April 22-27 (Detachments). Scout from Fort Laramie to Wind River May 3-21 (Detachment). Scout from Plum Creek to Midway Station, Wind River, May 8-20 (Detachment). Scout from Fort Kearny to Little Blue River, Nebraska May 9-June 2 (Detachment). Scout from Cottonwood May 12-14 (First Battalion). Scout from Plum Creek, Nebraska, May 26-27 (Detachment). Expedition to Platte River, Nebraska, June 12-July 5 (Detachment). Mustered out July 1, 1866.

Predecessor Unit:
Nebraska Volunteers First Regiment Infantry
Organized at Omaha June 11 to July 21, 1861. Attached to Department of Missouri to February, 1862. District of Cairo, Illinois, February, 1862. Second Brigade, Third Division, Army of the Tennessee, to July, 1862. Helena (Arkansas) District of Eastern

Arkansas to October, 1862. Second Brigade, Second Division, Army of Southeast Missouri, Department of Missouri to March 1863. District of Southeast Missouri to November, 1863.

SERVICE: Left state for St. Joseph, Missouri, July 30, 1861; moved to Independence, Missouri, August 3-5, and to St. Louis, Missouri, August 8-11. Moved to Pilot Knob, Missouri, August 13-14, and to Syracuse, Missouri, August 19. Duty there until October 21. Freeman's Campaign against Springfield, Missouri, October 21-November 2. March to Sedalia and Georgetown November 9-16. Campaign against Bushwhackers December 8-15. Pope's Expedition to Warrensburg and Milford December 15-27. Action at Shawnee Mound, Milford, and Blackwater, December 18. (Capture of 1,300 prisoners.) Duty at Georgetown until February 2, 1862. Moved to Fort Donelson, Tennessee, February 2-13. Investment and capture of Fort Donelson, February 13-16. At Fort Henry February 17-March 6. Moved to Pittsburgh Landing, Tennessee, March 6-13. Battle of Shiloh, Tennessee, April 6-7. Advance on and siege of Corinth, Mississippi, April 29-May 30. March to Memphis, Tennessee, June 2-17; moved to Helena, Arkansas, July 24; with duty there until October. Expedition from Helena and capture of Steamer *Fair Play* August 4-19. Milliken's Bend August 18. Expedition up the Yazoo River August 20-27. Haines Bluff August 20. Bolivar August 22. Greenville August 23. Moved to Sulphur Springs, Missouri, October 5-11; moved to Pilot Knob October 28-30, and to Patterson November 2-4. Moved to Reeves Station December 9-10; returned to Patterson December 19. Moved to Van Buren December 21-24, and toward Doniphan January 9-10, 1863. Moved to Alton January 14-18; to West Plains and Salem, Arkansas, January 28-February 2. Moved to Pilot Knob and Ironton February 2-27. Moved to St. Genevieve and to Cape Girardeau March 8-12. Operations against Marmaduke April 21-May 2. Action at Cape Girardeau April 26. Pursuit of Marmaduke to St. Francis River April 29-May 5. Castor River, near Broomfield, April 29. Bloomfield April 30. Chalk Bluffs, St. Francis River April 29-May 5. Moved to Pilot Knob May 26-29 with duty there until August 28. At St. Louis, Missouri until November. Regiment ordered mounted October 11, 1863, and designation changed to First Nebraska Cavalry November 6, 1863.

277

Second Regiment, Nebraska Cavalry
Organized at Omaha October 23, 1862, and assigned to duty at Fort Kearny, Nebraska, guarding the Nebraska frontier, protecting emigrants, stage and telegraph lines and operating against Indians until April, 1863. Ordered to Sioux City. Attack on Pawnee Agency June 23, 1863 (Company D). Sully's Expedition against Indians in Dakota Territory August 23-September 11. Action at White Stone Hill Dakota Territory September 3. Skirmish at White Stone Hill September 5 (Company F). Company D on duty at Omaha and Fort Kearny, Nebraska. Mustered out December 23, 1863.

Omaha Scouts, Nebraska Cavalry
Organized at Omaha May 3, 1865. Attached to District of Nebraska. Scout from Fort Kearny, Nebraska, May 19-26, 1865. Powder River Expedition June 20-October 7. Actions on the Powder River September 1,2,4,5,7 and 8. Operated against Indians on the Plains and protected lines of communications and emigrants until July, 1866. Mustered out July 1, 1866.

Pawnee Scouts, Nebraska Cavalry
Organized at Columbus, Nebraska, January 13, 1865. Attached to District of Nebraska. At Fort Kearny, Nebraska, February, 1865. At Fort Rankin April 1865. Powder River Expedition June 20-October 7, 1865. Action at Tongue River August 28. Actions on Powder River September 1-8. Operations on the Plains against Indians; protected lines of communications and emigrants until April, 1866. Mustered out April 1, 1866.

Appendix D
Perspective:
Putting the numbers in context

Observations
"At the peak of the nineteenth-century Indian wars, the army had an effective strength of something less than fifteen thousand men, yet its soldiers manned one hundred thirty-six forts, posts, camps, and cantonments; sixteen arsenals and armories; and three recruiting and

one engineer depot. The troops guarded some three thousand miles of frontier and an equal length of seacoast. They scouted thousands of weary miles in uncharted territory. Besides its role as the agent of empire, the army physically attacked the wilderness, building forts, roads, and bridges, at times conducting extensive farming operations and gathering some of the first scientific data on the great hinterland. Troops watched over railroads and telegraph lines and escorted paymasters' and quartermasters' trains. They guarded parties surveying railway territories, boundary lines, and public lands."

Source: John D. McDermott, *A Guide to the Indian Wars of the West*, (Lincoln and London: University of Nebraska Press, 1998) p. xvii

Distribution of Regular Army Troops
{Note the small sizes of most frontier garrisons}

1822

Fort Atkinson 490*
* At its peak strength, Fort Atkinson housed about 1,000 soldiers

1850
Fort Kearny 101

1860
Fort Kearny 206

1867
Fort Kearny 72
Fort McPherson 332
Camp Sargent* 231
* Also called North Platte Station. Located at North Platte (1867-1881)

1870
Fort Kearny 49
Fort McPherson 500
Omaha Barracks 620

1878
Fort Hartsuff 37
Fort McPherson 109
Omaha Barracks 126

Red Cloud Agency 150 (Camp Sheridan)
Camp Robinson 68
Sidney Barracks 38

1885
Fort Niobrara 271
Fort Omaha 399
Fort Robinson 222
Fort Sidney 224

1895
Fort Niobrara 476
Fort Omaha 571
Fort Robinson 516

Source: Francis Paul Prucha, *Atlas of American Indian Affairs*, (Lincoln: University of Nebraska Press, 1990) p. 163-171

Native Populations

Estimated populations of the Plains tribes referenced in this book

Arapaho	3,000 (1780)
Cheyenne	4,000 (1875)
Comanche	6,000 (1816)
Crow	4,000 (1780)
Kiowa	2,000 (1780)
Omaha	3,000 (1802)
Oto	500 (1895)
Pawnee	1,440 (1879)
Ponca	800 (1780)
Sioux	40,000 (1870)
Utes	4,500 (1845)

Source: John D. McDermott, *A Guide to Indian Wars of the West*, (Lincoln and London: University of Nebraska Press, 1998) p. 14

Losses

"Between 1865 and 1891 the U.S. Army conducted 13 campaigns against (Native tribes), engaging them in 1,067 separate actions. One authority has tallied army casualties as 948 killed and 1,058 wounded. Meanwhile, Native American casualties in those battles have been estimated at 4,371 killed, 1,279 wounded, and 10,318 captured."

280

Source: Richard Sauers, *America's Battlegrounds*, (San Diego: Tehabi Books, 2005) p. 59

"During the twenty-five year period that followed the Civil War, 923 officers and enlisted men died, and 1,061 suffered wounds. Army records estimate 5,519 Indians killed and wounded. Also engaged were white civilians, 461 of whom died in these battles and 116 of whom were wounded. General Sheridan reported that the proportions of casualties to troops engaged on the Great Plains in 1876-1877 were greater than those of the Civil War or the Russo-Turkish war then being fought. It was an intense, dramatic confrontation, played out in a great, varied landscape."

Source: John D. McDermott, *A Guide to the Indian Wars of the West*, (Lincoln and London: University of Nebraska Press, 1998) p. 28

Endnotes
1 Merrill J. Mattes, *The Great Platte River Road*, (Lincoln: The Nebraska State Historical Society, 1964) p. 19.
2 Eugene F. Ware, *The Indian War of 1864*, (Lincoln: University of Nebraska Press, 1960) p. 14.
3 Mattes p. 20,21.
4 Margaret E. Wagner, Editor, *The Library of Congress Civil War Desk Reference*, (New York: Simon & Schuster, 2002) p. 587 .
5 Merrill J. Mattes, *The Great Platte River Road* (Lincoln: The Nebraska State Historical Society, 1964) p.18.
6 Mattes p. 270.
7 Mattes p. 271.
8 Ibid.
9 I am grateful to Margaret E. Wagner, Editor, Publishing Office, The Library of Congress, for providing this information.

APPENDIX E

MEDALS OF HONOR EARNED IN NEBRASKA

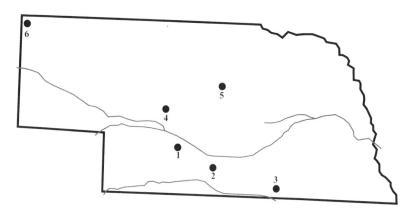

1. Pvt. Francis W. Lohnes
   Co. H 1st Nebraska Cavalry   May 12, 1865   Near Gothenburg

2. Lt. John Babcock
   Co. M, 5th Cavalry   May 16, 1868   Phelps County (Spring Creek)

3. Sgt. Patrick J. Leonard
   Co. C, 2nd Cavalry   May 17, 1870   Nuckolls County W. of Ruskin
   Pvt. Heath Canfield   (Spring Creek)
   Pvt. Thomas Hubbard
   Pvt. Michael Himmelsbach
   Pvt. George W. Thompson

4. Scout "Buffalo Bill" Cody
   Co. B, 3rd Cavalry   April 26, 1872   Near Stapleton
   Sgt. John H. Foley
   Sgt. Leroy Vokes
   Pvt. William H. Strayer

5. Lt. Charles Heyl
   Co. A 23rd Infantry   April 28, 1876   Near Burwell
   Cpl. Patrick T. Leonard   (Battle of the Blowout)
   Pvt. Jeptha Lytton

6. Sgt. William B. Lewis
   Co. B, 3rd Cavalry   January 20, 1879   NW of Fort Robinson
                                                       (Cheyenne outbreak)

APPENDIX F

PONY EXPRESS STATIONS IN NEBRASKA

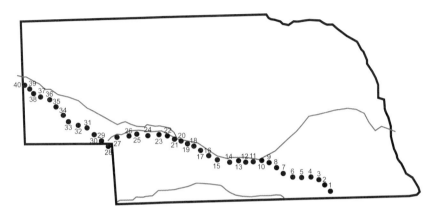

1. Rock Creek
    Virginia City [1]
2. Big Sandy
3. Kiowa/Millersville
4. Little Blue/Oak Creek
5. Liberty Farm
6. Spring Ranch/Lone Tree
7. Thirty-two Mile
8. Summit/Sand Hill
9. Fairfield [2]
10. Hooks/Kearney/Valley
11. Fort Kearney
12. Platte/Seventeen Mile
13. Craig's [3]
14. Plum Creek
15. Willow Island/Willow Bend
16. Midway Ranch/Cold Water
17. Gilman's Ranch
18. Sam Mettache's [4]
19. Cottonwood Springs

20. Cold Springs
21 Fremont Springs
22. O'Fallon's Bluff/Dansey's/Elkhorn
23. Alkali Lake
24. Sand Hill/Gill's
25. Diamond Springs
26. Beauvais Ranch
27. South Platte
28. Julesburg (Colorado)
29. Nine Mile
30. Pole Creek #2
31. Pole Creek #3
32. Midway
33. Mud Springs
34. Courthouse Rock
35. Chimney Rock
36. Ficklin's Spring
33. Scottsbluff
38. Horse Creek [5]

1. Not identified in Nebraska Stations website.
2. Not identified in Pony Express National Historic Trails: National Resources Study.
3. Identified as "Garden Station" in Pony Express National Historic Trails: National Resources Study.
4. Identified as "Machette's Station" in Pony Express National Historic Trails: National Resources Study.
5. Identified as "Fort Mitchell Station" in Pony Express National Historic Trails: Natural Resources Study.

Sources include Pony Express National Historic Trail: National Resource Study (www.nps.gov/archive/poex/hrs/ hrst.html) and Nebraska Stations (www.xphomestation.com/nesta.html). Some stations were known at times by different names or underwent location changes.

APPENDIX G

LOCATIONS OF NEBRASKA MILITARY POSTS MENTIONED IN THIS BOOK.

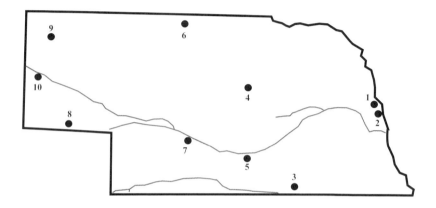

1. **Fort Atkinson.** One mile east of Fort Calhoun, nine miles north of Omaha. (Washington County)
2. **Fort Omaha.** 30th and Fort Streets, Omaha. (Douglas County)
3. **Camp Bingham.** Temporary post established April – October 1870. Northeast of Ruskin on the Little Blue River. (Nuckolls County)
4. **Fort Hartsuff.** Ten miles southeast of Burwell, near Elyria. (Valley County)
5. **Fort Kearny.** Three miles south, four miles east of Kearney. (Kearney County)
6. **Fort Niobrara.** One and a half miles southeast of Valentine. (Cherry County)
7. **Fort McPherson.** Four miles south of Maxwell. (Lincoln County)
8. **Fort Sidney.** Inside Sidney city limits. Commandant's house is at 1108 Sixth Avenue. (Cheyenne County)
9. **Fort Robinson.** Three miles east of Crawford. (Dawes County)
10. **Fort Mitchell.** Four miles west of Scottsbluff. (Scottsbluff County)

APPENDIX H

General locations of the Plains tribes: Early to mid 1800s

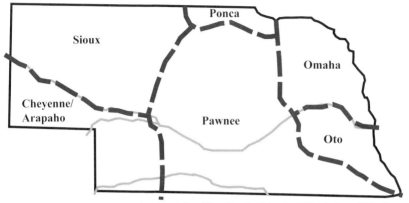

Source: Francis Paul Prucha, Atlas of American Indian Affairs, (Lincoln: University of Nebraska Press, 1990) p.6.

About The Author

A native Nebraskan, Tom Phillips developed an early fascination for the state's history while growing up on a farm near Lincoln. Soon after graduating from high school, he began a long, distinguished career in the armed forces. During the course of a thirty-six-year military career, he rose from enlisted recruit to colonel.

Phillips' assignments included running a "think tank" for the Commander-In-Chief, Strategic Air Command, serving as director, Air Force Personnel Readiness Center during Operation Desert Storm and commanding some of the first American troops sent to Sarajevo, Bosnia-Herzegovina. He received numerous awards and citations during his career and while in the Air Force earned degrees from Colorado State University and the University of Colorado.

Tom Phillips

After completing military service, Phillips worked as an administrator at the University of Nebraska, and as a free lance writer.

Tom and his wife Nita currently reside in Lincoln, Nebraska, where he writes about military and American history, defense issues and baseball.

Index

For a free catalog of Caxton titles write to:

CAXTON PRESS
312 Main Street
Caldwell, Idaho 83605-3299

or

Visit our Internet web site:

www.caxtonpress.com

Caxton Press is a division of THE CAXTON PRINTERS, Ltd.